LETTERS
FROM THE
SOUTHERN
HOME FRONT

Edited by
JOSEPH A. FRY

LETTERS
FROM THE
SOUTHERN
HOME FRONT

The American South
Responds to the
Vietnam War

LOUISIANA STATE UNIVERSITY PRESS
Baton Rouge

Published by Louisiana State University Press
lsupress.org

Manufactured in the United States of America
First printing

DESIGNER: Mandy McDonald Scallan
TYPEFACE: Minion

Jacket image: U.S. soldiers moving across a rice field in search of Viet
Cong, January 1966. Photograph by Robert C. Lafoon. National Archives
and Records Administration. ARC Identifier: 17331378.

Library of Congress Cataloging-in-Publication Data

Names: Fry, Joseph A., 1947– editor.
Title: Letters from the southern home front : the American South responds
   to the Vietnam War / edited by Joseph A. Fry.
Description: Baton Rouge : Louisiana State University Press, [2023] |
   Includes bibliographical references and index.
Identifiers: LCCN 2022011867 (print) | LCCN 2022011868 (ebook) | ISBN
   978-0-8071-7883-6 (paperback) | ISBN 978-0-8071-7856-0 (cloth) | ISBN
   978-0-8071-7882-9 (pdf) | ISBN 978-0-8071-7881-2 (epub)
Subjects: LCSH: Vietnam War, 1961–1975—Public opinion. | Public
   opinion—Southern States. | LCGFT: Business correspondence.
Classification: LCC DS559.62.U6 L48 2023 (print) | LCC DS559.62.U6
   (ebook) | DDC 959.704/3—dc23/eng/20220623
LC record available at https://lccn.loc.gov/2022011867
LC ebook record available at https://lccn.loc.gov/2022011868

For George C. Herring

CONTENTS

ACKNOWLEDGMENTS

Since this is my first serious editing project, I have needed significant help and guidance. Sheryl B. Vogt, director of the Richard B. Russell Jr. Library for Political Research and Studies at the University of Georgia, and Kathryn Stallard, the past director of Special Collections and Archives at Southwestern University, provided much of that crucial direction. In addition to facilitating my work in the Richard B. Russell Jr. and Herman E. Talmadge Papers (U. of Georgia) and the John G. Tower Papers (Southwestern), both educated me regarding privacy and copyright issues. I am much in their debt. That said, neither is responsible for my decisions or errors in either of these aspects of the project.

Although accumulating these letters in libraries across the South from 2000 through 2012 would not have been possible without the expert help of the staffs of all the archives cited in the "Sources of Letters" section, I would also like to specifically thank Mike Ballard, Craig Piper, and Betty Self at the Congressional and Political Research Center at Mississippi State University (John C. Stennis Collection) and Ethel B. (Betty) Austin at Special Collections at the University of Arkansas (J. William Fulbright Papers). All these wonderful professionals have since moved or retired, but they made my stays in Starkville and Fayetteville both enjoyable and productive. I am also grateful to the Long Family for permission to use materials from the Russell B. Long Papers in the Louisiana and Lower Mississippi Collection at Louisiana State University.

Yuko Shinozaki in the University of Nevada, Las Vegas Interlibrary Loan Department, provided timely and indispensable support for my efforts to include Black letters in this collection. Ms. Shinozaki worked tirelessly and successfully in identifying and obtaining microfilm copies of African American papers from across the South. Mike Green, an old friend, and UNLV History Department colleague; Priscilla Finley, UNLV Humanities Librarian; and Su Kim Chung, Head of UNLV's Special Collections Public Service Division, graciously tutored me on accessing and researching digital resources.

I have also received generous support from the University of Nevada, Las

Vegas Department of History. Prior to my retirement in 2013, the Department helped fund the research trips during which the senatorial letters were located and copied. Since my retirement, the Department has been equally gracious in affording me office space essential to my ongoing research and writing. As I have focused on this collection of letters over the past three years, Andy Kirk, the Department chair, and Annette Amdal, the Department's lead staff person, have carved out this office space in creative and thoughtful ways. Thank you. Annette and Shontai Zuniga, the Department's other primary staff person, have also helped me on numerous other technical and not-so-technical fronts. Finally, the opportunity to maintain contacts with the history faculty has been both personally enjoyable and professionally informative. I am fully aware that retired faculty at many universities are not always treated so well, and none of this good treatment has been taken for granted.

Thomas C. Wright, Distinguished Professor of History Emeritus at UNLV, and Jeffrey J. Matthews, George Frederick Jewett Distinguished Professor at Puget Sound University, have provided close readings of the entire manuscript. Their perceptive observations and keen editorial suggestions have significantly improved all aspects of this book. I am very fortunate to have Tom and Jeff as editors but even more fortunate to count them as valued friends.

I consider myself equally fortunate to be publishing this book with the Louisiana State University Press. I began systematic examination of the American South and U.S. foreign relations with *Dixie Looks Abroad*, which LSU published in 2002. To complete my work on this topic twenty years later, again with LSU, provides nice symmetry. Editor-in-Chief Rand Dotson has overseen this most recent experience with skill, patience, and professionalism. His responses to my queries and concerns have been unfailing thoughtful and his direction unerring. Senior editor Neal Novak has supervised the book's production with exemplary skill and much appreciated enthusiasm. Jo Ann Kiser skillfully copyedited the manuscript with just the proper balance of intervention and restraint. Of course, Tom, Jeff, Rand, Neal, and Jo Ann bear no responsibility for any remaining errors or shortcomings. They belong to me alone.

Before concluding with thanks to the person to whom this book is dedicated, I would once again like to thank my wife, Sandy, for not just her usual support for my scholarly indulgences but also the joy and love she brings to everyone in our family. There is no better wife, mother, and as of 2020, grandmother.

Finally, I am delighted to have the opportunity to dedicate this book to

George C. Herring, an exceptional historian and mentor, and even better friend. I shall not try to enumerate all the ways George has helped me over the past forty-plus years, and countless others could offer a comparable list. Suffice it to say that George demonstrated a confidence in me and a willingness to extend direction and friendship that were crucial to my development as a competent professional prepared to interact with the broader scholarly community.

LETTERS
FROM THE
SOUTHERN
HOME FRONT

Introduction

From 1963 to 1965, the United States committed to a war in Vietnam that ultimately claimed more than 58,000 American lives and at least two million Vietnamese fatalities. As the United States deployed advisers to aid the South Vietnamese government, initiated sustained bombing, and dispatched ground troops, both pro- and antiwar southern Americans expressed their opinions on the war by writing letters to their political representatives and to the editors of the South's newspapers.

A Georgia physician voiced majority southern opinion in favor of unrestrained military effort. The United States, he asserted, "should go to war" with "an effort to *win*." To do otherwise was "being dishonest and untrue to the youth of our nation whom we are sending to their death. . . . I feel we should bomb and destroy Hanoi and Haiphong and any other military target necessary to win. I think we should attempt to . . . obtain unconditional surrender with all means at our command, including atomic weapons."[1]

Other southerners expressed early, prescient, and probing qualms about the U.S. intervention. Writing in mid-1963, a Texan traveling in Europe urged Senator Ralph Yarborough (D/TX) to advocate "an end" to growing U.S. involvement, "a tragic situation, daily becoming more menacing." By following U.S. actions in the European press, this Austin resident concluded the United States was being "sucked into a debacle like that in Korea." According to another Texan, the United States had "obviously lost the initiative" in Vietnam by late 1963; therefore, as in football, the South's favorite sport, the "best answer" was to "quick kick" the problem back to France, the former colonial ruler of Vietnam.[2]

1. R.P.T. to Richard B. Russell Jr., December 6, 1965, series 16, box 40, folder 4, Richard B. Russell Jr. Papers, Richard B. Russell Library for Political Research and Studies, University of Georgia, Athens, GA (hereafter cited as Russell Papers, box:folder; all subsequent cites to series 16).

2. F.K.F. to Ralph W. Yarborough, July 29, 1963, Box 4Zd675: Folder August 10, 1964, Ralph W. Yarborough Papers, Briscoe Center for American History, University of Texas, Austin, TX; R.B.S. Jr. to John G. Tower, October 1, 1963, box 285, folder 4, John G. Tower Papers, Special Collections and Archives, Southwestern University, Georgetown, TX.

Southerners voiced even more specifically regional perspectives. An antiwar North Carolinian asked Senator Sam Ervin (D/NC) "what we would think of a foreign country" that landed "troops on our shore to settle the negro question." An Atlanta resident posed a similar question to Senator Richard B. Russell (D/GA): If southerners believed "that people as close as New York don't quite know enough to tell us how to run Georgia," how could the senator think that the United States knew "what is best" for a country "as far away" as Vietnam? Another Georgian provided a fitting sectional epitaph eight years later as the United States withdrew from Vietnam: "As Southerners we should know that the greatness of a people is not merely their ability to win, but their ability to accept defeat when defeat is inevitable."[3]

As the war continued for nearly a decade, southerners graphically described the conflict's mounting toll. Writing from Bethlehem, Georgia, a former sharecropper and World War II veteran had become "a very bitter man." He and his wife had struggled to provide their only child a "home and an Education," only to have him drafted into the military following his graduation from high school. Had he been a "man's son with money he could have gone on to school and stayed out of the army. . . . Why," the father asked, "must it always be the poor man that has to fight wars? And these bearded people that burn their draft cards and cause so much trouble, why aren't they in the army?" A J. William Fulbright constituent informed the senator of her nineteen-year-old son's death: "He hadn't even become a man yet, to us he was just a young boy and we never got to finish raising him . . . and now we must put everything away, as though we never had a son."[4]

In 1970 a Tennessee woman summarized the war's more general impact from the perspective of a majority of white southerners: "I am a 'tired' American. I am tired of the discrimination against the South. I am tired of the communist indoctrination of minority groups that have infiltrated our universities and campuses and created the unrest and riots. I am tired of the television networks and

3. H.H.H. to Sam J. Ervin Jr., March 19, 1964, box 97, folder 4336, Sam J. Ervin Papers, #3847A, Subgroup A: Senate Records, Series 1, Southern Historical Collection, Wilson Library, University of North Carolina, Chapel Hill, NC; Mrs. W.K.Z. to Russell, August 6, 1964, Russell Papers, 41:11; E.T.L. to Herman E. Talmadge, December 29, 1972, series XI, box 144, folder 2, Herman E. Talmadge Papers, Richard B. Russell Library for Political Research and Studies, University of Georgia, Athens, GA.

4. W.W.L. to Russell, January 15, 1968, Russell Papers, 33:7; Mrs. H.C. to J. William Fulbright, box 56: folder 3, J. William Fulbright Papers, Special Collections, University of Arkansas Libraries, Fayetteville, AR.

newspapers that present such biased view points and facts. I am tired of the members of Congress who are dividing our country instead of working to bring us together. I am tired of the lawlessness and crime in our country. . . . I am tired of the intellectuals in our colleges who are spreading the seeds of anarchy and revolution. Let me say in closing . . . that President Nixon is a very dedicated man and has made a right decision in Cambodia and should have the full support of every right thinking American."[5]

While expressing many of the same pro- and antiwar arguments and exhibiting similar war weariness as white southerners, the region's African Americans added a distinctive racial perspective. They debated whether opposing the war would hinder or advance the Civil Rights Movement and whether valiant service by Black soldiers in Vietnam would advance freedom at home; but virtually all Black letter writers agreed that the nation's primary focus should have been on domestic racial and economic equality. As one correspondent wrote in July 1967, "the callous treatment Negroes have received from this country for the past 400 years indicates our first concern ought to be with making democracy work here instead of in the rice-paddies of Southeast Asia." Other Blacks were even more pointed: "If tomorrow morning . . . Negroes should say, 'I shall not fight in Vietnam until I am accorded the same freedom as the white man in this country'; the war would be over in 24 hours, and why? The white men of the United States would rather lose a war in Asia than accord the black American the same status as his fellow whites have!"[6]

Over the course of the war from 1963 through 1973, white southerners wrote tens of thousands of letters like these to their congressmen and senators, to Presidents Johnson and Nixon, and to the editors of the South's daily newspapers. Southern letter writers extended in age from elementary school students to World War I veterans; included men and women and residents of the rural, small-town, and urban South; ranged from farmers and small-business owners to teachers, doctors, lawyers, and university professors; ran from persons of decidedly modest circumstances to the more affluent; and numbered students from a broad range of colleges and universities.

I collected more than 1,200 letters written to Presidents Johnson and Nixon;

5. S.S.M. to Albert Gore Sr., May 11, [1970], series 6, box B44:folder 8, Albert Gore Sr. Senate Papers, Albert Gore Research Center, Middle Tennessee State University, Murfreesboro, TN.

6. J.B. to Editor of the *Pittsburgh Courier,* July 22, 1967; R.T.P. to Editor of the *Louisville Defender,* February 23, 1967.

to U.S. senators from Alabama, Arkansas, Georgia, Kentucky, Louisiana, Mississippi, North Carolina, Tennessee, Texas, and Virginia; and to editors of several southern daily newspapers while researching *Dixie Looks Abroad: The South and U.S. Foreign Relations, 1789–1973* (2002), *Debating Vietnam: Fulbright, Stennis, and Their Senate Hearings* (2006), and *The American South and the Vietnam War: Belligerence, Protest, and Agony in Dixie* (2015). The letters included in chapters 1, 2, 4, 5, and 6 of this collection have been selected from that corpus of material.

Letters from southern African Americans are the conspicuous omission in this body of materials. In this time frame, Blacks do not appear to have written to their white, overwhelmingly Democratic and primarily segregationist political officials; and if Black southerners did write to these officials, their letters were not readily identifiable by race. I have attempted to provide Black voices and perspectives by researching Letters to the Editor sections of southern African American newspapers. Letters located in that research make up chapter 3.

Vietnam Veterans are the other prominent group whose letters have not been included in this collection, save in a few selective instances, such as responses to the U.S. military's My Lai massacre of South Vietnamese civilians in 1968 and the subsequent trial of Lieutenant William Calley for murder. I have elected not to include veterans' letters more generally because of the domestic, home-front focus of this collection.

Those southerners willing to invest the time and effort to write letters addressing the war in Vietnam allow readers to follow the ongoing debate over the war on the local, domestic level. They have also provided an essential, explanatory supplement to the data gathered from public opinion polling. The South's letter writers help explain *why* respondents to the Gallup and Harris polls answered questions as they did.[7] These authors added qualitative nuance, depth, and complexity to the quantitative results and trends reported by national and regional polls. They discussed an impressive range of war-related issues and topics, including U.S. geopolitical and strategic interests; U.S. standing in the world; opposition to and the containment of international communism; appropriate U.S. military strategies; civilian versus military oversight and control over those strategies; national honor; patriotism; religion and the war's moral implications; presidential versus congressional roles in declaring and waging war; the conflict's fiscal costs; the draft and its class and racial impacts; college

---

7. See the next section for a discussion of polling and the explanatory contributions of southern letter writers.

students and their obligations and choices relative to the war; domestic protests against the war and questions of law and order; My Lai and the Calley trial; the Civil Rights Movement and the war; American POWs; the job performance of national and regional leaders, such as Presidents Johnson and Nixon, Secretary of State Dean Rusk, Secretary of Defense Robert McNamara, and southern senators, such as Richard Russell, John C. Stennis, J. William Fulbright, and Albert Gore Sr.; the war's domestic agony and suffering; and the cumulative war weariness so crucial to U.S. withdrawal from Vietnam.

A collection of letters devoted exclusively to the South's domestic response to war is highly unusual and perhaps unique. There are multiple collections of letters from soldiers writing home while serving in American wars, including *Dear America: Letters Home from Vietnam*; and there are numerous oral histories and interviews with U.S. veterans of service abroad, such as *Landing Zones: Southern Veterans Remember Vietnam* and *A Time for Looking Back: Putnam County* [Tennessee] *Veterans, Their Families, and the Vietnam War*. Published collections of letters from the home front during U.S. wars are far less common. *The Lincoln Mailbox: America Writes to the President* and *Dear Harry . . . Truman's Mailroom, 1945–1953: The Truman Administration through Correspondence with "Everyday Americans"* afford two important examples, but neither focuses exclusively on the war in progress. Instead, the letters range broadly over both contemporary war-related topics and other domestic issues.[8]

Just as these Vietnam letters constitute a much-needed complement to public opinion polling, they also have certain advantages over oral histories. Unlike persons providing oral recollections, these southern authors registered real-time responses to the war based on their access to current, contemporary information. Although oral histories allow for subsequent contemplation and reflection, the recollections and opinions of the persons being interviewed can change over time and yield a less-than-accurate historical record of their earlier perceptions and positions.

8. Bernard Edelman, ed., *Dear America: Letters Home from Vietnam* (New York: W. W. Norton, 1985); James R. Wilson, ed., *Landing Zones: Southern Veterans Remember Vietnam* (Durham, NC: Duke University Press, 1990); William J. Brinker, ed., *A Time for Looking Back: Putnam County Veterans, Their Families, and the Vietnam War* (Cookeville, TN: Tennessee Technological University, 1990); Harold Holzer, ed., *The Lincoln Mailbag: America Writes to the President, 1861–1865* (Carbondale, IL: Southern Illinois University Press, 2006); D. M. Giangreco and Kathryn Moore, eds., *Dear Harry . . . Truman's Mailroom, 1945–1953: The Truman Administration through Correspondence with 'Everyday Americans'* (Mechanicsburg, PA: Stockpole Books, 1999).

By investing the time, thought, emotion, and energy to write to a political figure or newspaper editor, these southern authors demonstrated unusual concern over U.S. national policies and actions. They also exhibited a greater awareness and knowledge of foreign affairs than the general public. This attention, knowledge, and willingness to write rendered the authors a distinct minority within their communities and nation. Although many of their neighbors and fellow citizens nationally also followed the war carefully and held strong opinions regarding the conflict, relatively few of them took the initiative to put pen to paper or to sit before their typewriters. Given this level of attention and knowledge, civic commitment, and willingness to express personal opinions, these southerners and their perspectives deserve to be heard as the United States continues to grapple with the historical record and significance of the Vietnam ordeal.[9]

These southerners and their responses to the Vietnam War are also important as a vital contribution to a more general recounting and analysis of war-related U.S. public opinion from 1963 through 1973. Leslie H. Gelb, a Defense Department official in the Johnson administration from 1967 to 1969, has asserted that U.S. public opinion significantly influenced both Presidents Johnson's and Richard M. Nixon's policies for fighting the war. Gelb argued that "pubic support and opposition to the war" was "the key stress point"—the "*essential domino*" as both administrations considered diplomatic, strategic, and military strategies for waging and ending the conflict.[10]

During the period of the most intensive U.S. intervention from 1964 until 1973, the Gallup and Harris polls sought to ascertain and track the American public's attitudes toward the war. From the late 1960s to the present, scholars have employed these national polls and other, more regionally specific ones to analyze the public opinion Gelb deemed so important to policy formation. These scholars agree that the American public paid relatively scant attention to the war until mid-1965 when the United States had initiated sustained bombing of

9. On the American public's "rather monumental lack of knowledge and interest" regarding U.S. foreign relations, see, John E. Mueller, *War, Presidents, and Public Opinion* (Lanham, MD: University Press of America, 1985; originally published, 1973), 1–2; and Ole R. Holsti, *Public Opinion and American Foreign Policy* (Ann Arbor: University of Michigan Press, 1997), 215.

10. Louis Klarevas, "The 'Essential Domino' of Military Operations: American Public Opinion and the Use of Force," *International Studies Perspectives* 3 (2002): 417–37 (Gelb, 418). This article is an excellent overview and synthesis of studies of public opinion and the war.

North Vietnam and committed ground troops to fight in South Vietnam. Over the ensuing year, a patriotic rally-round-the-flag response produced the most robust public support of the war's nine-year duration. By mid-1966, that initial, majority prowar opinion had dissipated. When asked in August 1965 if U.S. intervention had been a mistake, 61 percent of respondents answered "no." In September 1966, 48 percent did so. Thereafter, Americans who did not judge the war a mistake declined to 28 percent in May 1971 when Gallup stopped posing the question. For a brief period in 1967, 55 percent of Americans polled endorsed military escalation as the preferred U.S. policy, but by March 1969, those supporting this option had fallen to 32 percent. As the United States withdrew from Vietnam in 1973, 79 percent of Americans rejected the use of U.S. troops even if North Vietnam sought "to take over South Vietnam."[11]

Students of wartime public opinion have reached a general consensus regarding the groups in American society most inclined to support and oppose the war. Americans under the age of thirty-five were more likely to back the war; those over thirty-five to oppose the conflict. Men were more prowar; women more antiwar. Whites were more supportive of the military intervention; Blacks by a significant margin disapproved. Better educated Americans with college degrees were more approving of the war than those with high school diplomas, and high school graduates more prowar than fellow citizens who had not completed the twelfth grade. The least well-educated were the least belligerent. In summary, women, the least well-educated, Black Americans, and by extension the least well-off socially and financially were the least prowar. Democrats were more opposed to the war than Republicans.[12]

Explanations of these demographic findings suggest that better-educated, more affluent, white men were more likely to have benefited from interactions with the American government at all levels, more likely to have been informed of the U.S. rationales and strategies for the war, and more likely to

11. William L. Lunch and Peter W. Sperlich, "American Public Opinion and the War in Vietnam," *Western Political Quarterly* 32 (March 1979): 22–32 (quote 25); John E. Mueller, "Trends in Popular Support for the Wars in Korea and Vietnam," *American Political Science Review* 65 (June 1971): 364–65; Mueller, *War, Presidents, and Public Opinion*, 53–56.

12. Lunch and Sperlich, "American Public Opinion and the War in Vietnam," 37–42; Mueller, *War, Presidents, and Public Opinion*, 122–23, 143, and "Trends in Popular Support for the Wars in Korea and Vietnam," 368; Howard Schuman, "Two Sources of Antiwar Sentiment in America," *American Journal of Sociology* 78 (Nov. 1972): 528.

have responded to prowar cues from national and state leaders. In contrast, women, minorities, the less well-educated, and the less affluent had exercised less political influence, had benefited less from government policies historically, and were, therefore, less inclined to endorse national explanations for the war, its conduct, or its costs.[13]

These macro polling results appear inconsistent with the prominent role of college students in opposing the war. If younger, better-educated Americans were, according to Gallup, more supportive of the war, how could college students have been the "foot soldiers" of the antiwar movement? This seeming paradox is explained by the concentration of student protests at "elite" private universities, such as Harvard, Columbia, or Yale, and major state universities, such as the University of California, Berkeley, University of Texas, University of Virginia, and University of Georgia. Smaller and less prestigious universities and colleges, both public and private, and junior colleges and their students far outnumbered those attending "quality" universities, and those students were much more prowar. Moreover, for polling purposes, "college-educated" included persons who had attended college but never graduated and many others who had graduated well before the war reached its peak but were not yet thirty-five years old. Therefore, "fewer than 25 percent of the college-educated members of the population" had any contact with the universities where antiwar protests were most common. Significantly, a clear majority of adult Americans polled had an unfavorable perception of protestors, and this majority included many respondents who also opposed the war.[14]

While analysts of Vietnam War–era public opinion and its demographic composition have largely agreed on the overall trends of support and opposition to the war, they have reached no consensus on how best to explain these findings. John E. Mueller established the parameters for much of the debate by arguing

---

13. Schuman, "Two Sources of Antiwar Sentiment in America," 528; Mueller, *War, Presidents, and Public Opinion,* 122–23, 143, and Lunch and Sperlich, "American Public Opinion and the War in Vietnam," 368.

14. Melvin Small, *Antiwarriors: The Vietnam War and the Battle for America's Hearts and Minds* (Wilmington, DE: Scholarly Resources, 2002): 85 (foot soldiers); Steven J. Kelman, "Youth and Foreign Policy," *Foreign Affairs* 48 (April 1970), 414 (elite); Lunch and Sperlich, "American Public Opinion and the War in Vietnam," 22–23 (38–39, quality); Philip E. Converse and Howard Schuman, "'Silent Majorities' and the Vietnam War," *Scientific American* 222 (June 1970): 22–23 (25 percent of the college-educated); Schuman, "Two Sources of Antiwar Sentiment in America," 516–18.

in 1971 that the number of American casualties (killed and wounded) was the primary determinant of declining public support for the war. Cumulative American casualties, rather than specific events, such as the North Vietnamese and Vietcong Tet Offensive of 1968 or the U.S. invasion of Cambodia in 1970, best explain the public's increasing distaste for the war. More recently, Scott Sigmund Gartner and Gary W. Segura have acknowledged the centrality of U.S. casualties but contended that "marginal" casualties or those suffered during a more limited period of the war, and therefore tied to important events, may provide greater insight. They have also argued that dead and injured soldiers from a local community had greater influence on opinion than aggregate national totals.[15]

Without endorsing the predominant influence of aggregate casualties over marginal or local ones, there is no doubt that mounting numbers of killed and injured American soldiers were a fundamental contributor to the nation's "war weariness" and the conflict's increased unpopularity after mid-1966. Scholars have linked war weariness to other "pragmatic" concerns such as the conflict's economic costs, domestic social divisions and turmoil, the lack of clear progress toward victory, and the frustrating strength and resilience of the North Vietnamese and Vietcong. In sum, Americans increasingly came to believe that the costs of the war far outweighed its ostensible benefits.[16]

While rejecting the influence of American casualties or day-to-day events, John R. Zaller and Adam J. Berinsky have cited "cues" from national leaders and the media as the most formative influence on U.S. public opinion. According to Berinsky, the vast majority of Americans lacked the "information needed to make cost/benefit calculations." Instead, the public listened to "trusted" political sources. This dynamic led the general public to follow the lead of national leaders and the media with whom citizens most closely identified and agreed. When elites were in general agreement on the need for war, the public tended to be

15. Mueller, "Trends in Popular Support for the Wars in Korea and Vietnam," 366 (quote), and *War, Presidents, and Public Opinion*, 57, 60, 62; Scott Sigmund Gartner and Gary M. Segura, "War, Casualties, and Public Opinion," *Journal of Conflict Resolution* 42 (June 1998): 279–98, and "Race, Casualties, and Opinion in the Vietnam War," *Journal of Politics* 62 (Feb. 2000): 138, 140.

16. Converse and Schuman, "'Silent Majorities' and the Vietnam War," 24 (war weariness); Schuman, "Two Sources of Antiwar Sentiment in America," 519 (pragmatic); Gartner and Segura, "War, Casualties, and Public Opinion," 280–81, 298; Harlan Hahn, "Correlates of Public Sentiment about War: Local Referenda on the Vietnam Issue," *American Political Science Review* 64 (Dec. 1970): 1186–98.

more supportive; when the elite consensus faltered, Americans became divided and responded along more politically partisan lines.[17]

These studies of public opinion provide instructive historical background and context for reading and contemplating southern responses to the Vietnam War, but quantitative analysis of polling data suffers from significant explanatory deficiencies. These shortcomings are evident in two of the most important questions posed to the American public. The first asked by Gallup from 1965 to 1971 inquired if sending "troops to fight in Vietnam" had been a "mistake." A "yes" response was generally interpreted as opposition to the war; however, supplemental polling in 1968 and 1969 revealed that nearly as many Americans who responded "yes" favored escalation of the war as those who endorsed U.S. withdrawal. A second question asked Americans whether they considered themselves a "dove" who favored a reduction of "our military effort in Vietnam" or a "hawk" who advocated a "step up" of U.S. military operations. As the misleading nature of the mistake question responses demonstrated, individual attitudes on the war were far more complex than the hawk-dove dichotomy could convey. Indeed, many Americans did not "cue on the issue" of hawk versus dove; instead, they tended to follow national leaders regarding the use of force.[18]

These two examples illustrate the limitations of mass surveys that asked only "closed-ended questions" requiring a "yes" or "no" response or an answer confined to a choice among several fixed options. Gallup and Harris surveys provided an excellent "understanding of the structure and distribution of public opinion on the war" but afforded "only the most indirect information on *why* people" supported or opposed the conflict or responded to how the U.S. government explained and the military conducted the war. Ascertaining "why" Americans answered polling queries as they did would have required "open-ended questions

17. John R. Zaller, *The Nature and Origins of Mass Opinion* (New York: Cambridge University Press, 1992), 275 (cues), 328; Adam J. Berinsky, "Assuming the Costs of War: Events, Elites, and American Public Support for Military Conflict," *Journal of Politics* 69 (Nov. 2007): 975 (other quotes), 977–78, 984, and *In Time of War: Understanding American Public Opinion from World War II to Iraq* (Chicago: University of Chicago Press, 2009), 4–9, 124–26, 202; Klarevas, "The 'Essential Domino' of Military Operations," 424–28; Michael Roskin, "From Pearl Harbor to Vietnam: Shifting Generational Paradigms and Foreign Policy," *Political Science Quarterly* 89 (Autumn 1974): 566.

18. Hazel Erskine, "The Polls: Is War a Mistake?" *Public Opinion Quarterly* 34 (Spring 1970): 134–50; Converse and Schuman, "'Silent Majorities' and the Vietnam War," 19–20; Lunch and Sperlich, "American Public Opinion and the Vietnam War," 24; Mueller, *War, Presidents, and Public Opinion,* 54–55, 106–8, 266–67 (cue).

that ask[ed] people to state in their own words why they" favored "a particular policy position." This collection of letters from diverse southerners helps provide answers to the vital "why" question as the letter writers elaborated on their assessments of and responses to the war.[19]

As southerners composed their letters in response to the Vietnam War, they did so against a backdrop of the South's long history of assessing U.S. foreign relations from a distinctly regional perspective. By 1963, when the United States moved toward military intervention in Vietnam, the South was unrivaled as the most coherent and self-conscious American region. For nearly two hundred years, southerners had employed a consistent set of regional assumptions and interests when evaluating and seeking to influence their nation's foreign policy.[20]

U.S. involvement in Vietnam was a key battleground and the nation's most disastrous military intervention during the broader Cold War—the post–World War II conflict between the United States and its allies and the Soviet Union

19. John P. Robinson and Solomon G. Jacobson, "American Public Opinion about Vietnam," in *Vietnam: Some Basic Issues and Alternatives*, ed. Walter Iscard (Cambridge, MA: Schenkman Publishing Co., 1969), 63; Schuman, "Two Sources of Antiwar Sentiment in America," 518.

20. This overview of the American South and U.S. foreign relations prior to the Vietnam War is drawn primarily from Joseph A. Fry, *Dixie Looks Abroad: The South and U.S. Foreign Relations, 1789–1973* (Baton Rouge: Louisiana State University Press, 2002), and *The American South and the Vietnam War: Belligerence, Protest, and Agony in Dixie* (Lexington: University Press of Kentucky, 2015), 1–49. For a discussion of the influence of domestic regionalism on U.S. foreign policy, see Joseph A. Fry, "Place Matters: Domestic Regionalism and the Formation of American Foreign Policy" *Diplomatic History* 36 (June 2012): 451–82, with commentaries and author's response, 483–514. For a comprehensive, analytical, and thoughtful assessment of the South's broader international involvement beyond foreign relations, see Tore C. Olsson, "The South in the World since 1865: A Review Essay," *Journal of Southern History* 87 (Feb. 2021): 67–108. For additional important work on the South and Vietnam, see John Ernst and Yvonne Baldwin, "The Not So Silent Minority: Louisville's Antiwar Movement,1966–1975," *Journal of Southern History* 73 (Feb. 2007): 105–42; Mark David Carson, "Beyond the Solid South: Southern Members of Congress and the Vietnam War," (Ph.D. dissertation, Louisiana State University, 2003); Lee Russell Dixon, "The Vietnam War and the U.S. South: Regional Perspectives on a National War," (Ph.D. dissertation, University of Manchester, 2015); Jessica F. Dirkson, "More Than a Conservative, Pro-War Narrative: Savannah, Georgia and the Vietnam War," (M.A. thesis, Georgia Southern University, 2018); Reynolds Stewart Kiefer, "Dissent in the Desert: The Vietnam Antiwar Movement in El Paso," (M.A. thesis, University of Texas, El Paso, 1997); Thomas N. Naquin, "The Big Muddy and the Bayou State," (M.A. thesis, University of Louisiana, Lafayette, 2005).

(USSR) and the People's Republic of China (PRC) and their backers. Although the United States, Great Britain, and the Soviet Union had been allies while defeating the Axis Powers in World War II, Soviet-American cooperation ended with the demise of their common enemies. During 1945–46, the USSR, led by Joseph Stalin and the Russian Communist Party, solidified control over Eastern Europe; probed militarily in Iran, Turkey, and Manchuria; and rejected international control of atomic power. A potential communist takeover in Greece followed in 1947 and the Soviet blockade hampered U.S.-British-French access to Berlin in 1948. The Cold War seemed to have become a worldwide struggle when Mao Zedong and the Chinese Communist Party (CCP) prevailed in the decades-long Chinese civil war in 1949 and communist North Korea invaded South Korea in 1950.

The United States responded to these developments by seeking to contain and at times to reverse communist expansion. The policy of containment began in Western Europe with the Truman Doctrine, which directed aid to noncommunist groups in Greece and Turkey (1947); the Marshall Plan, which sought to rebuild war-ravaged Western Europe (1947); and the North Atlantic Treaty Organization (NATO, 1949), a military alliance negotiated to block possible Soviet territorial expansion beyond Eastern Europe. With the CCP's victory in China and the onset of the Korean War, containment was expanded to Asia and beyond. This ambitious undertaking was codified in 1950 when President Harry S. Truman approved National Security Council document No. 68 (NSC-68), which asserted that the USSR sought to "impose its absolute authority in the rest of the world." All Soviet advances had to be rebuffed since "a defeat of free institutions anywhere" was equivalent to "a defeat everywhere." Given this assumption, all portions of the noncommunist world had to be defended. Following the CCP's victory and U.S. intervention in Korea, the application of NSC-68 seemingly rendered Vietnam and its defense as important as that of European nations, even though this small, poor nation had far less economic, strategic, or ideological significance.[21]

Conservative southerners, consistent with their denunciation of domestic social and racial reformers as communists, readily rallied to the cause of con-

---

21. For NSC-68, see George C. Herring, America's Longest War: The United States and Vietnam, 1950–1975 (New York: McGraw Hill, 2014), 21; John Lewis Gaddis, Strategies of Containment: A Critical Appraisal of American National Security Policy during the Cold War (New York: Oxford University Press, 2005), 89.

taining international communism. By the summer of 1947, 78 percent of Dixie's residents predicted another war within ten years, and southerners provided crucial congressional leadership and votes for the approval of the Truman Doctrine, Marshall Plan, and NATO. Although key southern senators such as J. William Fulbright (D/AR) and Harry Byrd Sr. (D/VA) supported these sweeping containment measures, they also worried about the costs. Byrd warned correctly that the Truman Doctrine funding for Greece and Turkey would lead to a "global policy . . . which will carry American dollars to many other foreign countries." Staunch anticommunism, the prospects of revived commerce with Western Europe, and partisan Democratic politics overcame southern fiscal reservations during the late 1940s, but the ever-mounting costs of Cold War U.S. foreign policies remained an important concern for Dixie's residents and representatives.[22]

The South's religious beliefs provided another strong motivation for opposing the USSR, PRC, and international communism. Billy Graham, a Southern Baptist minister from North Carolina and the era's foremost evangelist, spoke for fellow southerners when he portrayed the Cold War as a conflict with communism, which had "declared war against God, against Christ, against the Bible, and against all religion!" Since communism was "masterminded by Satan himself," religious southerners were obligated to join the battle between "Christian America and . . . atheistic Russia."[23]

As had been the case during the previous half-century, southerners garnered disproportionate economic benefits from national defense spending. The South made defense dollars a crucial and ongoing component of the region's economy during World War I. For example, six of fifteen new U.S. Army camps and thirteen of sixteen National Guard cantonments were built in the South; the Newport News Shipbuilding and Drydock Company became the nation's largest naval complex; and the war created unprecedented demand for southern cotton used

22. Ronald L. Heinemann, *Harry Byrd of Virginia* (Charlottesville: University of Virginia Press, 1996), 249; Jeff Woods, *Black Struggle, Red Scare: Segregation and Anticommunism in the South, 1948–1968* (Baton Rouge: Louisiana State University Press, 2004);Thomas Borstelman, "The Cold War and the American South," in *Local Consequences of the Global Cold War*, ed. Jeffrey A. Engel (Stanford, CA: Stanford University Press, 2008), 77–95; Fry, *Dixie Looks Abroad*, 226–30.

23. Stephen J. Whitfield, *The Culture of the Cold War* (Baltimore: Johns Hopkins University Press, 1996), 77, 80–81 (Graham); Fry, *American South and the Vietnam War*, 39; for religion and U.S. foreign relations, see Andrew Preston, *Sword of the Spirit, Shield of Faith: Religion in American War and Diplomacy* (New York: Knopf, 2012).

in textiles and explosives and for pine lumber needed for the construction of military camps and wooden ships.[24]

This trend continued during World War II. The war promised massive defense spending. In 1941 Congressman Pat Harrison (D/MS) envisioned "no limitation" on defense appropriations, save "what the job requires," and southerners aggressively pursued their portion of the national bounty. The South again received more than its share of military bases and training centers. Of the nation's 110 new camps, more than sixty were located in the South. When combined with the cost of refurbishing and expanding existing facilities, the spending on these bases totaled approximately 36 percent of funds dedicated to continental military installations. Huge outlays also built the Pentagon, then the world's largest office complex; expanded shipbuilding at Newport News-Norfolk, Charleston, and Houston; and developed aircraft plants in Dallas-Fort Worth and Marietta, Georgia.[25]

Over the twenty-five years after 1945, the South forged a "political alliance with the Pentagon" and continued to receive disproportionate regional benefits from national defense spending. Southerners such as Senators Russell and John C. Stennis (D/MS) and Congressmen Carl Vinson (D/GA) and L. Mendel Rivers (D/SC) consistently chaired the Senate and House Armed Services Committees and other key defense-related subcommittees. From these positions, they safeguarded Department of Defense (DOD) funding. In return, "fortress Dixie" became home to seven of the nation's ten largest defense contractors. By 1968, one of fourteen southerners worked directly for the Pentagon or indirectly via a DOD contractor. In 1971 40 percent of U.S.-assigned military personnel were stationed in the South, and southern companies produced 52 percent of DOD-contracted ships, 46 percent of its airframes, and 42 percent of its petroleum products.[26]

Several conspicuous examples typified these trends. The Savannah River Plant

24. Fry, *Dixie Looks Abroad*, 151–52, and *American South and the Vietnam War*, 28.

25. Martha H. Swain, *Pat Harrison: The New Deal Years* (Jackson: University of Mississippi Press, 1978), 243 (Harrison); Fry, *American South and the Vietnam War*, 35–36, and *Dixie Looks Abroad*, 209–14.

26. Bruce J. Schulman, *From Cotton Belt to Sunbelt: Federal Policy, Economic Development, and the Transformation of the South, 1938–1980* (New York: Oxford University Press, 1991), 142 (fortress Dixie), 145 (political alliance); David L. Carlton, "The American South and the U.S. Defense Economy: A Historical View," in *The South, the Nation, and the World: Perspectives on Southern Economic Development,* ed. David L. Carlton and Peter A. Coclanis (Charlottesville: University of Virginia Press, 2003), 151–62; Fry, *American South and the Vietnam War*, 40, 68–71.

for processing plutonium occupied parts of three counties in South Carolina, was built in 1951–52 by nearly fifty thousand workers, and was the largest U.S. construction project up to that time. In 1958 Lockheed-Georgia operated in 55 of the state's 159 counties and was the largest industrial corporation in the Southeast. Nor was it a coincidence that the National Aeronautics and Space Administration's Manned Spaceflight Center was located in Houston, or that NASA's launch site was at Cape Canaveral, Florida, and other installations were placed in New Orleans; Huntsville, Alabama; and Bay Saint Louis, Mississippi.[27]

The South's alliance with the Pentagon was not based solely on the region's dependence on defense spending. Southern support for America's Cold War military also derived from the region's longstanding defense of personal and national honor, vocal patriotism, and devotion to the warrior ethic. Heightened southern concern for personal and regional honor had been a central motivation in the South's secession from the Union in 1861 and its willingness to fight the disastrous Civil War. Four decades later, the region's devotion to honor, manhood, and patriotism were evident when the region rallied to the cause during the war with Spain and the suppression of Filipino insurgents. Military campaigns in Cuba and the Philippines provided southerners the opportunity to follow in the martial steps of their Confederate forebears and demonstrate their patriotic allegiance to the restored Union. The *Lynchburg [VA] News* declared, "The people of the South . . . [are] as loyal to the flag of the Union as the people of Massachusetts or Illinois," and in case of war, "the men of the South would rush to the defense of the country with as much promptness and enthusiasm as the men of any other section." And, the South readily answered President Woodrow Wilson's call to defend "our flag, our uniform and our national honor" as he dispatched troops to Mexico and the Caribbean and, most importantly, to Europe in World War I.[28]

---

27. Kari Frederickson, *Cold War Dixie: Militarization and Modernization in the American South* (Athens: University of Georgia Press, 2013); Fry, *Dixie Looks Abroad*, 237–40, and *American South and the Vietnam War*, 41.

28. Matthew Karp, *This Vast Southern Empire: Slaveholders at the Helm of American Foreign Policy* (Cambridge, MA: Harvard University Press, 2016), 173–250; Richard E. Wood, "The South and Reunion, 1898," *Historian* 31 (May 1969): 416 (*Lynchburg News*); Bertram Wyatt-Brown, "The Ethic of Honor in National Crises: The Civil War, Vietnam, Iraq, and the Southern Factor," *Journal of the Historical Society* 5 (2005): 431–60; Anthony Gaughan, "Woodrow Wilson and the Rise of Militant Interventionism in the South," *Journal of Southern History* 65 (Nov. 1999): 785–86 (Wilson); Tennant S. McWilliams, *The New South Faces the World: Foreign Affairs and the Southern Sense of Self* (Baton Rouge: Louisiana State University Press, 1988); 16–67; Fry, *Dixie Looks Abroad*, 111–74.

Echoing these themes, Senator Russell lectured a midwestern colleague in 1955 that he would "be more military minded too if Sherman" had devastated North Dakota; and nine years later the Georgia senator emphasized that when "national honor [was] at stake," the United States could only command "the respect of other nations, or . . . maintain its self-respect" by responding to "aggressive acts" with "calculated retaliation." Consistent with these values and assumptions, the majority of southerners expressed great respect for the military and subscribed to the axiom that military strength was the best guarantor of peace.[29]

This southern commitment to a strong military was evident in the region's ambivalent response to arms control treaties during the 1960s and 1970s. Southern senators were the strongest opponents of the Limited [Nuclear] Test Ban Treaty of 1963 and the 1968 Nuclear Nonproliferation Treaty and the strongest supporters of Anti-Ballistic Missile projects under both Presidents Johnson and Nixon. Distrustful of peaceful coexistence with the Soviets and Chinese, southerners cautioned against "unilateral disarmament" in a "world of international banditry." No "good fairy" on a "white horse" would "bring disarmament and peace with a wave of her magic wand." Far better to possess a robust military.[30]

The South's support for U.S. military interventions abroad after 1950 further illustrated the region's promilitary stance and inclination to settle international disputes through the use of force rather than diplomacy. The most significant of these pre-Vietnam interventions occurred in June 1950 when President Harry Truman dispatched U.S. troops to confront the North Korean invasion of South Korea. After the People's Republic of China intervened on the side of North Korea, Truman fought a limited war to restore the prewar boundary between the two Koreas at the 38th parallel. More than other Americans, southerners objected to this limited objective and restrained use of U.S. force and called instead for the pursuit of total victory through attacks north of the parallel, air and naval assaults on China, and even the use of nuclear weapons. Senator Stennis was especially outspoken in demanding that Truman strike "the enemy with everything we have until [our] terms are met." Despite this extreme rhetoric, Senators Stennis, Russell, and Byrd later pointed to U.S. frustrations

---

29. Gilbert C. Fite, *Richard B. Russell, Jr.* (Chapel Hill: University of North Carolina Press, 1991), 353 (Sherman); Fry, *American South and the Vietnam War,* 85 (self-respect).

30. Fry, *American South and the Vietnam War,* 44–45 (quote), and *Dixie Looks Abroad,* 240–43.

in Korea as a caution against any subsequent ground wars in Asia—including Vietnam.[31]

These and other southerners voiced this caution as the United States moved toward war in Vietnam from 1954 through 1964 but were far less restrained regarding other parts of the world, especially the Western Hemisphere. In 1954 southerners supported President Dwight D. Eisenhower's use of the CIA to over-throw a left-leaning government in Guatemala; the South was more willing than other American regions to confront the Soviet Union over access to Berlin in 1960; and southerners rallied behind President John F. Kennedy's abortive attempt to oust Fidel Castro with the Bay of Pigs invasion in 1961 and President Lyndon B. Johnson's use of U.S. and Organization of America States forces to prevent an alleged communist from gaining power in the Dominican Republic in 1965.[32]

Racial assumptions also shaped the South's foreign policy perspective. Put bluntly, the great majority of white southerners continued to consider nonwhites, whether they lived in the American South, Latin America, Africa, or Asia, in-ferior. This fundamental assumption led prominent southern segregationists to oppose Hawaii's admission as a state in 1959. It was also apparent in the South's increased disenchantment with the United Nations (UN) as its membership changed from one dominated by North American and European nations to one in which Africans and Asians were in the majority. The South's opposition to the Immigration Act of 1965 further illustrated the region's racial views. This law distressed southerners by revising the U.S. immigration system that dated from the 1920s, blatantly favored Western Europeans, and virtually excluded Asians.[33]

The South's racial beliefs were also central to the region's bitter opposition to the domestic Civil Rights Movement and African American demands for more equal political, social, educational, and economic treatment. This opposition demonstrated that maintaining white dominance at home took precedence over Cold War foreign policies. Racial prejudice and control trumped containing com-munism abroad. U.S. presidents from Truman through Johnson recognized that America's racial discrimination and violence against African Americans severely

31. Michael S. Downs, "A Matter of Conscience: John C. Stennis and the Vietnam War," (Ph.D. dissertation, Mississippi State University, 1989), 15 (Stennis); Fry, *Dixie Looks Abroad,* 231–36, and *American South and the Vietnam War,* 54–57.

32. Fry, *Dixie Looks Abroad,* 233–37.

33. Fry, *Dixie Looks Abroad,* 251, 255, and *American South and the Vietnam War,* 42–43.

compromised the nation's position in the Cold War world. From 1945 into the 1960s, Soviet officials delighted in charging the United States with hypocrisy. How, they asked, could Americans condemn the USSR's oppression of its citizens and persons in Eastern Europe while condoning the suppression of Blacks in the South? Was it not hypocritical for "white faced but black-souled gentlemen [to] commit their dark deeds in Arkansas, Alabama, and other Southern states, and then . . . put on white gloves and mount the rostrum in the UN General Assembly and hold forth about freedom and democracy?" In 1964 Secretary of State Dean Rusk acknowledged this glaring U.S. inconsistency when he told a Senate committee led by archsegregationist Strom Thurmond of South Carolina, "The biggest single burden we carry on our backs in our foreign relations in the 1960s is the problem of racial discrimination."[34]

Although southerners expressed a strong commitment to containing Soviet and Chinese communism, they deemed that principal component of Cold War foreign policy secondary to thwarting the domestic Civil Rights Movement. Repulsing changes to "the social order of the South" took precedence over combating international communism. In 1958 Senator Herman E. Talmadge (D/GA) likened President Eisenhower's deployment of U.S. troops to safeguard Black students entering a Little Rock, Arkansas, high school to the USSR's forceful suppression of protestors seeking national independence in Hungary. Like the Soviets, the U.S. president was using "tanks and troops . . . to destroy" local "sovereignty"—this time in "the state of Arkansas." Alabama governor George Wallace was equally dismissive of international repercussions when he decried the Civil Rights Movement as a communist plot, asserted that the Civil Rights Act of 1964 had been lifted directly from *The Communist Manifesto,* and charged that Reverend Martin Luther King Jr. and his "procommunist friends and associates" had maintained that "Castro was a 'good Democratic soul,' that Mao Tse-tung was only an 'Agrarian Reformer.'"[35]

Given this persistent white southern disregard for the welfare and basic rights

---

34. Michael L. Krenn, "'Unfinished Business': Segregation and U.S. Diplomacy at the 1958 World's Fair," *Diplomatic History* 20 (Fall 1999): 593 (black-souled); Paul G. Lauren, *Power and Prejudice: The Politics and Diplomacy of Racial Discrimination* (Boulder, CO: Westview Press, 1996), 244 (Rusk).

35. Mary L. Dudziak, "The Little Rock Crisis and Foreign Affairs: Race, Resistance, and the Image of American Democracy," *Southern California Law Review* 70 (Sept. 1997): 1685 ("social order" and Talmadge); Dan T. Carter, *The Politics of Rage: George Wallace, the Origins of the New Conservatism, and the Transformation of American Politics* (Baton Rouge: Louisiana State University Press, 1995), 161 (Wallace).

of Blacks, it is not surprising that African Americans adopted different foreign policy priorities than those of their white neighbors. From the turn of the twentieth century prominent Black leaders and editors consistently highlighted the same inconsistency and hypocrisy that the Soviets emphasized in their Cold War propaganda. While opposing territorial expansion following the 1898 war with Spain, Booker T. Washington had Black segregation, disfranchisement, and lynching in mind when he questioned whether the U.S. government could do "for the millions of dark-skinned races . . . in Cuba, Porto Rico, Hawaii and the Philippine Islands that which it had not been able to do for nearly 10,000,000 negroes and Indians" already living under American jurisdiction. James Weldon Johnson voiced similar concerns during World War I when he gave priority to domestic racial conditions over foreign involvements and castigated the United States for expressing "horror at German 'atrocities'" while ignoring "the wholesale murder of American citizens on American soil by bloodthirsty American mobs."[36]

Southern Blacks voiced comparable reservations following World War II and were decidedly less committed than whites to anticommunist, interventionist foreign policies. Consistent with earlier priorities, African Americans considered domestic reform far more important than containing communism abroad. In 1947 the National Association for the Advancement of Colored People proclaimed, "It's not Russia that threatens the United States so much as Mississippi; not Stalin and Molotov but [U.S Senators Theodore G.] Bilbo and [John E.] Rankin." Reverend Martin Luther King Jr. later asserted that the U.S. military interventions applauded by southern whites derived from "racist decision making" since American leaders had no "respect [for] anyone who is not white." When looking abroad, Blacks frequently identified with other nonwhites who were being held as colonial subjects by anticommunist U.S. allies in Europe such as Britain, France, or Portugal.[37]

36. Willard B. Gatewood Jr., *Black Americans and the White Man's Burden, 1898–1903* (Urbana: University of Illinois Press, 1973), 190 (Washington); Jonathan S. Rosenberg, *How Far the Promised Land? World Affairs and the American Civil Rights Movement from the First World War to Vietnam* (Princeton: Princeton University Press, 2006), 35 (Johnson).

37. Thomas Borstelmann, *The Cold War and the Color Line: American Race Relations in the Global Arena* (Cambridge, MA: Harvard University Press, 2001), 77 (NAACP); Brenda Gayle Plummer, *Rising Wind: Black Americans and U.S. Foreign Relations, 1935–1960* (Chapel Hill: University of North Carolina Press, 1996), 296, 305, and *In Search of Power: African Americans in the Era of Decolonization* (New York: Cambridge University Press, 2012); James H. Cone, "Martin Luther King Jr. and the Third World," *Journal of American History* 74 (Sept. 1987): 462.

Therefore, as the United States approached war in Vietnam in the early and mid-1960s, southerners wrote their letters from the historical context of the South's well-established practice of assessing U.S. foreign relations from a distinctly regional perspective. This majority, white southern outlook featured great concern for personal and national honor; demonstrative patriotism; devotion to the warrior ethic; and great respect for military service and the military as an institution. The region's functional alliance with the DOD and vital economic gains from national defense spending reinforced these ideological traits and southern preferences for a strong military and forceful solutions for international problems. The section's belief in evangelical Christianity often cast U.S. foreign relations goals as God's will and American adversaries, particularly communists, as tools of the devil. The South's political conservatism furthered strengthened the region's commitment to containing communism as a threat to U.S. representative government and capitalism. While this anticommunist impulse included a preference for unrestricted, frequently unilateral, military interventions in pursuit of decisive victories, it did not include a willingness to reform southern racial practices as a means of enhancing America's international standing. The same assumption of nonwhite inferiority that fueled domestic racial repression explained the South's belief that alleged inferiors should not be allowed a major voice in the UN, granted equal immigration rights, or viewed as capable of governing their own countries.

White racial prejudices and discrimination against African Americans goes far toward explaining why Black southerners were much more focused on domestic reform and equality than on pursuing diplomatic and military objective abroad. Beginning with the Spanish-Cuban-American War of 1898, the South's Black leaders repeatedly cited the hypocrisy in the United States' stated devotion to furthering freedom and democracy abroad while simultaneously oppressing minorities at home. Given their primarily domestic focus and identification with people of color abroad, who were often seeking to escape European colonial control, African Americans were less rigidly anticommunist and less supportive of U.S. military interventions in Latin America, Africa, or Asia.

As U.S. intervention in Vietnam evolved and solidified in the twenty-five years after World War II, southerners, like other Americans, responded to the urging of national leaders to contain international communism, to defend America's strategic and economic interests in Southeast Asia, to uphold U.S. honor and credibility, to exhibit patriotism and national unity, and to repulse atheistic attacks upon Christianity.

With these foreign policy interests at stake, U.S. involvement in Vietnam dated from the mid-1940s. As World War II ended, France, which had held this small country as a colony from the 1880s until 1941when Japan invaded, sought to reestablish imperial control. French efforts were frustrated and ultimately defeated by Ho Chi Minh and his followers, known as the Vietminh. Ho and the Vietminh were Vietnamese nationalists who had sought independence from France since at least the 1930s, fought the Japanese during World War II, and challenged the French again after Japan's defeat. Ho proclaimed the independent Democratic Republic of Vietnam (DRV) in September 1945. Given the United States' revolutionary past and repeated declarations in the twentieth century favoring national self-determination, Vietnamese independence from France appeared to align with longstanding U.S. ideological and foreign policy positions.[38]

Although the Vietminh had aided U.S. military operations against the Japanese during World War II and President Franklin D. Roosevelt had criticized France's imperial record in Southeast Asia, the emerging Cold War led the United States to side with France. Ho was not just a nationalist fighting for independence from France; he was also a devoted communist with well-established ties to the Soviet Union and to Mao Zedong, the leader of the Chinese Communist Party. As the United States installed containment in Europe and the Middle East, Roosevelt's successor, Harry Truman opted to aid France, an anticommunist ally in Europe. Ensuring French participation in the Marshall Plan and NATO and blocking Soviet expansion into Western Europe took precedence over supporting Ho and his band of guerrilla fighters. When Mao and the CCP won the Chinese civil war in 1949 and North Korea, with Chinese and Soviet backing, attacked noncommunist South Korea in 1950, Ho and the Vietminh appeared to be another adversary in the worldwide Cold War.

During the 1950s, the United States solidified its opposition to Ho and the Vietminh and helped transform what essentially had been a local war against French colonial domination into an increasingly important part of the larger international Cold War. In 1950 Truman endorsed NSC-68, which committed the United States to a zero-sum dynamic that defined a communist victory anywhere, including Vietnam, as a U.S. defeat. The same year, the United States extended diplomatic recognition to the Vietnamese government of Bao Dai, a noncommu-

---

38. This overview of U.S. involvement in Vietnam is based on Herring, *America's Longest War;* John Prados, *Vietnam: The History of an Unwinnable War, 1945–1975* (Lawrence: University Press of Kansas, 2009); Mark Atwood Lawrence, *The Vietnam War: A Concise International History* (New York: Oxford University Press, 2008).

nist French puppet. By 1953, the United States was paying 40 percent of French war costs in Vietnam. The following year President Dwight D. Eisenhower cited the "falling domino" principle as the rationale for U.S. involvement. The domino theory, on which the United States had been acting since at least 1947, held that a communist victory in Vietnam could lead to the loss of neighboring Southeast Asian countries and even trigger similar loses across the world.[39]

Neither a decade of French military efforts nor significant U.S. aid proved effective. Ho and the Vietminh won the First Indochina War on May 7, 1954, by defeating the French in the fifty-five-day battle of Dien Bien Phu. Although the Eisenhower administration was alarmed by the French loss and considered military intervention to rescue its NATO ally, the president decided against either the deployment of U.S. ground troops or an airstrike against Vietminh forces. The Vietminh's victory was codified at the Geneva Convention that met from April 26 through July 20, 1954. The Geneva Agreements called for the temporary division of Vietnam at the 17th parallel with Ho and the Vietminh controlling the DRV in the North and the French and their Vietnamese successors ruling the South. Elections were to be held in 1956 to unite the country into one nation. In the interim, neither the DRV nor those overseeing South Vietnam were to join military alliances. Despite participating in the Geneva talks, the United States refused to sign the final accords. Instead, the Eisenhower administration pledged not to "disturb" the agreements through force and endorsed the use of "free elections supervised by the United Nations" to decide the future government of a united Vietnam.[40]

The United States failed to honor either of these pledges. Over the second half of the 1950s, the Eisenhower administration supported Ngo Dinh Diem, the leader of the Republic of Vietnam (GVN), as a noncommunist alternative to Ho and the DRV. The United States offered no objection when Diem refused to participate in the election to reunite the country, and Eisenhower violated the spirit of the Geneva accords by negotiating the Southeast Asia Treaty Organization (SEATO). A military alliance, SEATO was designed to preclude communist expansion in Southeast Asia as NATO had done in Europe. But unlike NATO, this alliance had no standing army, and the United States was not obligated to come to the aid of other members facing aggressive attacks. Since South Vietnam

---

39. www.speeches--usa.com/Transcripts/dwight_eisenhower-domino.html, accessed January 24, 2021.

40. Prados, *Vietnam*, 37.

was not a member, the United States attempted to circumvent this omission by enrolling the Saigon government as a "protocol" state. While SEATO was designed to prevent the spread of communism in the region, the United States had no treaty obligations to intervene militarily in Vietnam. By reinforcing Diem's refusal to hold elections and organizing SEATO, the United States had intentionally disturbed the Geneva Agreements.

During Eisenhower's second term, the United States also sought to strengthen Diem by financing approximately 80 percent of the GVN's expenses with $2 billion in economic and military aid. In early 1956 the United States established a Military Assistance and Advisory Group to assist and train the South Vietnamese Army (ARVN), and by the end of the decade more than 1,500 Americans were in Vietnam in various civilian and military capacities. Much of this support went toward combating a growing insurgency in rural South Vietnam. Vietminh cadre who had remained in the South following the Geneva Conference initiated an armed insurrection against the GVN after 1956 when the promised elections were not held. Ho and the DRV endorsed the struggle and oversaw the formation in 1960 of the National Liberation Front (NLF), a communist-directed and controlled organization open to all Diem opponents. By the time President John F. Kennedy took office in January 1960, the NLF (derisively labeled the Vietcong (VC) or "Vietnam Communists" by the GVN) numbered ten thousand guerrilla fighters and controlled much of the Mekong Delta.

Acting on the Cold War assumptions embedded in NSC-68 and the domino theory, Kennedy; his Secretary of Defense, Robert S. McNamara; and his Secretary of State, Dean Rusk sustained and escalated the U.S. presence in Vietnam. The number of U.S. military personnel increased from 685 in January 1961 to more than fifteen thousand at the time of Kennedy's assassination in November 1963. Although technically advisors, American ground troops were often involved in combat and U.S. pilots periodically flew the planes assigned to Vietnamese students on missions attacking the Vietcong. The U.S. Military Assistance and Advisory Group was upgraded to the Military Assistance Command Vietnam (MACV), and the United States introduced defoliants (such as Agent Orange) and helicopters to the war. None of these actions thwarted the NLF's steady growth, which imperiled the Diem government. When the Saigon government proved incapable of subduing the Vietcong or responding to the antiwar protests of Buddhist monks in the South Vietnamese cities, the Kennedy administration gave indirect permission to a clique of South Vietnamese generals who overthrew the government on November 1, 1963. Although Kennedy had sanctioned the coup, he had not endorsed the subsequent murder of Diem and his brother Ngo Dinh Nhu. After Kennedy's assassination three weeks later, Lyndon B. Johnson inherited South Vietnam's surging rural insurgency, urban discontent, and governmental chaos.

Faced with the real possibility of a North Vietnamese/NLF takeover of South Vietnam, Johnson, who retained McNamara and Rusk in his cabinet, committed the United States to war and vastly escalated American involvement. Like his predecessors, the new president and his key advisors subscribed to the domino theory, the NSC-68 tenet of a worldwide communist threat, and the importance of defending U.S. credibility as an effective and dependable ally of noncommunist nations and opponent of Soviet and Chinese expansion. President Johnson believed that his personal honor and manhood were on trial and that the failure to contain communism in Southeast Asia would devastate his political future and imperil his domestic reform agenda.

Johnson secured congressional authorization for a massive U.S. intervention in Vietnam by manipulating the Gulf of Tonkin Affair. On August 2, 1964, a North Vietnamese PT boat fired on the *USS Maddox,* an American destroyer sailing along the coast of North Vietnam in the South China Sea. Citing this attack and a second alleged one on August 4, Johnson, Rusk, and McNamara persuaded the Senate to pass the Gulf of Tonkin Resolution by a vote of 99–2. Subsequent evidence revealed that the second attack did not occur; moreover, the Johnson administration had misled Congress regarding covert U.S. and South Vietnamese operations that likely provoked the August 2 attacks. This crucial resolution authorized Johnson to take "all necessary measures to repel any armed attack against the forces of the United States" and "all necessary steps, including the use of armed force, to assist any member or protocol state [South Vietnam]" of SEATO that requested aid. The president had secured a functional proxy for a formal declaration of war—in essence a blank check for future Vietnam decisions.[41]

Johnson drew on this resolution in February 1965 to initiate the Rolling Thunder bombing campaign against North Vietnam. This operation ended in October 1968 after the United States had dropped 643,000 tons of bombs on the North. Over the entire span of the U.S. military intervention in Vietnam (1962–75), the United States employed more than 7 million tons of bombs in North and South Vietnam, Cambodia, and Laos. The 4 million tons directed at targets in South Vietnam were decisively greater than the 1 million used against the North, and these bombing totals far exceeded U.S. bombing in all theaters

---

41. Fry, *American South and the Vietnam War,* 84 (quotes).

of World War II. In addition to the 500- and 750-pound bombs carried by B-52s, the U.S. bombing arsenal included napalm (jellied gasoline that stuck to targets, including humans) and antipersonnel cluster bombs utilized to destroy enemy soldiers with steel pellets and fiberglass darts. Bombing and long-range artillery attacks by the United States were primarily responsible for the estimated death of as many as 1.1 million Vietcong and North Vietnamese fighters and more than one million civilians in the two countries. Rolling Thunder also led to the loss of 950 U.S. aircraft and many captured pilots who were held as POWs in Hanoi. This unprecedented use of sophisticated technological equipment against a small, underdeveloped country and the resulting death and destruction on all sides was an important motivator of the American antiwar movement.

Beginning in March 1965, Johnson also dispatched U.S. ground troops to Vietnam. By the end of the year, 200,000 American soldiers were assigned to Vietnam. This massive American presence had increased to approximately 385,000 as 1966 ended and grew to more than 530,000 by the time Johnson left office in January 1969. Along with this growing deployment came a steadily increasing number of American deaths: 216 in 1964, 1,928 in 1965, 6,350 in 1966, 11,363 in 1967, and 16,899 in 1968.

Under the direction of USA General William C. Westmoreland, the American commander, U.S. soldiers implemented the "search and destroy" strategy. Like bombing and artillery fire, this strategy embodied the "American way of war"— an approach that sought to employ superior technology to minimize American casualties. Small units of U.S. ground troops were sent to "find, fix, and finish" the Vietcong or North Vietnamese Army (NVA). In reality American ground troops sought to find and fix. Once the enemy had been located, bombing and artillery would be used for the finish. By mid-1967, search and destroy, which essentially offered U.S. soldiers as bait to entice the enemy into battle, comprised 86 percent of American ground operations.[42]

Even with the use of this massive fire power and the deployment of hundreds of thousands of U.S. military personnel, the Johnson administration "limited" its

---

42. For the term "American way of war," see Russell F. Weigley, *The American Way of War* (Bloomington: Indiana University Press, 1973); for its application in Vietnam, see James William Gibson, *The Perfect War: Technowar in Vietnam* (Boston: Atlantic Monthly Press, 1986); Nick Turse, *Kill Anything That Moves: The Real American War in Vietnam* (New York: Metropolitan Books, 2013), 51 (find, fix, and finish); and Adrian R. Lewis, *The American Culture of War: The History of U.S. Military Force from World War II to Operation Enduring Freedom* (2d. ed., New York: Routledge, 2012), 2, 3, 259.

prosecution of the war in several important ways. The president's and his advisors' overall strategy was designed to inflict a level of pain sufficient to force North Vietnam and the NLF to abandon their campaign to defeat South Vietnam and unite the country under communist rule. Johnson and Rusk emphasized that the United States sought to preserve an independent, noncommunist South Vietnam but not to overthrow North Vietnam's communist government or eradicate its national sovereignty.

Rather than seeking to apply an immediate knockout blow with bombing, Johnson and McNamara gradually escalated the intensity but refused to target Hanoi and Haiphong, North Vietnam's two most populous cities; restricted operations near the Chinese border; and avoided bombing or mining Haiphong harbor, the entry point for critical, imported war materiel. The administration also declined to order U.S. ground troops into North Vietnam or to invade neighboring Cambodia or Laos, which the Vietcong and NVA periodically used as sanctuaries from the battle in South Vietnam. On the U.S. domestic front, Johnson never asked Congress for an official declaration of war and declined to activate the National Guard or reserves.

Both international and domestic considerations drove Johnson's limited war strategy. The administration feared that overly aggressive bombing or an invasion of North Vietnam could draw China or the Soviet Union into the war and even provoke a nuclear conflict. In July 1965 the president pondered, "What will be enough and not too much?" What application of U.S. force would safeguard South Vietnam without leading to a bigger war? He never found the answer. Johnson feared an all-out war and the ensuing debate on the home front would block the passage of his Great Society reform agenda—especially civil rights legislation, Medicare, and antipoverty measures. Asking Congress for a declaration of war and activating the Guard and reserves could further that debate, divert attention from domestic legislation, and provide conservative opponents arguments for giving the war fiscal priority over domestic projects.[43]

On January 30, 1968, as Johnson began his final year in office, the Vietcong and NVA attacked every major urban area and numerous key military installations in South Vietnam. Although the Tet Offensive failed to capture and retain control of any major South Vietnamese city, the breadth of the offensive, including the siege of the U.S. embassy in Saigon, graphically revealed that the American air and ground strategies had failed. Both the Vietcong and NVA remained

43. Fry, *American South and the Vietnam War*, 99 (enough).

formidable adversaries with a robust nationalist and ideological dedication to the pursuit of an independent, united Vietnam.

Bombing had reinforced, rather than diminished this zeal in both North and South Vietnam. American attacks had destroyed the North's industrial capacity and much of its military equipment, but aid from the Soviet Union and China had compensated for these losses. Russia provided materiel ranging from rifles to fighter planes, surface-to-air antiaircraft missiles, and tanks. Bombing also failed to stop the flow of material into North Vietnam and from the North into South Vietnam along a complex of jungle paths known as the Ho Chi Minh Trail. China deployed approximately 320,000 troops to North Vietnam where they did not engage in combat but freed up North Vietnamese soldiers by helping to rebuild and maintain the North's transportation and defense infrastructure.

The search and destroy ground strategy was no more successful in forcing the enemy to yield to U.S. pressure. American soldiers had great difficulty distinguishing the Vietcong guerrilla fighters from South Vietnamese villagers, all of whom wore the same peasant garb. Moreover, the Vietcong maintained a viable, covert political and intelligence presence throughout South Vietnam. They used this intelligence, together with the noise from U.S. soldiers and equipment and the predictable patrolling patterns of American soldiers and flight patterns of American helicopters, to maintain the combat initiative and to avoid most large battles. Indeed, the Pentagon found that at least 75 percent of the firefights were initiated at the time and locations chosen by the enemy. By determining when to engage and by fighting a much simpler, less technologically dependent war in the South, the Vietcong and NVA soldiers survived the massive onslaught of U.S. power.

In April 1969, soon after Richard M. Nixon began his presidency, U.S. troop strength in Vietnam reached its peak of 543,000. Since national disillusionment with the war had risen steadily after mid-1967 and the new president had campaigned on a purposefully vague plan to end the war honorably, Nixon confronted the daunting task of both winding down and winning the conflict. Like his predecessors, Nixon and his Secretary of State, Henry Kissinger, believed that U.S. credibility and international standing were on the line in Vietnam. They also shared the Johnson administration's fundamental assumption that the application of superior U.S. force and technology would compel the DRV and NLF to bow to U.S. dictates.

Expecting to prevail where Eisenhower, Kennedy, and Johnson had failed, Nixon adopted three interlocking tactics: Vietnamization, linkage, and the "madman" theory. Vietnamization, or the progressive shifting of responsibility for the war from the United States to the South Vietnam, was meant to gain time to implement the other two strategies. The United States' troop strength was reduced to 475,200 by the end of 1969; to 334,000 by the close of 1970; to 156,800 by December 31, 1971; and to approximately 24,000 as the country negotiated the end of American involvement in December 1972 and January 1973. The troop drawdown dramatically cut the number of American deaths from 11,780 in 1969 to 6,173 in 1970, 2,414 in 1971, and 759 in 1972. A brilliant domestic political strategy, Vietnamization did provide Nixon time and room for maneuver by steadily reducing American casualties and by seeming to respond to the nation's desire to escape the unpopular war. There was no comparable progress in Vietnam, where South Vietnam's military and political capacity fell far short of compensating for U.S. withdrawal. By mid-1972, both Washington and Hanoi recognized this deficiency.

Through linkage, Nixon and Kissinger sought to tie big power relations to the war by pressing China and the Soviet Union to help force North Vietnam and the NLF to end the conflict. By 1972, Nixon and Kissinger achieved a stunning diplomatic breakthrough with China, made progress with the USSR, and moved toward détente and saner relations with both major adversaries. But neither of these nations was willing to put decisive pressure on North Vietnam, and the improvement of relations with China and Russia called into question the reality of a worldwide communist threat, the validity of the domino theory, and the necessity of continued war against communists in Vietnam.

When neither Vietnamization nor linkage achieved an honorable peace, Nixon was left with the madman theory. He had coined this term to describe his desire to be seen by the Vietnamese adversaries as unpredictable and willing to use greater force than Johnson—to "do *anything*"—perhaps even use nuclear weapons to win the war. Nixon initiated this approach in the spring of 1969 by ordering the secret bombing of communist sanctuaries and supply routes in Cambodia. During the ensuing summer, he threatened Hanoi with the bombing of major population centers, the blockading of Haiphong, and even the potential employment of tactical nuclear weapons. The stunning, nationwide Vietnam Moratorium Day antiwar protests on October 15, 1969, have been credited with dissuading Nixon from going forward with these threats.[44]

These protests did not prompt the president to scrap this third portion of his effort to achieve victory. The following spring, he sent U.S. troops on a two-month

44. Joseph DiMona, *The Ends of Power* (New York: Times Books, 1978), 83 (quote); Fry, *American South and the Vietnam War*, 254.

incursion into Cambodia seeking to eliminate an enemy command center, sanc-tuaries, and supply depots. In February 1971 the Nixon administration directed the joint U.S.-South Vietnamese invasion of Laos. No American ground troops were involved, but the United States provided vital air and artillery support for the ARVN forces. When none of these operations deterred the NVA or Vietcong, Nixon doubled down in 1972. He responded to North Vietnam's 120,000-troop invasion of South Vietnam with the Linebacker I bombing campaign. From May through October, the United States dropped approximately 150,000 tons of bombs, or about one-quarter of the three years of tonnage used in Rolling Thunder. The president also ordered the mining of Haiphong harbor and a naval blockade of North Vietnam. These actions helped lead to negotiations with Hanoi and the NLF. When those talks stalled in November, Nixon unleashed Linebacker II from December 18 to 29, 1972, against the Hanoi-Haiphong area. The 20,000 tons of ordinance consumed in those twelve days exceeded the tonnage employed by the Nixon administration from 1969–1971.

The continued North Vietnamese refusal to capitulate marked Nixon's final failure to impose American will on the enemy. The subsequent "peace" settlement of January 1973 embodied the U.S. loss of the Vietnam War. More than 58,000 Americans had died, but little honor accompanied an agreement that granted political legitimacy to the NLF, now called the Peoples' Revolutionary Govern-ment, or allowed 150,000 North Vietnamese troops to remain in the South below the 17th parallel. In return for halting the bombing and agreeing to withdraw its remaining troops from South Vietnam, the United States secured the release of its 591 POWs being held in Hanoi. Nor was there peace, as the fighting between South Vietnam and its DRV and NLF adversaries continued until NVA troops overran Saigon in April 1975 and the United States evacuated its embassy in an inglorious and embarrassing fashion.

Before turning to these letters from the southern home front, three explanatory issues must be addressed: First, a working definition of the American South; second, a discussion of how the southerners who authored these letters will be identified; and third, an explanation of my assumptions and methodologies in editing the letters.

Some scholars have objected to the concept of a historically distinctive or exceptional South. While acknowledging that the South is obviously part of the United States and that regional and national histories, values, and cultures have converged and overlapped, I remain convinced that the South has been the nation's most self-conscious, coherent, and persistent region. Much of the

South's sense of self derived from its white population's unwavering belief in its superiority, slavery, and segregation and the "siege mentality" that accompanied the defense of this conviction and these institutions. The region's disproportionate concern for honor and manhood, proclivity for violence, and pursuit of personal and sectional equality and independence reinforced this mentality, as did the devastating loss in the Civil War and the northern-led national government's attempt to force social, political, and economic change in the South during Reconstruction. Southern dependence on staple agriculture and low-wage, first-stage processing industries and the section's pervasive post-Civil War poverty also set the South apart from other parts of the country. The region's adherence to evangelical Christianity has appropriately earned the region's designation as the nation's "Bible belt," and these religious beliefs have had profound social and political implications. Finally, the South's one-party, primarily Democratic politics distinguished the region until the 1970s.

Over the final quarter of the twentieth century, the South became less distinctive as Republicans became the majority party, the population moved from rural to urban areas, and the economy diversified. Still, the South remains the nation's poorest, most religious, most vocally patriotic, most violent, least well-schooled, and most culturally conservative region. As the twenty-first century began, prominent students of the South predicted that southerners would "keep inventing new ways to be different," that "the South actually *is* constantly disappearing, only to be replaced by another South, also distinct but distinct in a different way." And a recent analysis presents a persuasive argument "that the South remains culturally and politically distinct and that the *perception* of distinctiveness is a particularly important component of southern identity."[45]

Assuming there has been a distinct South, there have been varying geographical definitions of the region, with some scholars and pollsters at various times

45. John Shelton Reed, "If I'd Just Waken up From a Thirty-six-year Sleep," *Southern Cultures* 7 (Spring 2001): 108 (inventing); Sheldon Hackney, "The Contradictory South," *Southern Cultures* 7 (Winter 2001): 72 (disappearing); Christopher A. Cooper and H. Gibbs Knotts, *The Resilience of Southern Identity: Why the South Still Matters in the Minds of Its* People (Chapel Hill: University of North Carolina Press, 2017), 7; see also David L. Carlton, "Rethinking Southern History," *Southern Cultures* 7 (Spring 2001): 38–49, esp. 48; for strong objections to the idea of southern exceptionalism or an overly distinctive South, see Laura F. Edwards, "Southern History as U.S. History," *Journal of Southern History* 75 (Aug. 2009): 533–64; and Matthew D. Lassiter and Joseph Crespino, "Introduction: The End of Southern History," in *The Myth of Southern Exceptionalism,* ed. Matthew D. Lassiter and Joseph Crespino (New York: Oxford University Press, 2009), 3–23.

including West Virginia, Oklahoma, Maryland, and Missouri. Cases can be made for all or portions of each of these states as southern, but based on the foregoing historical characteristics and experiences, I shall define the South as the eleven states of the Confederacy—Alabama, Arkansas, Georgia, Florida, Louisiana, Mississippi, North Carolina, South Carolina, Tennessee, Texas, and Virginia, plus Kentucky. The latter is included because of geographical proximity, long dependence on staple agriculture and low-wage industries, racial attitudes and practices, pervasive rural poverty, concern for personal and national honor, vocal patriotism, devotion to a Confederate-related military tradition and symbolism, and religious practices.

Having stipulated a working definition of the South and its geographical boundaries, I shall explain how the writers will be identified and my basic editorial approach. After much contemplation and experimentation, I settled on a thematic chapter organization with the letters therein presented chronologically. Based on the advice of several very knowledgeable and helpful archivists and employing Robert S. McElvaine's *Down and Out in the Great Depression: Letters from the Forgotten Man* as a model, I have identified southern letter writers with initials and place of residence. Where possible and not clear from the letter's content, I have also noted the author's gender. The use of initials rather than full names and the exclusion of inside addresses responds to the potential privacy expectations of persons writing to public officials and avoids the possible connection of a letter writer or his/her family to embarrassing language or positions on public issues. Moreover, many letters, especially those from family members in chapter 4, were deeply personal. For purposes of consistency, this practice of initials only has been applied to authors of letters to the editors of newspapers as well, even though those southerners had elected to engage publicly in the debate over the war. This form of identification also embodies the assumption that the sentiments and arguments expressed in all of these letters were more revealing and instructive than the individual identity of the authors. When letter writers noted the location from which they wrote, I have included it together with their initials; if no location has been cited, the author did not provide that information.[46]

While adopting a minimalist approach to editing these letters, I have not corrected spelling, grammatical errors, or punctuation; nor have I inserted "sic" as an

---

46. Robert S. McElvaine, *Down and Out in the Great Depression: Letters from the Forgotten Man* (Chapel Hill: University of North Carolina Press, 2008; orig. published, 1983).

indication of such errors. In the one exception to this approach, I have moved all commas and periods within quotation marks to conform to standard U.S. usage. For purposes of consistency of presentation, I have indented the first sentence of all paragraphs, rather than reproducing originals in which authors wrote single-spaced letters with no indentation of first sentences and double-spaces between paragraphs. Where I have omitted portions of letters unrelated to the war or to limit the length of individual letters and the overall collection, I have inserted ellipses (. . .); where the letter writers inserted ellipses, I have employed asterisks (* * *). I have retained the underlining employed by the authors rather than employing italics. In letters to the editors, I have corrected obvious typos or words omitted by the paper. Finally, I have identified important persons or events cited in the letters via the following **Key** or explanatory footnotes.

Key to Persons Mentioned in the Letters

Jack Anderson, a syndicated newspaper columnist; **William F. Buckley Jr.,** a conservative author, commentator, and television host; **Ellsworth Bunker**, U.S. ambassador to South Vietnam, 1967–1973; **Neville Chamberlain,** British prime minister who became synonymous with "appeasement" of an aggressor by surrendering a portion of Czechoslovakia to Adolph Hitler at the 1938 Munich Conference; **Rap Brown** and **Stokely Carmichael**, both civil rights activists who chaired the Student Nonviolent Coordinating Committee. Brown also became president of the Black Panthers; Carmichael has been credited with popularizing the tern "black power." Both were charged with inciting antiwar riots at the 1968 Democratic Convention in Chicago; **USA General Lewis B. Hershey**, director of the Selective Service System (draft), 1946–1970; **Abbie Hoffman and Jerry Rubin**, cofounders of the Youth International Party (Yippies), which opposed the war; **J. Edgar Hoover**, director of the Federal Bureau of Investigation, 1935–1972; **Henry Cabot Lodge Jr.,** U.S. ambassador to South Vietnam, 1963–1964, 1965; **Ronald Reagan**, governor of California, 1967–1975 and later U.S. president, 1981–1989; **Walt Rostow**, national security advisor to President Johnson, 1966–1969; **Bertrand Russell**, British philosopher and pacifist who favored world government and opposed the war; **USA General Maxwell Taylor**, U.S. ambassador to South Vietnam, 1964–65, and Vietnam advisor to LBJ thereafter; **U Thant,** secretary general of the United Nations, 1961–1971; **Lurleen Wallace**, wife of George Wallace and governor of Alabama, 1967–1968; **George Wallace**, three-time governor of Alabama between 1962 and 1976, presidential candidate 1964, 1968, and 1972, and outspoken opponent of Black rights; **USA General Earle Wheeler**, chairman of the Joint Chiefs of Staff, 1964–1970.

U.S. Senators **Birch Bayh** (D/IN), **Frank Church** (D/ID), **John Sherman Cooper** (R/KY), **Everett Dirksen** (R/IL), **Mark G. Hatfield,** (R/OR), **Jacob Javits** (R/NY), **Edward M. Kennedy** (D/MA), **Russell B. Long** (D/LA), **Eugene McCarthy** (D/MN), **George McGovern** (D/SD), **Edmund S. Muskie** (D/ME), **Charles H. (Chuck) Percy** (R/IL), **Stuart Symington** (D/MO), and **Strom Thurmond** (R/SC) are also referenced in the letters. All of these senators except Long, Symington, and Thurmond opposed the war. Symington, a strong proponent of the U.S. air war, altered his position and opposed bombing of North Vietnam in late 1967. McGovern ran against Nixon in the 1972 presidential election and lost overwhelmingly. Thurmond was a staunch opponent of the Civil Rights Movement.

1. Prowar Southerners

From 1965 through 1973 the South was the nation's most consistently prowar region. Gallup polling documented this southern perspective and highlighted several of the region's longstanding foreign policy positions. Compared to other Americans, southerners were most likely to agree that "wars are sometimes necessary to settle differences" and least willing to allow the United Nations or World Court to oversee elections in Vietnam or to mediate the conflict. As the war escalated sharply in 1966, southerners were most likely to predict that the conflict would end in a clear-cut U.S. victory rather than a negotiated compromise and most in favor of going "all-out to win a military victory." The South's preference for military solutions to international problems and endorsement of all-out, unilateral U.S. actions were also evident in the region's dissatisfaction with President Lyndon Johnson's limited war policies, a dissatisfaction that prompted the South to lead the nation in expressed dislike for Defense Secretary Robert McNamara's civilian direction of the Department of Defense and the war in Vietnam. These propensities were clear in October 1967 when the South was the region most supportive of an escalation plan that would "let the heads of the army run the war as they see fit, giving them all the men they say they need. Increase the pressure on the enemy troops and step up the bombing of North Vietnam. Add new targets that have not been bombed thus far, such as the harbor of Haiphong. Go all out and use atomic weapons and bombs if the army believes we should."[1]

This endorsement of bombing was consistent with the South's strategic perspective over the course of the war. Southerners were most in favor of bombing large North Vietnamese cities in November 1966 and most opposed to halting the bombing of North Vietnam in November 1967. The South was the Democratic

1. *Gallup Opinion Index*, no. 2 (July 1965): 17 (hereafter cited as *GOI*, no. [date]: page); *GOI*, no. 13 (June 1966): 3; *GOI*, no. 10 (March 1966): 16–17; GOI, no. 16 (Sept. 1966): 10; GOI, no. 24 (June 1967): 7; *GOI*, no. 29 (Nov. 1967): 16; *GOI*, no. 53 (Nov. 1969): 3; *GOI*, no. 74 (Aug. 1971): 24.

region least supportive of Johnson's suspension of bombing the North in April and May 1968; most supportive of President Richard Nixon's renewal of the bombing of North Vietnam including Hanoi and Haiphong in 1972; and most in favor of resuming that bombing in January 1973, if the pause after Christmas did not achieve a peace settlement.[2]

In an additional reflection of the South's respect for the military and proclivity for the use of force to resolve international disputes, southerners preferred their sons serve in the military rather than devote two years to some form of alternate national service, were most willing in 1967 to pay higher taxes to support the war, most inclined to increase defense spending in March 1971 and August 1972, and most opposed during 1969 to 1972 to a series of congressional attempts to legislate a specific date for the withdrawal of all U.S. troops.[3]

Southern responses to the mistake question were more ambiguous. From November 1965 through March 1969, the region did not differ appreciably from the national figures. Those national poll results embodied the growing disillusionment as Americans went from 25 percent who deemed U.S. intervention a mistake in November 1965 to 53 percent in September 1968. The South's 53 percent in the fall 1968 likely reflected its residents taking cues from important public figures ranging from hawks, such as Senator Richard Russell and Senator John C. Stennis, to doves, such as Senator J. William Fulbright and Senator Albert Gore Sr. (D/TN), all of whom agreed that intervention with ground troops was a mistake, even if they disagreed profoundly on how best to wage and end the war. Moreover, the majority of white southerners strongly opposed Johnson's limited war, which may have helped prompt their perception of the war as a mistake. Southern opponents of the war, who certainly viewed U.S. intervention as mistaken, augmented the South's "yes" responses. As the national consensus on the war as a mistake continued to grow through May 1973, the South consistently provided a smaller "yes" percentage than other regions or the nation as a whole. The South's heightened sense of patriotism, respect for the military, and reluctance to admit defeat help to explain this response, as did the region's support for President Nixon, whose bombing and invasion of Cambodia and

2. *GOI*, no. 9 (Feb. 1966): 6; *GOI*, no. 29 (Nov. 1967): 18; *GOI*, no. 34 (April 1968): 17; *GOI*, no. 35 (May 1968): 18; *GOI*, no. 88 (Oct. 1972): 20; *GOI*, no. 92 (Feb. 1973): 12.

3. *GOI*, no. 13 (June 1966): 13; *GOI*, no. 26 (Aug. 1967): 7; *GOI*, no. 53 (Nov. 1969): 5; *GOI*, no. 65 (Nov. 1970): 23; *GOI*, no. 69 (March 1971): 11; *GOI*, no. 71 (May 1971): 23; *GOI*, no. 74 (Aug. 1971): 23; *GOI*, no. 86 (Aug. 1972): 20; *GOI*, no. 88 (Oct. 1972): 21.

renewed bombing of North Vietnam were far more palatable than Johnson's ostensible restraint.[4]

The South's contrasting evaluations of Johnson and Nixon afford additional perspective on the region's foreign policy assumptions, racial beliefs, and response to the Vietnam War. The South was the region most critical of Johnson's performance as president and of his handling of the war. This disapproval derived from not only the region's rejection of his limited war strategy but also its opposition to his Great Society social programs aimed at the less fortunate and his civil rights legislation. Southerners consistently told pollsters that LBJ was "pushing integration too fast." The South's estimate of the president was evident in February 1966 when only 42 percent of southerners approved of his performance as chief executive versus 59 percent of Americans generally. This pattern persisted over the next two years. In January 1967 38 percent of southerners (versus 46 percent nationally) approved of his work as president; by November, only 32 percent viewed his presidential performance favorably. Similarly, only 32 percent of southerners endorsed his handling of Vietnam in January 1967, and their positive assessment had declined to 25 percent in September. In January 1968 the South's approval of LBJ's handling of his "job as president" was 11 percent lower than the national average.[5]

The Democratic South was far more supportive of Richard Nixon's management of the Vietnam War. Here again, regional racial views and aversion to antiwar protestors reinforced foreign policy preferences and prevailed over party politics. Nixon, a Republican, had run for president promising minimalist enforcement of civil rights laws, a return to "law and order," and the pursuit of an honorable peace—all promises that appealed to the South. As Nixon assumed office, 78 percent of southerners' "best guess" was that integration would be pushed "not so fast" or "about right," and the new president did not disappoint them. On the foreign policy front, Nixon's bombing and invasion of Cambodia

4. Erskine, "The Polls: Is War a Mistake?" 141–50; *GOI*, no. 1 (June 1965): 3; *GOI*, no. 6 (Nov. 1965): 10; *GOI*, no. 10 (March 1966): 7; *GOI*, no. 12 (May 1966): 6; *GOI*, no. 16 (Sept. 1966): 8; *GOI*, no. 18 (Nov.–Dec 1966): 11; *GOI*, no. 24 (June 1967): 5; *GOI*, no. 26 (Aug. 1967): 4; *GOI*, no. 29 (Nov. 1967): 4; *GOI*, no. 33 (March 1968): 6; *GOI*, no. 35 (May 1968): 21; *GOI*, no. 39 (Sept. 1968): 3; *GOI*, no. 45 (March 1969): 11; *GOI*, no. 52 (Oct. 1969): 14; *GOI*, no. 56 (Feb. 1970): 2; *GOI*, no. 69 (March 1971): 12; *GOI*, no. 73 (July 1971): 3.

5. *GOI*, no. 8 (Jan. 1966): 3; GOI, no. 10 (March 1966): 5; GOI, no. 14 (July 1966): 17; *GOI*, no. 19 (Jan. 1967): 3–4; *GOI*, no. 27 (Sept. 1967): 13; *GOI*, no. 28 (Oct. 1967): 2–3; *GOI*, no. 32 (Feb. 1968): 3; *GOI*, no. 40 (Oct. 1968): 30.

in 1969 and 1970, the U.S./ARVN invasion of Laos in 1971, renewed U.S. bombing of North Vietnam in 1972, and assurances of an honorable peace and American victory all appealed to southern patriotism and rejection of limited war.[6]

The South's support for the Nixon administration's war policies was especially important at crucial junctures such as the U.S. invasion of Cambodia in May–June 1970; the renewed bombing of North Vietnam, especially the Hanoi-Haiphong area, and blockading of Haiphong harbor in June 1972; and the intense Christmas bombing of these same cities in December 1972. Following each of these highly controversial military escalations, the South was the Democratic region most supportive of the Republican president. In both early May 1970 and June 1970, the South's approval of Nixon's Vietnam policy ran 6–7 percent ahead of the national average.[7]

Prowar southern letter writers amplified and elaborated on the Gallup polling data. In so doing, they added nuance and texture to our understanding of the South's response to the war. Southerners adopted a strong anticommunist position from which they endorsed containment, the domino theory, and the U.S. need to maintain credibility by keeping its commitment to defend noncommunist South Vietnam. The South's residents who supported the war viewed the Vietnam conflict as part of a worldwide struggle between good and evil—between democracy and despotism, between capitalism and communism, between Christianity and atheism.

Therefore, prowar southerners advised their political leaders that war was necessary and should be fought all-out, without restraints imposed by politics or public opinion—either domestic or international. The U.S military should be empowered to direct the war; U.S. troops should be afforded all needed resources

---

6. *GOI*, no. 45 (March 1969): 2.

7. *GOI*, no. 52 (Oct. 1969): 14; *GOI*, no. 56 (Feb. 1970): 2; *GOI*, no. 60 (June 1970): 1–2, 4–5; *GOI*, no. 69 (March 1971): 12; *GOI*, no. 84 (June 1972): 3–4; see also surveys of Texas public opinion, Dec. 1969, June 1970, and March 1971, box 883: folders 3–4, Tower Papers; and surveys of Virginia voters, conducted by Oliver Quale and Company, September 1970, October 1971, box 12: folder 1971: Campaign Surveys, Political Climate in VA, William B. Spong Papers, Albert and Shirley Small Special Collections Library, University of Virginia, Charlottesville, VA. The polling of Southern Baptist ministers and Presbyterian Church in the United States ministers and laity yielded similar prowar results. See Gregory D. Tomlin, "Hawks and Doves: Southern Baptist Responses to Military Intervention in Southeast Asia, 1965–1973," (Ph.D. dissertation, Southwestern Baptist Theological Seminar, 2003), 6–7, 144; and David J. Settje, *Faith and War: How Christians Debated the Cold and Vietnam Wars* (New York: New York University Press, 2011), 68–69 (for Southern Baptists); and Richard L. Nutt, *Toward Peacemaking: Presbyterians in the South and National Security, 1945–1983* (Tuscaloosa: University of Alabama Press, 1994), 125–27.

and be allowed to invade North Vietnam, Cambodia, and Laos; superior U.S. technology should be employed to full advantage, including the bombing of all military targets in both North and South Vietnam; and Haiphong harbor should be blockaded. Neither the impact on Vietnamese civilians nor the threat of Chinese or Soviet intervention on the side of the NLF and DRV should inhibit the U.S. measures required to preserve American lives and secure a military victory. Indeed, many prowar southerners advocated preemptive action, perhaps even a nuclear strike, against China before that nation developed a more robust nuclear capacity. Limited war in Korea and the extended postwar occupation were often cited as the unacceptable outcomes that accompanied the U.S. failure to pursue a decisive victory by utilizing superior power and technology to the fullest.

Just as the vital importance of the issues in question dictated war, they rendered a negotiated compromise anathema to prowar southerners. Compromise with evil was simply unacceptable; and, even if it were acceptable, no true compromise was possible since the communists could not be trusted to negotiate in good faith. Victory and an honorable conclusion of the war were the only satisfactory outcomes.

As the war dragged on and the national and southern agony mounted, prowar southerners emphasized that not fighting to win or failing to extend full support to U.S. troops was immoral. Their conception of full support demanded unity on the home front. Prowar southerners condemned critics of the war whether prominent public figures such as Senator Bill Fulbright; peaceful adult protestors who marched in a weekly peace vigil in Chapel Hill, North Carolina; or more boisterous, rowdy, student protestors. All were charged with betraying U.S. soldiers by giving aid and comfort to the enemy and by leading the Vietnamese communists to believe they could outlast a divided United States. Southerners argued further that losing the war would dishonor the Americans who had died in Vietnam and waste the lives and resources devoted to the conflict. Until the end of U.S. combat involvement in the spring of 1973, these southerners remained adamantly opposed to any legislation specifying a set date for the withdrawal of American troops and continued to argue that military action was the key to forcing North Vietnam to release American POWs.[8]

8. Southerners' prowar arguments paralleled those made by conservative, primarily Republicans or Republican-leaning activists and organizations. See Sandra Scanlon, *The Pro-War Movement: Domestic Support for the Vietnam War and the Making of Modern American Conservatism* (Amherst: University of Massachusetts Press, 2013).

1

To the Editor of the *Louisville Courier-Journal*:

June 7, 1964

It seems our government is content to add just enough fuel to the brush fire wars to keep them slowly burning while we continue to lose the lives of our servicemen, our material, money, face, prestige and friends.

If we must stick our nose in every war that comes up, for Pete's sake let's go all out with all means at our command and strike the enemy wherever he is or goes and with a few wars, gain the respect and confidence of our friends, and put fear in the minds of our enemies. Then we won't have so many wars.

We've been pushed around until we're the laughing stock of the whole world. We've been bled to death and losing every day. A red foe is planted and financed by Mr. K[hrushchev] in Cuba, and he dares us to do anything about it. He carries an olive branch in one hand and a dagger in the other. . . .

We don't want wars, but, we have them and will continue to have them until we cause our friends to respect us and our enemies to fear us enough to treat us with some common decency.

J.B.N. Sr. (Grand Rivers, KY)

2

Dear Senator [Ralph W. Yarborough],

July 14, 1964

I am deeply troubled by the state of affairs in S.E. Asia. I wonder, are we going to continue with our do the bare minimum attitude or are we going to win. One day the word is we are winning, the next we are losing. I know for a fact that we are not winning from personal contact with the returning troops.

. . . What does it take to get us on the wagon? The Spanish sank the Maine and we went to war. These Viet Cong are killing our boys every day and we do just the bare minimum. The Asian is not impressed with talk. We should know that by now. He respects action. Let's do something other than sitting on our behinds. . . .

My father fought in World War II for a cause. My uncle died for the cause. The guys in Viet Nam are dying for nothing. It is a waste. Let's get it over with.

The French dragged it out for months and years and they lost. It is inevitable that we too will lose the way things are going. Let us do something harsh and brash liking to kick the stuffings out of the Commies. Or don't you believe that is nice? . . . So let's stop being the guy in the white hat with the two guns and be big and bad * * * * *

Yours truly,
C.L. (Texan writing from San Francisco)

3

My dear Senator [Ralph W. Yarborough],

August 2, 1964

. . . I have just heard on the radio that one of our naval vessels was attacked by a Communists' PT boat off Viet Nam. I also hear almost daily about one of our soldiers or other military persons getting killed over in that area.

I am not in favor of going to war over every incident BUT I think if we are going to try to keep the Reds out of South East Asia, as we have stated we will do, then we should either turn our military forces loose and win that battle or we should get out!

It appears to me that we are in the same position we were in Korea—we allowed the Reds to hit and run behind their border and then do the same thing time after time.

Strong men must temper their strength with good judgement and the same applies to strong nations. However if we let these little countries push us around as they seem able to do we will continue to be the laughing stock of the world.

We have very little to show for the millions we have spent in South East Asia.

Sincerely,
N.D.M. (San Antonio, TX)

4

Dear Mr. President [Lyndon B. Johnson]:

November 1, 1964

As I write this letter two days before our National Election I do not know which of the two men running for this high office will receive and read this letter. I could not wait until after the election to write this letter in behalf of myself, my husband and thousands of other parents who must feel as we do.

Our pleas are for a strong definite stand on our Country's foreign policy. We are the parents of a 21 year old son who is at present serving in the Air Force of our Country. At present time he has 18 months left of his first hitch in the Air Force. We also have another son 16 years old and who will be facing a draft or enlistment into our Armed Forces in two years. Our greatest concern is the well being and welfare of these two God given sons of ours.

As I sat before my television set on this past Friday Night and watched a newscast, I was moved to tears by the pictures of the Services for the 8 United States Airmen shot down last week over Cambodia. I watched, moved, as the medals were pinned on the Flag draped caskets of these fine young men, but my tears of sympathy and concern turned to tears of anger as the Commentator announced in the next breath, that the United States had apologized to Cambodia because this unarmed Transport Supply plane had strayed over into their skies and was shot down.

Where in the world is our backbone when an incident such as this takes place? How can we hold our heads up and be an inspiration as a strong nation to the other weak and small countries of the World when we apologize for the lives of 8 young men being wantonly destroyed by an act such as this?

You may say "She's an isolationist." Maybe I am, but if our sons are going to be asked to give their lives for their country then we want to know why and for what they died.

Back in April of 1943, I stood on a train platform and watched my only brother leave for the Armed Forces. The following Tuesday I . . . watched my husband leave for the Armed Forces. . . . Four months later, I with the help of God, brought into the world this 21 year old son of ours. This son was almost 3 years old when his Daddy and two Uncles returned home.

This matter of service and war is nothing new to me, but at least back in 1943 we knew who we were at war with and for what we were fighting. Today we do not even admit to being at war.

This is my plea! Either take a firm stand on foreign policy even at the risk of all out war, or pull out of Viet Nam completely. For a change let us show some strength on the part of our State Department or this action may drag out until the next generation is old enough for the draft.

A concerned Mother,
Mrs. I.J.W. (Humboldt, TN)

5

Dear Senator [Albert] Gore [Sr.],

February 5, 1965

I read with dismay that you had called for a negotiated settlement of the war in Viet Nam which would permit withdrawal of U.S. troops in order to avert total war with Red China. Apparently, you have very little understanding of the danger of communism, not only in countries such as Viet Nam, but also here in the states. . . .

None of us can deny that we, as Americans, have sat by while millions of our Christian neighbors have been trampled under the yoke of communism. . . . We seem to have developed a policy of continual retreat. I would like to ask you if we will also retreat when we, as a Christian nation, finally face up to the fact that communism is our enemy too. It is *not* just a foreign disease. . . .

Now, I am heartsick at the thought of the boys who die regularly in Viet Nam, but history tells us that sacrifice is the price of liberty. . . . The thought of my own son going to war is frightening to me, but the thought that my own government might some day send him to a foreign land to fight and then refuse him the backing he needs to win, is abominable and makes me ashamed as an American. To send boys to fight for freedom is one thing, but to send them to fight with one hand tied behind their back is disgraceful and inexcusable.

. . . I just cannot see that the appeasement and back up policy that we have held in regard to the ever spreading communism and its terrors is going to accomplish anything. . . .

This is the first year in my life that I have ever undertaken the responsibility of writing to our law makers. I do it only after careful consideration, and genuine concern for the future of my two children. . . .

Your very truly,
Y.B.S. and Mrs. Y.B.S. (Oak Ridge, TN)

6

Dear Senator [Albert] Gore [Sr.]:

February 18, 1965

I do not claim to be an expert on foreign affairs, nor am I trained in military affairs. But I am an American, and as such, I want to express an opinion. . . .

As I understand it, we have agreed to protect South Viet-Nam against aggression, under the Geneva Treaty. If we see fit to negotiate our way out of this agreement, then what fool, either Asian or Russian, would ever believe anything we said?

Granted that this undeclared war in Viet-Nam is a mess, fraught with great danger, we are already in it. We have signed our honor as a nation to a treaty, and have agreed to do certain things. Then it seems to me that we have only two alternatives—surrender another country to communism, or continue to fight for the freedom of these people. . . .

I realize that my one letter will not change the course of history. . . . But as one who will be affected in the event of a major war, I cast my vote for the right for freedom and for living up to our commitments. . . . In this day when honor has become a forgotten word, even in our service academy, the honor of all of us is at stake. Perhaps few people think of it anymore, but I still want to be able to know that my country has done what is *right*, not merely what is expedient. . . .

Sincerely,

N.M.H. (female, Nashville, TN)

7

My dear Senator [Richard B.] Russell [Jr]:

July 15, 1965

When President Johnson took a firm stand in Vietnam and the Dominican Republic, millions of Americans were cheering because LBJ had shown some guts. . . .

The first and second world wars were directed by our military command, and both were won decisively. The Korean War and the Cuban fiasco were run by the State Department, and we lost both. Our State Department is again in full charge of the Viet Nam debacle, and under its "No Win" policy, we will lose this one, too. It is disgusting and humiliating when the President of the most powerful nation in the world stoops to offer a small Asian gangster nation a billion dollar bribe to stop fighting us, instead of issuing an order to bomb Hanoi and Haiphong; thus stopping this war within 24 hours. . . . [9]

Sincerely,

W.B.Z. (Atlanta, GA)

9. "Cuban fiasco" refers to the CIA-directed invasion of Cuba in April 1961, which failed to overthrow Fidel Castro. "Offer to a small Asian gangster" refers to President Johnson's offer in April 1965 of a $1 billion development plan for the Mekong River as part of potential peace negotiations.

8

Dear Sir [Senator Richard B. Russell Jr.]:

July 28, 1965

... Today Mr. Johnson called for an increase in the draft and reiterated the firmness of our stand in Viet Nam. He repeated that we would not retreat. I hope he means this. If he does, he is contradicting the predictions of most of the liberal wing of his own party. ...

... For years it has seemed that it has been American policy to overlook what was best for the American people to follow what passed for our image abroad. ...

What these so-called men are saying to the youth who will be called up and activated to make the show look good is: We will send you to a dirty place where you will probably receive some injury (if you are lucky) or have your head blown off (if you are unlucky). When you die, you will have the comfort of knowing that your death serves much the same purpose as that of a sacrificial goat on a pagan altar. You will have been merely a token appeasement to world opinion. ...

You no doubt think you have happened upon the letter of a card-carrying member of Bertrand Russell's little clique, a died in the wool pacifist. Nothing could be further from the truth. If the Army would recognize the fact that women would make much sneakier fighters than men (which they would), I would dearly love to be in the fray myself. And I have a husband who will no doubt find himself in the unenviable position of seeing the world the Air Force way. He is not dreading this, and neither am I *if it will do any good at all*. We are young and newly wed, and such an interruption in our lives will be inconvenient, to say the least, but we feel it a small price to enjoy the heritage of freedom so painstakingly won and given to us by prior generations. That, no doubt, is corny. But we believe it, and so do a lot of other Americans. ...

If we are going to continue the war in Viet Nam (and it looks as if we are), then in God's name let us go in it to win. If we cannot approach it in that spirit, then let us get out—now. ...

Sincerely,
Mrs. R.G.H. (Savannah, GA)

9

My Dear Senator [Richard B.] Russell [Jr.]:

December 6, 1965

... I feel we should go to war with an effort to *win* the war. I also feel we are being dishonest and untrue to the youth of our nation whom we are sending to their death. I could not sit down with a clear conscience and enjoy my Thanksgiving dinner on the same day we had 240 odd casualties announced. It was both revolting and nauseating to me that we were not supporting our men in action. I was ashamed to be an American.

I feel we should bomb and destroy Hanoi and Haiphong and any other military target necessary to win the war. I think we should attempt to . . . obtain unconditional surrender with all means at our command, including atomic weapons. I recognize that this places my family and me in the front line of fire, but I feel that this is only right since I am sending the children of other men into the front line. Any other course of action is morally wrong as well as militarily foolish, and is dishonorable and unworthy of a great nation such as ours.

Sincerely,
R.P.T. (East Point, GA)

10

Dear Senator [John C. Stennis]:

December 7, 1965

. . . How long would the war with Germany and Japan lasted, had we conducted it in the unrealistic way that this one is being conducted? What is sacred about the Industrial cities of North Vietnam that was not sacred about the cities of Germany and Japan? I think we have the best chance of getting many millions of American soldiers killed that we have ever had. It is a tragedy that the administration seems to believe that we can bring an end to the war without destroying their ability to make war.

I do not believe that we may expect any help from anyone, so it appears that we have two choices. One is to make total war against every source of supply (China, Cambodia, Laos and any other country) the other choice is to serve notice on our allies that equal help must come from them or we are getting out. And of course, there is the choice of our present policy of just replacing dead soldiers with live ones for many years to come.

When the United States has spent all of it's resources in policing the world who then will defend us?

Sincerely your friend,
C.P. (Belen, MS)

11

Dear [Senator] Harry [F. Byrd Jr.],

December 17, 1965

. . . I would like to give you a few of my observations on South Viet Nam. First, I would like to say that I think our country has gone ahead of the rest of the World because of its form of government, and I believe that our government is good, because it is based on the importance of the individual, and this comes primarily, I believe, from the fundamental concept of the Christian religion. Probably many other religions have the same concept. It is my opinion that fundamentally, we are no better or worse people than other peoples of the World, but we have forged ahead in a very short time to become the greatest country in the World, and I believe the reasons that I have given above can explain it to a large extent.

If our principles are right and those of communism are wrong, then I think we have no choice except to go ahead and do whatever is necessary in South Viet Nam to stop communism, and give these fine, bright, ambitious people an opportunity to have a good government like ours, if they want it, or any other kind that they want. If we do not stop communism in South Viet Nam, then I feel that we might as well just give up and let communism take over Asia and probably most of the rest of the World. As you know, sixty-five percent of the population of the World lives in Asia, and once they become communist with communication and travel what it is now, it will not be long until they will have the scientific knowledge and materials that we have, and they may possibly go way beyond us with all their people and natural resources, and when that happens, we will be a very minor consideration in the World because there are so many more people there than there are here. I feel very strongly about our obligations to these people, and incidentally in the long run to our own people in carrying this war through to a satisfactory conclusion. . . .

Sincerely,

J.McL.A. (Winchester, VA)

12

Dear Senator [John C.] Stennis,

February 16, 1966

I am writing to agree wholeheartedly with your stand on the war in South Viet Nam. I wish you would remind those bleeding hearts who are crying because we are bombing North Viet Nam because innocent men, women and children are being killed that these so-called innocents are the backbone of the North Viet Nam war effort. They supply the food for the Viet Cong and North Viet Nam soldiers. They work in the plants making war supplies for the soldiers. I wonder how long the Second World War would have lasted if we hadn't bombed Germany out of existence. I for one do not believe Germany would have been defeated had we not bombed their munition plants, their oil refineries, and their oil fields. I do not think I heard any of these bleeding hearts crying because German men, women, and children were being killed by these bombs. This killing of so-called innocents usually aids in shortening a war. Because the people lose faith in their Government because it doesn't protect them and cause the overthrow of the government.

I notice where McNamara says we are not going to overthrow the North Viet Nam Government. How stupid can you get. If you have a cancer which is eating you up you don't just try to contain it, you try to remove it. . . .

Sincerely,
C.L.W. (Jackson, MS)

13

Dear Senator [J. William Fulbright]:

February 25, 1966

. . . My position is rather simple, my primary concern is not over who is right nor who is wrong over Vietnam, my primary concern is for the Serviceman in Vietnam. I say we should do one of two things: Either give the Serviceman all munitions, the necessary personnel, logistical support, the right to bomb Hanoi, or any other place in North Vietnam. Let's clobber them quick and get this war over and come home. I do not share the views of those who say this would cause World War III, I think that is a calculated Risk anyway. I am not concerned over what the "Bleeding Hearts" would think. I am not concerned over the ethics of this nor whether it is the Christian thing to do; Stephen Decatur is supposed to have said, "Our Country, may it always be right, but our Country, right or wrong." Those are my sentiments exactly, and I would believe this though America stood alone against the world! . . .

Sincerely,
M.E.R. (female)

14

Dear Senator [Richard B.] Russell [Jr.]:

March 24, 1966

. . . How our military personnel in Viet Nam manages to maintain their morale and perseverance under the circumstances is beyond comprehension. For Johnson, Rusk, and McNamara to elect that Hanoi and Haiphong be made privileged sanctuaries is asinine and incredible. In wars that are directed by rational and competent men *all* of the enemies territory immediately becomes subject to the necessary application of military power deemed advisable to render it impotent. . . . Every day, yes every hour, that Johnson, Rusk, and McNamara prolong this war and contribute to the unnecessary death and disablement of innocent American soldiers compounds the murder and misery they insist upon perpetrating. The successful operation of any enterprise is usually performed by experienced and qualified men and wars are no exception. In our opinion the disgraceful fiasco that exists in Viet Nam will not materially change until the three ostentatious civilian buffoons in Washington cease and desist and direction and control of our armed forces is placed in the hands of military men where it belongs. The debacle in Korea is proof enough for any one to see, MacArthur was 100 per cent right and had he prevailed over 100 per cent wrong Harry Truman, we would have had a total victory and honorable peace instead of the preposterous and untenable situation that exists there to this day. The same result will inevitably take place in Viet Nam if the American people don't arise from their complacency and demand unconditional victory and in the minimum of time. . . .

Very truly yours,
C.A. L. and F. L. (female, Atlanta, GA)

15

Dear Senator [Richard B. Russell Jr.]:

May 17, 1966

. . . The city of Baxley, Georgia, was thrown into a state of shock by the news that a mere boy of approximately 21 years of age was killed in Viet Nam. He was a life long resident of Baxley, Georgia, and was known by many.

I have a good idea why we are in Viet Nam. I am more than sure that this young Marine knew why he was there, since he volunteered. Are we going to continue to receive notice of the deaths of young Americans in Viet Nam, or are we going to end this war in one way or another?

If we are there to win, why don't we use our weapons? Should we use knives when we have firearms? Should we use cannon against cannon when we have rockets and missiles? What kind of strategy is it to fight a man in his back yard on his terms? . . . I think I share the sentiment of the majority of the people of this country; i.e., get out of Viet Nam, or go ahead and use what we have, win the war, and send our young people back home. . . .

Can you not use your influence to best the situation in this war so that our young men will have the best equipment and training with which to win this war? I guess I am asking you to pull rabbits out of a hat; however, there should be some practical solution to end this slaughter. . . . There will be no hurt feelings as a result of this boy's death. Only everlasting grief. There will be no funeral. There is nothing left to bury. You see, he was fighting in the other man's back yard, a well placed jungle mine field. One that neither you nor I know who placed there. It could, in light of the unrest in Viet Nam, have been placed there by our little South Viet Nam helpers. It could have been the Viet Cong. . . .

The letter may be confusing, but my understanding and many other peoples' understanding is confused by the complexity of the situation. All Americans believe in aid to foreign countries who need help and want it. We are not sure about Viet Nam. The death of a local youth causes more thinking thus more confusion. . . .

Warmest person regards, and again, my apologies for taking up your time.
E.P.J. (Baxley, GA)

16

Dear [Senator] Harry [F. Byrd Jr.],

October 13, 1966

For some years I have been increasingly concerned about the part that our country is playing in the war with North Viet Nam and the Viet Cong. . . .

In my own mind, I feel that we are dealing with a much more wily enemy than we fought in World War II against Germany and Japan. The Viet Cong guerrillas fight in ways which we do not seem to understand or to know how to combat. In my view escalation is a nasty word and I believe that if the United States is to be involved in such a war it is the duty of the whole country, including the President and the present Administration, to go at the thing with all forces available. Just at the present moment I feel that the policies of Mr. Johnson and Mr. Rusk will in the future prove disastrous, not only to this country as a whole but to the peace of the world as well. This crisis in Southeast Asia must . . . be settled with the least possible delay and I am heartily in favor of sending all the necessary forces and equipment to this area without further delay and getting on with the job to be done.

There is one further matter which concerns me deeply and this is the development by Red China of the nuclear bomb with the probability that within three to five years they will have developed the thermonuclear explosive weapons which we now possess. I feel that once the Red Chinese possess such weapons there is nothing that will deter them from beginning a surprise thermonuclear war and if they strike first, our country is going to be in a lot of trouble.

I am not an advocate of mass slaughter of civilian populations but . . . I sincerely feel that our government should seriously consider the use of thermonuclear devices against strategic points in North Viet Nam and in Red China in order to forestall a probable nuclear holocaust which may be directed against the entire free world by the Red Chinese within three to five years. . . .

Sincerely,
W.P.McG. (Winchester, VA)

17

Dear Sir [Senator John C. Stennis]:

January 2, 1967

I wish to express my wholehearted approval of the report your Armed Forces Committee is preparing . . . on the Viet Nam war.[10]

Nobody objects to the very slight burden the people at home must bear when a war is being fought, but no one wants anything to do with a *war of attrition,* which our troops are not allowed to win. If the current attitude about the Viet Nam War prevails, and it is still going on when my son reaches draft age, then *I will join forces with those who seek to help young people "beat the draft."* I am a veteran of WW II & Korea. While I feel that those wars could have been prevented, I am not bitter about my part in them. Literally millions had it a thousand times worse than I did. But this utter nonsense of an inconclusive and everlasting "war of maneuver" is a communist device to destroy our country.

10. From his chairmanship of the Preparedness Investigating Subcommittee of the Senate Armed Services Committee, Stennis oversaw the preparations of several reports advocating the unrestricted bombing of North Vietnam.

The weak guts in our state department and "defense" department need to be told *now* that the American people are up to their ears in the liberal frightened communist vomit that says we must allow Russia and even our allies to prolong this senseless fight. . . .

Very truly yours,

J.K.P. (Baton Rouge, LA)

18

Dear Senator [John C.] Stennis,

January 5, 1967

This is just a brief note to extend you our support and assure you of our complete agreement with your recent statements defending the bombing of North Vietnam. This is a most peculiar war, when such a fuss is made over civilian casualties in the enemy camp. Nobody to my knowledge shed any tears when we were bombing German, Italian, and Japanese cities during World War II, or North Korean cities in the Korean War.

The American people—the vast majority at any rate—want to see *maximum* force brought to bear to win this war at *minimum* cost to our boys in the field. The pacifists and pro-North Vietnamese among us may have the most powerful set of lungs, but they do not have the backing of most of the American people.

. . . The object of war is to break the enemy's will to continue to fight, and we ought to bend every effort in that direction, including bombing of the Red River dikes, mining of Haiphong harbor, etc. When have we done anything different in past wars? How many Americans wept bitter tears in public over civilian casualties from our raids over Hitler's Germany?

I also wish Congress would bring some pressure to bear against allowing Hanoi to handpick American correspondents to come and accept their guided tours of North Vietnam and to swallow their propaganda statistics, etc. Who would have thought of allowing Americans to go over to Germany . . . and file dispatches on the war from Hitler's point of view? . . . [11]

Sincerely yours,

J.K.McL. (Alexandra, VA)

11. The correspondent in question was Harrison Salisbury, a Pulitzer Prize–winning *New York Times* correspondent, who traveled throughout North Vietnam in January 1967. His dispatches documented the massive destruction and extensive civilian deaths resulting from U.S. bombing.

19

Dear Senator [Harry F.] Byrd [Jr.],

October 18, 1967

I believe I am writing you today as any average American taxpayer would, provided, he took the time to do so. My background includes a college degree, a junior manager of a large corporation, a father, a homeowner, and an independent voter with a brother in Vietnam. . . .

First, I am gravely concerned about the situation we find ourselves in Vietnam. I do not have all the facts, nor do I have the answers to it. I can only write as an observer and the only information on the matter comes from the newspaper, radio, Television, and a weekly letter from my brother in Vietnam. I am mostly concerned about the news that I get from my brother . . . , which is pretty dismal. It seems to me that we are again fighting another Korean type "No win Vietnam War," & as a taxpayer, I want to serve notice now that I am pretty dissatisfied with the National Democratic Party and their sorry leadership.

I have no doubt that if our National leaders had the intestinal fortitude that John Kennedy had when he stood Khrushchev off in Cuba, we could end this conflict in short order.[12] I am also well aware of the political implications, however, I want to point out that the last war we won in Asia was the result of some A bombs. . . . Again, I point out that if the communists are strong enough to challenge our national security today, what can we look forward to when China develops a nuclear arsenal. . . .

I do know that everyday middle class Americans like myself are fed up with the Johnson administration. We also know that our present "No Win Policy" is deteriorating the moral support of many good democratic citizens. In addition, it is causing a division in our country, it is causing a gathering storm that no one can see the ultimate consequences of and in so many words, someone has got to do something now! . . .

The more I think of this whole situation, the more ridiculous it seems, and this brings me to the proposed increase in taxes (Surtax). If it means winning in Vietnam & restoring our national prestige, I would gladly obtain a second job just to donate the entire salary to the war effort, however, what good would it really do if our government continues to spend like money grows on trees. . . .

Yours very truly,

J.F.J. (Richmond, VA)

---

12. The Kennedy-Khrushchev reference is to the Cuban missile crisis of October 1962 which ended when Khrushchev withdrew Soviet missiles under pressure from the United States and in response to a then-undisclosed U.S. promise to withdraw U.S. missiles from Turkey.

20

Dear Senator [Harry F. Byrd Jr.],

November 22, 1967

Many persons familiar with the Vietnam War believe that something about it is wrong. . . . All the might of America's forces is proving insufficient to stop the aggression of little North Vietnam against the South. It is insufficient because we are not using our power as we ought. It is immoral to fight a war unless we intend to win. . . .

We could easily win in Vietnam, but we are not winning as I see it. As long as we keep granting sanctuary and cease fire days to the enemy he can continue to make us bleed and die. We have deliberately avoided a policy of winning because we feel that we do not have to win. We think that all we have to do is "negotiate." Once Ho Chi Minh sits down to talk, we fancy that all our troubles will be over. We think that he is going to be fair and square, once we get together. We imagine that he will give up his life long ambition of conquering the South, once we talk things over. We are laboring under an illusion that is more costly than we can afford.

We think that aggression has changed since Hitler's time, and that aggressors do not have to be defeated any more. We only have to get them to the table. The fact we negotiated with this same aggressor [Ho] in 1954 and again in 1962 never occurs to us. In 1954 we found Hanoi so unfair . . . that we refused to sign the treaty. Ho Chi Minh signed, promising to leave South Vietnam alone. But he never kept his word. . . .

We do not need another negotiation. . . . Negotiations are meaningless unless there is good will. And it is highly improbable that negotiations would ever bring about a reconciliation between two ideologies so adverse as those in the present conflict. . . .

Sincerely yours,
E.T.S. (Danville, VA)

21

To the Editor of the *Atlanta Constitution:*

February 16, 1968

. . . Most genuinely religious people know man is engaged in eternal combat, whether he likes it or not. This combat results in far more casualties than all the wars in which America has ever fought, at home or abroad. It is the conflict between right and wrong, good and evil, law and anarchy.

Surely those churchmen and others who cry for a pullout from Asia know there can be no peace with men who pursue ways which would deny all personal, political and spiritual freedom. They say we cannot win the war in Vietnam, therefore should get out. Into whose crystal ball are they gazing?

As a clergyman who was privileged to give his country eight years of service in and before World War II, I say we dare not pull out of our moral responsibility to combat communism any more than we dare pull out of our moral commitment against every form of evil which threatens to destroy free government and the hope of a moral human society.

. . . Would any of the good doctors of divinity have us close the churches, temples and synagogues because it "appears" the war cannot be won? . . .

J.A.R.

22

Mr. President [Lyndon B. Johnson]:

March 1, 1968

The Veterans Coordinating Council of the Shreveport-Bossier City Area desire to convey to you the support of it's members in the prosecution of the war in Vietnam, by every means necessary to bring a just and honorable peace.

At no time in the past one hundred years have the people of this great Nation been so divided, nor has the reason why we are involved been so misunderstood. We feel the two main reasons are: First, the television and other news media have played into the hands of our enemies by giving the peaceniks and other dissenters very wide coverage, which the enemy has used to bolster the morale of their people, and to a certain degree has had a bad effect on the morale of some of the people here at home. Second, our Government has been reluctant to take action against subversion and civil disobedience. Many people are beginning to wonder if they are being told the whole truth about the war. When the people lose faith in their leaders, patriotism soon becomes a dirty word. Mr. President how can you explain to a mother that has lost a son in Vietnam, or has a son that is being held a prisoner of war, that we are not officially at war, therefore, there are no laws to curb acts of sedition and treason, that she can see on television most every day.

There is no segment of the American people who are more concerned with the war or the manner in which it is fought, than we Veterans and I hope you won't consider the men who were at Chateau-Thierry and Meuse Argonne, Guadacanal and Normandy, Heart Break Ridge and Pork Chop Hill, men that did not shed their patriotism with their uniform, as being presumptuous in saying, we should step up the bombing of the North. We should blockade Haiphong Harbor and destroy their lines of supply wherever we find them. We should pursue the enemy into neighboring countries, if those counties allow them sanctuary. We should fight this war just as we have fought all previous wars, fight it to win, with whatever it takes. . . .

Most respectfully yours,
The Veterans Coordinating Council of the Shreveport-Bossier City [LA] Area

23

Dear Mr. [Henry E.] Niles [antiwar Baltimore insurance executive]:

March 28, 1968

. . . We all agree that our being in Viet Nam is an error. In fact, it is immoral. It is immoral because we are asking Americans to lay down their lives and then we fight a limited war. It is immoral because our Government is sending foreign aid to nations who are doing business and supplying materiel and munitions to the North Vietnamese. It is immoral for you and I to be conducting business "as usual."

Furthermore, it is immoral for us to even consider pussyfooting around with a bunch of criminals and the idea of sitting down at the peace table and talking is ridiculous. We should talk peace after victory. Then and only then, should we adopt the spirit of Christian charity. . . .

Yours truly,
E.D.M.

24

Dear Senator [Sam J. Ervin Jr.]:

July 30, 1968

First of all, I want to make it clear that I am not a Dove. I would never take part in any protest groups. I am not opposed to the draft. I have no desire to create a rebellion or a revolution. I realize that the Communist threat is a serious one and I believe that our country has a duty to resist it. However, I do have some protests to make and I hope you will listen to them. . . .

Everywhere one goes, he hears this disgraceful war discussed. And everyone is against it, in some way or another. Many think we should never have gone into Viet Nam; now that we are in, we should get out; or we should bomb the enemy and get it over with. Well, we're already in it, so that eliminates the first choice. . . . But—and this is, of course, the situation that puzzles, confuses, and saddens everyone—must our "presence" there go on forever? If we really wanted to deter the spread of Communism, wasn't the best way to show a firm, forceful attitude right at the start? But because we have been so vacillating about assuming that attitude, do we have to vacillate forever? We certainly aren't doing the South Vietnamese any favor by overrunning their country and keeping it in a state of siege. If we had *fought* this war in the beginning they could have had their peace, restored order to their country, and been on their own long ago. . . . The idea of laymen running the war is absurd. We spend millions to train and support the military and then when we are engaged in a military procedure, we let the civilians run it, completely disregarding the advice of the experts. If we *are* in a war, then we must *fight* it—not play at it as if it were a game. . . .

I have a son in the Army who probably will go to Viet Nam. The thought of his giving his life in a half-war, shackled by political palaver, makes me tremble with frustration. If our boys *must* die, let it be for an active cause. . . .

The American public wants this war ended. Our foreign policy won't let us pull out. Negotiations have already proven to be . . . a waste of everybody's time. . . . So there remains only the one other solution—bomb North Viet Nam wherever and with whatever it takes to defeat them—and *end this war!* . . .

Most sincerely,
F.M.N. (female, Durham, NC)

25

Dear Senator [Richard B. Russell Jr.]:

October 16, 1968

On behalf of my family and myself, I deeply appreciate your letter of condolence on the recent loss of my son, First Lieutenant D.R.S., in Vietnam. . . .

At the time of my son's arrival in the Mekong Delta area, enemy activity was relatively quiet. However, it is a documented fact that after the "limited bombing" went into effect, the enemy increased its flow of men and supplies to the South by several hundred percent. I know there is a great possibility that with unrestrained bombing my son could still be alive today.

Now there are proposals to stop all bombing of North Vietnam. I have no other sons to lose in the war, but my heart goes out to those who do. So I most strongly urge you to use all of the influence and pressure you possess not only to continue the bombing, but to allow the military to engage in unrestricted bombing in any and all parts of Vietnam.

I feel we owe an obligation to the over 28,000 who have already died to successfully conclude this war as soon as possible. How many more lives must we lose before we realize that the only way to reason with Asiatics is with force?

Sincerely,

D.D.S. (Atlanta, GA)

26

Dear Sir [Senator Sam J. Ervin Jr.]:

February 25, 1969

. . . Will you please give me some answer, I don't think there is a really legitimate one, as to why—after almost a year of Peace Talks . . . a group of men must wait a week in between sessions? This, while men are dying in Viet Nam. What would we think if these war weary soldiers took a day, much less a week, off after each battle? . . . [13]

We, the people, know that one thing that is happening is that the enemy is constantly building up and moving supplies straight through into South Vietnam. Too, it is not logical that with all the infiltration and building up by North Vietnam and the Viet Cong during cease fire—that this too has completely benefitted them? We honor cease fire and they go right on full blast—boys are killed and yet our authorities say that it isn't significant enough to be alarmed or to bomb. . . .

Bombs and fighting scare me to death; after all, we have a son there, and we'd like it the easiest way possible for him and thousands of others, but many of these boys are dying by degrees from anxiety, emotions, nerves, dope and alcohol, as well as slowly decreasing troops by unnecessary deaths by action. . . .

Too, I feel that it is the duty of our government to forbid these Hippies, and demonstrators who have burned draft cards or completely evaded the draft, to lie around on street corners near embarkation points and approach scared and emotionally concerned Vietnam bound boys—offering them papers and ways to defect to Canada. AND, the straw that breaks the camel's back is proposed

13. U.S.–North Vietnamese/Viet Cong peace talks began in May 1968 and continued periodically, privately, and publicly until the final "peace" agreement was reached on January 27, 1973.

legislation to grant amnesty to citizens who fled to Canada and other countries, shirking their duty as an American. . . .

Sincerely,

Mrs. T.G.Y. (Winston-Salem, NC)

27

Dear Senator [Richard B. Russell Jr.]:

August 10, 1969

Don't you think we have "dillydallied" long enough with this war in Vietnam? If it is an undeclared war and all of you Senators are opposed to it, we ought to pull out or go full out.

I have a son over there, and I feel he should be helping to protect American fighters from the enemy—but not fighting a South Vietnamese political problem. . . .

In regard to pulling troops out, who ever heard of reducing forces until the battle was won? Would any of you like to be on the front lines and have your country withdrawing help from you? Wouldn't Bobby Dodd look awfully funny pulling out 2 Georgia Tech guards when he was ahead 7 to 6 over Alabama?. . . [14]

This letter may seem to be written by a crank, but have any of you men ever had to wait and listen to a phone that rang at night, answer the front doorbell and not know what to expect to hear? . . .

L.J.F. (Atlanta, GA)

28

Dear Mr. President [Richard M. Nixon]:

September 29, 1969

I am seriously concerned lest the recent troop withdrawals you have ordered presage the withdrawal of all United States forces from Viet Nam under conditions that permit the communists to take over the government of South Viet Nam. Should this take place, no matter how well camouflaged by political "doubletalk," I foresee the following consequences: 1. All the suffering and loss of life both by the South Vietnamese and by our own boys will have been wasted. 2. There will be a slaughter of thousands of South Vietnamese as the communists consolidate their position. 3. All of Southeast Asia will be taken over by the communists. . . . 4. It will be proved to the world that the united States does not have the will to back up its allies.

14. Pulling out troops refers to Nixon's policy of Vietnamization.

. . . I urge you to announce to the world that our sole aim is to stop aggression against South Vietnam, and then order the military to win the war using whatever military moves are indicated, including bombing of North Viet Nam and closing of the Haiphong harbor. I personally believe that the start of such a campaign would bring a rush of the North Vietnamese to the negotiating table. . . .

I consider the fear of Russian intervention as being a bugaboo. I do not for a minute believe that Russia will go to war with us until she is good and ready and has an overwhelming nuclear superiority. Nor should "world opinion" deter us; it never deters the communists. . . .

Sincerely yours,
J.R.L.

29

Dear Senator [Albert] Gore [Sr.]:

November 14, 1969

. . . I cannot approve of your position, action, or words relative to the Viet Nam war. While I initially questioned our involvement in this war, I realize that we are deeply involved and must leave only under honorable conditions. To leave under any other conditions would inflict such a stigma on our national image that no one, foreign or domestic, could continue to respect this nation. I believe the policy as recently outlined by the President is the only workable solution that would permit us to withdraw from this war under honorable conditions. . . .

I am also convinced that President Nixon will not permit us to be dishonored by simply walking out without regard to the consequences. At the same time, it is my opinion that those who oppose this policy and insist that we withdraw immediately are giving the North Vietnamese the support they need, and will in turn tend to prolong the stay and increase the casualties suffered by Americans. In short, such actions are without doubt giving aid and comfort to the enemy. . . .

Recently ten of the eleven members of the Tennessee Congressional delegation signed a resolution of support for the President's policy. You, of course, were the only member who failed to sign this resolution. I believe if you were to poll your constituents, you would find the overwhelming majority of Tennesseans support this policy. . . .

Very truly yours,
L.L. (Nashville, TN)

30

Dear Sir [Senator Richard B. Russell Jr.]:

November 15, 1969

... The American people waited patiently for the President's speech, hoping that he would have some clear cut plan to end this conflict. Perhaps many of the silent majority have been satisfied that he is doing his best. No doubt about that. But let's be realistic.[15] It is safe to assume that the war will go on as before, with about the same number of casualties . . . according to the whims of the enemy. Isn't it about time that we realized we cannot deal with this enemy for an honorable peace? . . . The previous administration has lulled the people with false hopes for peace, constantly hoping that the enemy would be willing to sit down and talk. The only thing that came out of Paris were the words, "some progress is being made." This has turned out to be a lie. . . .

The American people want this war ended as soon as possible with honorable conditions that are right with all the people involved. We cannot run out or leave this situation unfinished. President Nixon's plan of troop withdrawal may satisfy some people, but this seems a dangerous plan, courting disaster for the few that will have to remain, unless it is a mutual agreement, for it is unrealistic to believe that once the bulk of our forces are out of Vietnam, the enemy will not try a swift and complete take over. . . .

With this dark picture facing us, it seems to me that there is only one course left, one that for some unknown reason has been written off by President Nixon. It is high time that we realize there is no other way to win this war, but to force the enemy at the conference table, with an ultimatum that unless he agrees to a swift and peaceful solution of this war, it will be necessary for the United States to initiate unrestricted major military operations to conclude this war as soon as possible. . . .

... Let's forget the politics. Let's win this war and unify our country. There is a longing for a strong leadership, to show the world we stand for righteousness and will fight for it. President Nixon needs to show the strength of men like Roosevelt, Churchill, with strong words and positive action to unite all the people. We need the military genius of a McArthur on the field to beat the enemy at his own game. . . .

15. In his November 3, 1969, speech Nixon disparaged war protestors, defended his conduct of the war, and appealed to the "great silent majority" of presumably prowar Americans to support him and the war.

Respectfully,

F.A.A. (Atlanta, GA)

31

Dear Senator [Albert] Gore [Sr.]:

[1970]

Would you please respond to this letter personally to help restore some of my faith in the United States. My problem is this: I am 22 and very confused. The U.S. is the most powerful country in the world & we have gotten ourselves into a position of fighting a 10th rate power at *their* terms. If we must send our men to Vietnam to fight then why can't *we* set the rules? Wouldn't it save face & lives on both sides if we gave an ultimatum or two? Couldn't we say all North Vietnamese troops will leave the south or we use nuclear weapons? Why don't we bomb the cities of Haiphong and Hanoi? Why don't we get rid of the Ky government (surely one of the most corrupt in history)? After we send our boys over there, how can we justify putting them on trial for killing the enemy? What good are billions of $ of nuclear weapons if even one American loses his life in a two-bit war? If we are not going to use these weapons to save American lives why have them? Couldn't you personally get up before the Senate and advocate an all out decisive war or no war at all? By all out I mean a war with a definite goal in mind. Our goal in Vietnam is supposedly free elections, well they had a free election & that is where they got their corrupt govt. What's the use??? I am not a hippie, don't resemble a hippie, have never picketed anything, have held my present job for 5 years, the SDS repulses me, Jerry Rubin repulses me, and stupid political wars repulse me. The current tactics of my country in waging this ridiculous police action are making patriotism very difficult. Can't something be done? And please don't say you advocate Pres. Nixon's Vietnamization plan because I consider the plan one of the current ridiculous tactics.[16]

Thank you very much for reading this,

T.C. (Memphis, TN)

16. "Putting soldiers on trial" refers to the My Lai massacre; see chapter five. SDS was the acronym for Students for a Democratic Society, a left-leaning student group that favored the Civil Rights Movement and opposed the war.

32

Mr. President [Richard M. Nixon]:

May 5, 1970

I am a twenty-seven year old pharmacist and a recent college graduate who supports your recent change in strategy in Viet Nam. My stomach is turned by watching most of the bleeding-heart news media bemoaning the fact that this country's leadership is finally showing some backbone. You will probably ignore this letter as just another from a redneck warmonger racist from Mississippi, for this is the picture most people from other sections of the country paint. A sad state of affairs is in existence when one who shows a respect for the flag is labeled a flag waving idiot. Student mobs call for a Viet Cong victory while Senator Halfbright from Arkansas is calling another Senate hearing about the war. If he had his way we would withdraw and give the communists everything west of the Arkansas line. Old-fashioned American patriotism, from all appearances, is dead. During World War II, anyone demanding a German Victory would have been tried for treason. Today he would be a celebrity and a prime candidate for a guest appearance on the Tonight Show or Merv Griffin (e.g. Abbie Hoffman). . . . It is regrettable that students were killed at Kent State, but if they had not been part of a mob and in their dorms they would be alive today. We have no mob action in Mississippi because we enforce laws and everyone, be he black, white, or assorted colors knows this. . . . While I was attending college the mere sighting of your face at a panty raid was grounds for suspension. . . . These days a group of well meaning students can burn buildings, ransack offices and pelt guardsmen with rocks with the full knowledge that they will receive amnesty and newsmen will discover a deprived childhood as the root cause of the unrest. . . .

Yours sincerely,
A.W. (Columbus, MS)

33

Dear [Senator] Sam [J. Ervin Jr.]:

May 7, 1970

It is my opinion that President Nixon and his advisors were correct in order-ing the invasion of Cambodia which had for years been a sanctuary for the North Vietnamese. Personally, I think this action should have been ordered at least five years ago. I believe that many an American has died because the enemy, while staying in Cambodia, could cross over into South Vietnam, make his attack and cross back into a sanctuary.

I have made it a point for the past week to talk to possibly twenty prominent men and without an exception they agree with the position I have expressed above. The only exception was my Pastor whom I regard very highly and who is a very able Methodist Minister. In the Church bulletin of last Sunday he requested all who believed that entering Cambodia was wrong to write our Senators. He also made a five minute talk to the same effect. I do not know how many letters you have received from this locality, but I did want to go on record as supporting Mr. Nixon in what he is doing. . . .

Cordially yours,
H.G. (Belmont, NC)

34

Dear President [Richard M.] Nixon:

May 8, 1970

I merely wish to let you know that I agree 100% with your Vietnamization Program, as I understand it; and also with the action that you have taken with regard to the communist position and presence in Cambodia. You are correct in concluding that there can be no prospect of peace in Southeast Asia, or anywhere else in the world, until the communists are convinced that America has the "will to win." . . . I am convinced that many American lives have been lost and the war has been extended uselessly because this country has failed in driving this fact of "will" home to the communists. Your move into Cambodia, and your TV presentation explaining it has done so———AND IT IS ABOUT TIME. I hope and pray that its effect will not be weaken by reaction to the obviously planned antiwar demonstrations within this country.

The "silent majority" in this country are beginning to awaken. I believe that they would have awakened long ago, if they had had a leader they could follow. Americans do not understand the concept of a "limited war." The only rational purpose of war, if it becomes necessary, is to win it. The fact that we have been in Vietnam so long and, until recently, were apparently pursuing an official policy of "no win" has been a major factor in convincing many Americans of good faith that we should get out. The reasoning is obvious—why should American youth be shot and shattered and killed year after year in a war America did not intend to go all-out and win? . . . I believe that your recent action has tended to clear the air in this regard. . . .

Sincerely yours,
F.E.S. Jr. (Vicksburg, MS)

35

Dear Senator [Albert] Gore [Sr.]:

May 18, 1970

. . . Please believe me that I do not doubt your sincerity in the least.

Again, let me agree with you that insofar as domestic policies are concerned, President Nixon and Vice President Agnew are tearing the country apart and I am frankly fearful that the desire of the majority for law and order and peace on the college campus could well tempt us to set up a totalitarian state as was the case in Germany under Hitler and, of course, this must not happen.

Mr. Ellenburg makes the point that the domino theory is invalid. If this is true, then I pose the following questions:

1. Why did North Korea, with the blessing of China, attack South Korea and why did China send troops to fight in that war? . . .
2. Why did North Vietnam, with the blessing of China, invade and occupy portions of Laos and Cambodia?
3. Why the support of both Russia and China of the military effort of North Vietnam? . . .
4. Why did the Communists try a takeover of Indonesia and Malaysia? . . .
5. Why the Russian support of Cuba and the Russian, Cuban and Chinese support of African militants? . . .

Now, turning to our own protestors:

1. Why do they condone rocket attacks on the civilian population of South Vietnam and raise a howl of protest over bombing of military targets in Cambodia, Laos, South Vietnam and North Vietnam?
2. Why do they condone the murder of South Vietnamese civilians by the Viet Cong and howl when we knock out a village that is a Viet Cong stronghold?

3. Why do they say nothing about our prisoners of war held by Hanoi and why do they carry Viet Cong flags in their protest marches? . . .

Turning to Mr. Ellenburg's recommendation that we simply . . . leave Vietnam:

1. What happens to those South Vietnamese who have fought the Communists?
2. If the South Vietnamese are as spineless, corrupt, . . . and unpatriotic as Mr. Ellenburg implies, how have they managed to create a nation under war time conditions and why do they now fight? . . .
3. If we leave Vietnam what will be the final result in Southeast Asia?

In your letter you state you recommend an appropriate and honorable negotiated settlement and I am certain that 100% of the American people join with you in this recommendation. But, my final question is, how can that be accomplished? For two years all that has happened in Paris has been for the North Vietnamese negotiators to insult us and use the conference for a sounding board to try to encourage violent dissent in America. . . .

My own view is that if the present Cambodian campaign can effectively restore Cambodian authority throughout Cambodia and get the Viet Cong and North Vietnamese out of Cambodia, then the war could be brought to a quick conclusion through negotiation, and our servicemen in Vietnam will be a lot safer than they are now. . . .

Yours very truly,
E.R.T. (Morristown, TN)

36

Dear Mr. [Herman E.] Talmadge:

June 8, 1970

. . . Our son, C.W.B., has returned from Viet Nam after spending some 19 months. Our other son takes his physical for Selective Service in July. In spite of these facts, I believe that the war has been prolonged far too long. The stalemate is costing us men every day. Surely this must be brought to a halt. I have a hard time finding a category to fit into. I want peace for Indo-China and could never be identified as those who are called Anti-War Demonstrators. Yet I could never march in a parade such as the one held in St. Louis yesterday supporting the war. Surely there is some in-between place that people could stand who simply want it to end.

Perhaps legislation such as you mentioned in your press conference would hasten the day when a way would be found to get out of Viet Nam and Cambodia with a degree of honor—but above all—to get out.

Sincerely yours,
R.D.B. (female, Decatur, GA)

37

Dear [Senator] Russell [B. Long]:

March 15, 1971

The purpose of this letter is to voice opposition to the McGovern-Hatfield Resolution, S 376, which calls for withdrawal of all American forces from South Vietnam by December 31, 1971, and to strongly urge that you oppose its passage.[17]

Partisan politics aside, it seems to me that since Mr. Nixon took office he has done a magnificent job in reducing our casualties and troop commitments in Vietnam, at the same time greatly strengthening the South Vietnamese forces to the point where they are now bearing the brunt of the fighting. In my opinion, the Commander-in-Chief should not be hamstrung by further Congressional intervention in his program. "Too many cooks spoil the broth."

If this resolution can be beaten, it will be by the Southern Democrats plus the Republicans in Congress (excluding such as Hatfield, Percy and Javits). . . .

Sincerely yours,
V.Y. (Bogalusa, LA)

38

My Dear Senator [Herman E.] Talmadge:

April 8, 1971

I urge you to resist in every way possible the movement now underway to

17. The Mc-Govern-Hatfield Resolution was one of the congressional attempts to legislate an end to the war by ending funding. The Cooper-Church Amendment would have forced Nixon to withdraw U.S. troops from Cambodia by June 30, 1970; the McGovern-Hatfield measure would have required the withdrawal of all U.S. troops from Vietnam by the end of 1971. Neither secured congressional approval. The author of the previous letter (#36) was also referring to end-the-war legislation.

bring about a surrender to North Vietnam by setting a definite date for withdrawal of our forces. . . .

Mankind the world over made progress in 1776 when a new form of government was instituted by wise men. . . . Greatest progress was in the area of religious freedom and it pains me to think that we could abandon the far east or any other part of the world to atheistic communism for no reason but that we lack the courage of our forebears.

I would expect Christians to be the last to agree to turn the world over to atheists. . . .

The only course of action worthy of the greatness of this country and the God we worship is to abandon our "no win" policy and get out of Asia by defeating the atheists who seek to impose their will on the entire world. This not being politically feasible, the next best is President Nixon's policy of Vietnamization and a withdrawal without abandoning South Vietnam to communism. . . .

Sincerely yours,
W.F.B. (Atlanta, GA)

39

Dear Mr. President [Richard M. Nixon]:

June 17, 1971

Few American Presidents in our history have known the abuse and vilification that you have endured in your pursuit of an honorable and satisfactory conclusion to our nation's involvement in a war which was undertaken long before you came into office. . . .

This letter is offered in behalf of the Raleigh, North Carolina, American Legion Post #1, and is intended to express our strong support for your Vietnam policies and specifically to commend you and your Administration for:

1. Your refusal to establish a definite date for final withdrawal of all American military personnel from South Vietnam. It should be obvious to everyone that alerting Hanoi to such a deadline would pose a great and immediate and unnecessary danger to our own forces and to the Republic of South Vietnam. . . .
2. Your refusal to come to any formal peace terms with Hanoi which do not absolutely guarantee the safe and prompt repatriation of all American military prisoners now held in the prison camps of North Vietnam.
3. Your steadfast adherence to a policy of concluding America's part in the

war in a way which will not abandon our South Vietnamese allies without a fighting chance of successfully resisting Hanoi's aggression.

4. Your undeviating pursuit of these policies in the face of unrelenting abuse from those who, out of ignorance, political motivation or disloyalty would summarily abandon the South Vietnamese to Communist conquest, American prisoners to their fate, and America to a dishonorable history of having expended billions of dollars and thousands of brave young lives in vain. . . .

Yours very sincerely,
W.F.H. (Raleigh, NC)

40

Dear Senator [Herman E.] Talmadge:

April 1972

I am writing you to let you know that here is one of your supporters who is very much *in favor* of what President Nixon is doing in North Vietnam. I emphatically support bombing the hell out of Hanoi & Haiphong—McGovern, Muskie and Humphrey not withstanding—they can go to hell! Senator Fulbright, Senator Church and those other doves can go to hell too! I for one am fed up to here! with doves—they, in my opinion, are the real reason the war has lasted so long. Had Hanoi not had their support down thru the years the war would have been over long ago. . . .

Sincerely yours,
G.M. (Athens, GA)

41

Dear Mr. [J. William] Fulbright:

April 18, 1972

. . . You seem at a complete loss to understand the bombing of Hanoi and Haiphong, contending that since it is the President's avowed intention to withdraw, this can only mean an escalation of the war. You keep trying to ignore the fact that the North Vietnamese launched a major attack across the demilitarized zone, and also that we still have approximately 100,000 men in South Vietnam. What do you propose that we do? Abandon them? Pull all of them out overnight? Or put the pressure on them where it hurts most?

I believe that Mr. Nixon has been doing all that any reasonable man can do to *honorably* extricate us from this no-win war and I believe that you and some of your fellow senators (McGovern, Muskie, E. Kennedy and others) are taking stands that come dangerously close to giving aid and comfort to the enemy. If the purpose of the questions you have been asking concerning our future moves is actually to obtain information, why should this not be done in closed hearings so that we will not telegraph our every move to the enemy?

I am a veteran of World War II, which I believe we would never have won if we had always kept the enemy informed as to our next move. . . .

Sincerely,

R.L.B. (Hot Springs, AR)

42

Dear Sir [Senator Herman E. Talmadge]:

May 12, 1972

I have been disappointed in the weak and feeble position you are taking in response to the President's recent action in blocking the ports of North Vietnam. . . .[18]

The President has brought home some 500,000 men from Vietnam and although I have been disappointed in many phases of our involvement in trying to leave Vietnam, I am still convinced the President is doing what is best for the country. It is strange that those who acclaimed President Kennedy for his bold actions in confronting the Russians in Cuba should now condemn President Nixon for his actions to stop naked aggression by the North Vietnamese.

By blocking the ports of North Vietnam we now have the one bargaining point with which to demand the release of our prisoners. Without this bargaining point, I believe the North Vietnamese will hold our prisoners until we crawl out of every part of Southeast Asia. . . .

Sincerely yours,

M.J.B. (Decatur, GA)

---

18. Talmadge, an earlier proponent of the domino theory and aggressive prosecution of the war, declared after the U.S. invasion of Cambodia in May 1970 that Nixon should have consulted Congress and that U.S. withdrawal was "just a matter of time" and should be implemented as rapidly "as possible."

43

Dear Senator [Herman E.] Talmadge,

May 13, 1972

 I would like to go on record as being very strong *in favor* of President Nixon's action in mining NVN Ports. I want to see SVN survive as an independent nation . . . but even more important—I want to see our POW's released. Those brave guys have been in the "Hanoi Hilton" too long already. Now—if it takes even stronger military action to get them out—then I approve of that also. If that means completely destroying NVN—then so be it!! We are not going to get them out by *begging* those damned communists to release them. It is *either or!* Release those POW's or face utter devastation. . . .

 . . . Senator—one more thing though I must tell you—*many of us Conservative Demo's have been concerned about your increasingly Dovish stands lately* * * *

Sincerely yours,
G.M. (Athens, GA)

44

Dear Senator [David H. Gambrell]:

June 12, 1972

Vietnam
Military Pressure and Blockage

 . . . please stand firm behind the conviction that *we cannot afford* . . . stopping our military pressure and blockade against North Vietnam. We can only afford to stop when: (1) The North Vietnamese cease their shameful act of aggression and pull back out of South Vietnam; (2) release our POW's; and (3) agree to an internationally supervised determination of the "color" of the future South Vietnamese political structure—if they warrant any consideration whatsoever. . . .

Public Notice of Deadlines

 Revealing of any deadline for our disengagement from South Vietnam is like a poker player showing his opponents his trump card. He's a fool; he's asking to be "clobbered" good. . . .

Very truly yours,
J.A.H. (Atlanta, GA)

45

Dear Senator [Herman E.] Talmadge:

January 5, 1973

This letter is to urge you to use your total influence in opposing any effort that the Congress might make to cut off support of our efforts in Vietnam.

It seems fairly certain that the war in Vietnam will be settled one way or another in a very few months. The important question now is, "What kind of settlement?" If North Vietnam were convinced that the President could continue to use whatever force is needed, they would most likely agree to a settlement that would discourage further aggression and give the independent countries of Asia a measure of security. But if the kind of peace that comes is one that permits them to continue their aggression, we can look for a tremendous bloodbath of South Vietnam as they take over, and further aggression into other countries. Through some ridiculous twisted reasoning, a group in the Senate and in the House seem determined that it will be the latter kind of "peace," rather than the former. They continue to assure Hanoi: "Don't agree to a thing. We'll cut off funds for American support, and then you can take what you want." . . .

If the people of this country had wanted an unconditional sellout to the Communists, they would have voted for Senator McGovern, since that is what he promised. The peace and security of the entire non-Communist world may depend on the kind of settlement that is obtained in Vietnam, and the kind of settlement will depend on what Congress does—or leads Hanoi to believe they might do. Let me urge you to speak in no uncertain terms in support of the negotiations for peace and *against* the sabotaging of these talks by the promise of an American withdrawal.

Sincerely yours,
J.T.C. (Birmingham, AL)

46

My dear Senator [J. William Fulbright]:

January 8, 1973

It is my wish that the Congress take no action to restrict President Nixon in his conducting of the Indo-China conflict.

It is apparent that the President has a better comprehension of what is required to restore and to maintain peace in Indo-China than most of the Congressmen who are attempting to restrain his freedom of choice.

I think the so-called "Doves" are indirectly responsible for the loss of thousands of lives. Their raucous "cooing" indicated their strength to be far beyond their actual numbers.

When Senator McGovern and his "unconditional surrender" policy was met with such a thunderous *NO* at the polls, President Nixon realized what the real wishes of the nation are. And he has the courage to act, even though he knew that those enamored with Communism will try to nail him to a gibbet.

Had this intense bombing been carried out years ago, countless lives would have been spared, and the small countries been given years, free from the fear of Communist aggression, to build their nations.

Please consider the moral caliber of those who are noisily condemning the bombing of North Vietnam. Strangely, they do not seem to grieve about the murder and terrorism the North Vietnamese wreck on South Vietnam. . . .

I wish that a firm warning go out to all nations in Indo-China that future aggression will not succeed. You should know from past history that Communists' promises and treaties are worthless, except when they are enforced by stronger nations who are ready to go to the defense of helpless people.

Very truly yours,
Mrs. C.L.B. (Mena, AR)

2. Antiwar Southerners

Just as Gallup polling demonstrated that the South was the nation's most prowar region and that the clear majority of white southerners supported the war, these polls also revealed a substantial southern antiwar minority. For example, in June 1966 Americans were asked how they would vote on the "question of continuing the war in Vietnam or withdrawing our troops during the next few months." Forty-five percent of southerners favored continuing, but 37 percent endorsed withdrawal. Eleven months later in May 1967, Gallup inquired if the United States should go "all-out to win a military victory in Vietnam, using atom bombs and weapons." Although the South led the nation with a third of respondents agreeing (versus 26 percent nationally), 52 percent of Dixie's residents disagreed. This response ran 8 percent fewer than the national average, but, once again, revealed a significant antiwar segment of southern society.[1]

Southern antiwar inclinations were also evident in responses to the bombing of North Vietnam. In October 1967 51 percent of southerners favored continued bombing, but 38 percent were opposed. In March 1968 during the Tet Offensive, 35 percent of Dixie's residents endorsed a bombing halt if North Vietnam agreed to peace talks, compared to 52 percent who objected. A month later, after President Johnson stopped the bombing of North Vietnam, 59 percent of southerners approved of his action; 29 percent disapproved. Following President Nixon's resumption of U.S. bombing of the DRV in 1972, 45 percent of those southerners questioned backed the decision; 36 percent demurred.[2]

The responses of the South's residents to the hawk/dove question also indicated a persistent and, by 1968, growing southern antiwar contingent. In February 1968 as the Tet Offensive began, 22 percent of southerners considered themselves doves, as opposed to 63 percent who self-identified as hawks. By April, as the

---

1. *GOI*, no. 13 (June 1966): 7; *GOI*, no. 24 (June 1967): 7.

2. *GOI*, no. 29 (Nov. 1967): 3; *GOI*, no. 34 (April 1968): 17; *GOI*, no. 35 (May 1968): 18; *GOI*, no. 88 (Oct. 1972): 20.

communist offensive was being repulsed, the percentage of southern doves had increased to 38. This figure was unchanged in October 1968 and grew to 52 percent in December 1969.[3]

Like the remainder of the nation, the South's mounting disillusionment with the war was expressed through an increasing willingness to declare U.S. military intervention a mistake. This perspective reflected both the assessment of the South's antiwar residents and that of disaffected prowar southerners who believed the war was not being waged with sufficient vigor. Even with this qualification, the pattern of southern responses affords additional evidence of the South's clear antiwar voices. When Gallup first posed this query in May 1965, 28 percent of southerners deemed intervention a mistake; by April 1968, the percentage had increased to 52. At the beginning of the Nixon administration, 50 percent of southerners were in the mistake column; during 1970 the response rose to 54 percent and peaked at 59 percent in May 1971 when Gallup stopped asking this question.[4]

Antiwar southern letter writers addressed most of the same issues as their prowar neighbors, but they expressed very different perspectives and reached sharply contrasting conclusions. Most fundamentally, the South's doves did not consider the war essential to U.S. national security. Rather than viewing the conflict as a crucial part of America's worldwide struggle against communism, antiwar southerners characterized the struggle as a civil war among the Vietnamese and argued that Ho Chi Minh and his followers were primarily nationalists seeking a united, independent Vietnam.

Working from this premise, southern opponents of the war argued that the domino theory was not applicable; that U.S. international credibility was not dependent upon winning the war; that the threat from a small, poor, nonindustrial North Vietnam was hardly comparable to that posed by Germany and Japan in World War II; and that Vietnamese communists did not endanger American democracy, capitalism, and Christianity. Had the Vietnamese posed an actual threat to U.S. interests and world stability, major U.S. allies in Europe and Asia

3. *GOI*, no. 33 (March 1968): 8; *GOI*, no. 35 (May 1968): 2; *GOI*, no. 40 (Oct. 1968): 25; *GOI*, no. 54 (Dec. 1969): 8.

4. *GOI*, no. 1 (June 1965): 3; *GOI*, no. 12 (May 1966): 6; *GOI*, no. 26 (Aug. 1967): 4; *GOI*, no. 29 (Nov. 1967): 4; *GOI*, no. 35 (May 1968): 21; *GOI*, no. 45 (March 1969): 11; *GOI*, no. 56 (Feb. 1970): 2; *GOI*, no. 73 (July 1971): 3.

would have come to America's aid rather than opposing the war. Opponents of the war emphasized President Nixon's efforts to achieve détente and the lowering of Cold War tensions with China and the Soviet Union in 1972. How, they asked, could the Vietnam War be of such great geopolitical importance if Nixon were seeking more friendly relations with the two nations that ostensibly had the most to gain from a U.S. defeat in Southeast Asia?

Antiwar southerners advanced a series of related arguments for ending U.S. military involvement in Vietnam. Not only was the U.S. intervention unnecessary, it was also unconstitutional and illegal since Congress had not officially declared that a war existed. These southern critics reprimanded their senators and congressmen for allowing Johnson and Nixon to wield dangerous and unilateral executive authority. Congress should reclaim its constitutional role by passing legislation to end funding for the war and to set a date for U.S. military withdrawal.

In addition to being unnecessary and unconstitutional, the war was immoral and un-Christian. Citing U.S. carpet bombing and use of chemical weapons, such as napalm and agent orange; the massive loss of civilian life; and the devastating destruction inflicted across both North and South Vietnam, antiwar southerners asked how an ostensibly civilized, Christian nation could devastate a small, poor country on the other side of the world. Some southern critics characterized U.S. actions as genocide and equated them with Nazi Germany's attempt to exterminate European Jews. While opposing increases in U.S. troop strength and more widespread bombing, southern doves contended that American escalations after 1964 had failed to end the war while simultaneously risking a nuclear conflict with the USSR or the PRC. Negotiations with the DRV and NLF, working with the UN, or reconvening the Geneva meeting of 1954 to end the conflict were far preferable. Moreover, ending the war was essential to redirecting resources to much-needed domestic reforms, to curbing the wasteful spending that primarily benefited big business, to restoring order and progress at home, and to securing the release of American POWs. Antiwar southerners voiced great frustration when their arguments against the war and pleas for peace failed for nearly ten years to change U.S. policy.

From a more peculiarly regional perspective, antiwar southerners asserted that it would be far more honorable for the United States to admit its mistake and withdraw than to continue a fruitless war to save face. Other southerners cited their section's history while arguing against any attempt to impose outside values and institutions on others. Finally, southern critics of the Vietnam conflict frequently commented on the difficulties and social pressures that came with speaking out against the war in the South. These pressures were evident as the South's doves proclaimed their patriotism; denied being radicals, isolationists, pacifists, or beatniks; and emphasized that their criticism of the war did not mean they opposed American soldiers who had been placed in an impossible situation by being drafted and sent to Vietnam.

1

My Dear Senator [Ralph W. Yarborough],

July 29, 1963

The European press carries disturbing reports of the Administration's buildup of American forces in Vietnam. . . .

It looks to me as though the United States is allowing itself to be sucked into a debacle like that in Korea, perhaps a worse one. And what was the result of our Korean intervention?—some tens of thousands of American dead, some tens of billions of dollars spent, an ignominious defeat, and an occupation that has so far lasted 14 years and has tied up a good portion of our army.

All this talk by the President (and I don't mean only Johnson,—Eisenhower and Kennedy have been equally guilty) about our determination to defend the "freedom" and the "liberty" of the Far East is pure hogwash. In the first place, the American people have never declared such determination; in the second place, "freedom" and "liberty" are unknown concepts in the Far East—the people there have never had either of them and show no signs of craving them now. If such desires existed among the Vietnamese, they would have obtained them by themselves. . . .

I hope you will do all you can to urge an end to this tragic situation, daily becoming more menacing. Our intervention should be stopped, quickly, and our forces taken out of Vietnam.

Very truly yours,

F.K.F. (Austin, TX)

2

Dear Senator [John G. Tower]:

October 2, 1963

I am a Housewife-Secretary—just one of a group of ordinary citizens who are becoming increasingly concerned about our Government's foreign policy which condones sending American servicemen to a foreign country where they are subjected to vilification and harassment, pouring untold millions of our tax dollars into a "non-war" and have little or no hope of doing more than losing face and eventually the war. How can you help a people who refuse to let you help them headed by a government most of them hate and which, in turn, states you are not doing much more than causing them trouble? When we back a government where 30% of the people (Catholic) are allowed to force their way of thinking on the other 70%, how can we say that is any better than the Communists? Whatever happened to religious freedom we so strongly advocate? . . .

When are we going to objectively look at our foreign policy and realize that the biggest debt the U.S. Government owes is to the *American* people. I'm no isolationist but I believe the best interests of our people can be served by . . . giving help to those people *deserving* of that help and who are willing to *help themselves*. . . . Unless there is a better argument for continuing this WAR than I have been able to ascertain from the newspapers and other articles . . . , I would be of the opinion that we should make some changes—and fast—in our policies regarding Vietnam. . . .

Very truly yours,
E.L. (Dallas, TX)

3

Dear Mr. President [Lyndon B. Johnson]:

March 23, 1964

The crucial situation of the war in South Vietnam is of such a vital nature right now that our leaders, such as you, should be informed on the opinions of individual citizens, such as myself.

1. First I wish to register my objection to supporting a government which was not elected and is not representative of the people.
2. Second it seems to me intolerable that we can sanction the cruelty of killing in order to settle differences.

3. Truly you must realize, Mr. President, that, in continuing this losing war, we are as well losing our moral leadership in the eyes of the world.

4. Would it not be far better to obtain a settlement in this tangled question by *negotiation*, working toward a demilitarized and neutralized Southeast Asia?

5. Would it not be possible and advisable at this point (before any further deterioration of the conditions sets in) to put an end to our destructive military operations and *honorably remove* our *forces?* This seems to me the only humane, sensible, and honorable thing to do; the only action worthy of our country as a world leader.

I urge you, before it is too late, to support the reconvening of the Geneva Powers—the countries which settled the French Indochina war in 1954. The People's Republic of China should be included if a satisfactory settlement is to be achieved. . . .

Sincerely yours,
J.S.H. (female, Chapel Hill, NC)

4

Dear Senator [Richard B.] Russell [Jr.]:

July 21, 1964

It is becoming increasingly clear that the United States government is guilty of hateful and imperialistic acts against the people of the Indochinese peninsula, particularly Viet Nam and Laos, and I am extremely disturbed by the assertions of Secretary McNamara, Secretary Rusk, and others that the longsuffering people of this area of Southeast Asia are to continue to be the victims of a war of annihilation which is to be carried forward henceforth on an even more intensified scale.

The South Vietnamese National Liberation Front is by all evidence an authentic independence movement, dedicated to free the people of South Viet Nam from a cruel and despotic regime and from foreign domination. Though President Ho Chi Minh of North Viet Nam might be described as a Marxist--Leninist, I believe it is an utter distortion to refer to the NLF as being the front line in Southeast Asia of an international communist conspiracy.

The United States should abide by the Geneva agreements of 1954 and withdraw its forces from the Indochinese peninsula. I am in agreement with the stand which you have taken in the Senate opposing the involvement of United States forces in Viet Nam and Laos.

Sincerely yours,
M.T.R. (Atlanta, GA)

5

Dear Senator [Sam J.] Ervin [Jr.],

April 16, 1965

. . . One of your statements bothers me greatly: "Under the Constitution, the power to conduct our foreign relations belongs to the President and not to individual Senators and Representatives." While this is a fact, the implication is that the people through their elected representatives in Congress actually have no voice in our country's conduct of foreign relations. In a democracy people have the right and the *responsibility* to keep vigilance over government, and, may I add, the Pentagon. I regret the extent to which military influence prevails over civilian in matters of foreign policy.

I disagree with the thinking in your letter justifying our continued and expanded war in Vietnam. You mention it as a struggle between the righteous and the evil * * * that we are there to defend freedom-loving people * * * that the trouble is because of Vietcong infiltration.

. . . Our very presence in Vietnam is on [a] flimsy base: we are there by invitation of the very unpopular and cruel Diem regime. . . .

We have ineptly gotten ourselves mixed up in perpetuating and feeding a Vietnamese *Civil* War. We are told that the only way to stamp out Communism is by more bombings and extension of the war to the North; yet . . . it seems like Communism *grows best* in the social disturbance which is made worse by war. I can't believe that the war-weary Vietnamese love us or freedom and democracy *more* as we continue to feed into their country the funds and weapons to keep the civil strife going. . . .

Sincerely,
R.G. (female, Franklin, NC)

6

To the Editor of the *Louisville Courier-Journal*:

July 2, 1965

. . . In U.S. military power, the world apparently has a Frankenstein on its hands. Nothing short of violations of international law, invasion of our soil, or depriving us of freedom of the seas should provoke us to war. And yet we find ourselves in the embarrassing position of waging undeclared war on two small nations, neither of which has committed an unfriendly act against our nation.

Apparently there is something wrong with our leadership, and until Congress makes these wars legal by a declaration, . . . the people have a right to appeal for honor, and more sanity in government administration. We cannot continue indefinitely, to swallow the "domino theory," that if South Viet Nam falls, all Asia will go Communistic, and our way of life, 8,000 miles away, will vanish. A more sensible theory is: If we don't stop interfering in the affairs of other nations, and giving them our assets in billion-dollar parcels, we will not have a nation to defend.

The Truman Doctrine is the gimmick that tripped us. We must learn anew that we are merely one sovereign nation in a big world, with no authority whatsoever to mess with world problems, or to tell other nations what type of government they shall or shall not have. Viet Nam has a right to engage in civil war, but we have no authority to occupy their territory, establish military bases, destroy their property or murder their people.

W.F.S. (Shelbyville, KY)

7

Dear Senator [Richard B. Russell Jr.]:

July 12, 1965

I am not much of a letter writer but as the father of a fifteen year old son, I feel compelled to write you my views on the spread of the Viet Nam war. The papers have painted the person that opposes this war as an unwashed beatnik and some kind of a subversive. I bathe, am a college graduate and have been fortunate in making well in the upper five figures for the last five years. The only organizations I belong to is the Baptist Church and the Human Race.

It seems everyone is now rationalizing a land war commitment eventually with China. We have done an excellent job of awakening the giant. I have endeavored without success to understand this miserable mess. . . . I would like to know why we cannot at least declare a moratorium and refer this mess to the United Nations. . . .

Respectfully,
J.W.T. (Atlanta, GA)

8

Dear Senator [A. Willis] Robertson:

July 19, 1965

. . . Sir, I don't understand what we are doing now. As I was on my way back from Europe, we dropped our first bombs on N. Vietnam. The horror of protest was so great in the next months that it seemed . . . like a battle between the American military seducing the government on the one hand and the American people and in fact the whole free and unfree world on the other. I watched the numbers change from 12,000 troops to help secure and counsel S. Vietnam units to the present almost 100,000 engaged in active offensive which (even when quoting the soldiers doing the bombing, admittedly destroys more women and children than Vietcong. And of course villages, even those just built with US aid. . .) convinces no one else but perhaps some of us that we are "winning anything of value. . . .

. . . some 6,000,000 Jews and our justified wrath and damnation at their destruction haunt me when I see what measures and price we levy at a "communist threat." Forgetting Hiroshima and Nagasaki, forgetting the phosphor bombs in Germany about which we "can do nothing," I ask you and myself, Senator Robertson, what is the . . . difference between blind determination to destroy Communists at all cost or to destroy Jews at all costs?. . .

Very sincerely yours,
L.H. (female, Manassas, VA)

9

To the Editor of the *Louisville Courier-Journal:*

July 28, 1965

In a July 19 editorial The Courier-Journal deplored the atrocities of the Viet Cong. No mention was made of the bombing of Vietnamese civilians by U.S. planes. . . . Perhaps the murder of women and children is more humane with a bomb than with a knife; better wholesale than piecemeal. . . .

We are told that these villages are being bombed at the request of the South

Vietnamese government, our ally. It is all to keep the people from going Communist. Just as there are no atheists in foxholes, there are no Communists in graveyards. And the people are going Communist. Does anyone really believe the quaint fiction that a guerrilla army can win support through terror? It is 20 per cent terror, perhaps, but 80 per cent sympathy.

For our ally is a reactionary military dictatorship, representing not the people but only the dregs of French colonialism—with American support. We are fighting against Communism, but is that enough? What are we fighting for?

T.B. (Louisville, KY)

10

Dear Senator [Albert] Gore [Sr.],

January 29, 1966

. . . This week I wrote Secretary Rusk and sent him a copy of the original 1954 Geneva Agreement . . . because I really don't think the man has ever read it! He so piously talks about "aggressors" in their own country * * * the Agreement mentions only *one Vietnam (two temporary zones),* the zones to have been reunified by a general, all-Vietnam election in July 1956. America backed Ngo Dinh Diem in his refusal to hold those elections which was clearly a violation of the Agreement; . . . Yet Mr. Rusk has the nerve to talk about living up to "our commitment"! . . .

. . . Frankly, I'd rather negotiate in humility than be guilty of committing genocide against those people who have never done a thing to us. Ho Chi Minh could be no more brutal than Curtis LeMay or Wallace Greene * * * * at least Ho used discrimination in whom he killed! I see no difference in the attitudes of these generals toward the Viet Cong and North Vietnamese than in Hitler's attitude toward Jews. What makes a war criminal anyway? It appears that napalm in Vietnam is at least as effective as were gas-ovens at Auschwitz! . . . [5]

Sincerely,

Mrs. A.H.K. (Oak Ridge, TN)

---

5. U.S.A.F. General Curtis LeMay was Chief of Staff of the U.S. Air Force from 1961 through 1965 and advocated unrestrained bombing of North Vietnam. U.S. Marine Corps General Wallace Greene Jr. was Commandant of the Marine Corps from 1964 through 1967.

11

Dear Senator [John C. Stennis]:

[February 1966]

. . . Much has been said about the brutality practiced by the Communists in So. Vietnam. . . . I fail to see how the Communists' brutality there differs from the same as experienced in Hungary and Cuba and other places including inside Red China and the Soviet [Union]. Yet we overlook elsewhere and travel . . . to a distant small country to put things in order there. . . .

Having pointed out that heretofore the military has many times said that a land war on the mainland of Asia is the very last thing we should engage in, I wish to follow this up by saying that a military win by the U.S. in So. Vietnam bodes more disaster to us than would an immediate withdrawal without further loss of our boys . . . I see in a win our forever occupying of the country, . . . and our military forever on the alert that 700 millions of Chinks just across the border do not invade to commence a new war all over again. . . .

. . . The Administrating Washington office holders (Feds) seek to have each and every foreign country, and our South, have the form of government and "way of life," as desired and dictated by these Washington office holders. . . . It is but natural that this has boomeranged to where the rank & file thruout the World detest our Washington government, and can we in our South blame them, when we are in the same boat and have experienced the same thing? The assault that has been made upon the South, in view of our heritage and tradition which were well known and established, thru the 1964–1965 Civil Rights Acts . . . seems to me to preclude any boy from the South participating in wars brought on by the Feds, and even that our South[ern] Draft Boards should cooperate to that end. . . .

Yours very truly,
J.E.P. (Falls Glade, FL)

12

Dear Senator [John C.] Stennis:

February 2, 1966

I heard your speech to the Mississippi legislature last week and I must admit that it disturbed me greatly. . . . Your gross misrepresentation and distortion of the facts was shocking. . . .

Only after we broke the Geneva agreements did any large scale rebellion arise. It was not a unilateral invasion from the North, as you would have us believe. At first, the government of North Vietnam was even opposed to the rebellion. It was not until much later that Ho Chi Minh began to give the rebels even moral support.

Now you claim that it doesn't matter how we got there. The only issue is that "our honor is at stake." I maintain that it is a mark of maturity and honor to recognize our mistakes . . , and that it would be more honorable to admit now that we were wrong rather than to continue to carry on this immoral, illegal war. You yourself complained that we were not getting help from our allies. Could it not be that they think we're doing the wrong thing? It seems to me that if no one else is on our side, it's time to reexamine our policy.

In conclusion, the cry of defending freedom half way around the world rings hollow to a large segment of the people of Mississippi. Negroes wonder what kind of freedom we're defending in Vietnam when they don't even have the freedom to listen to your speech from the galleries of the Mississippi House of Representatives.

Sincerely,
J.W. (Tugaloo, MS)

13

Mr. [Albert] Gore [Sr.],

February 4, 1966

I feel it is my duty to write in regards to the war in Viet Nam. I am not a communist, nor do I sympathize with them, I am just a hard working citizen trying to make ends meet in a Great Society that is apparently the greatest hoax the American public has ever had pulled on them. . . .

I Don't approve of this drain on my tax dollars that the Viet Nam war is causing and all this aid. I have some sick relatives here at home that could use some of this help from the Great Society. . . .

In regards to our war on poverty, this is another drain on the taxpayer and I have yet to see a person in poverty that has received any benefit from this. . . .

I think our Senators and Congressmen should unite and stop this drain on the taxpayer. An Illegal war in Viet Nam that should be stopped and a Bogus war on poverty in the U.S. is causing me some concern. . . .

Please help us . . . to bring our men home from Viet Nam, call a halt to wasteful spending in the Gov't agencies on useless projects, and reestablish some of the defense bases that Mr. McNamara has closed. To reopen them and build a stout defense for this country would be a good way to spend my tax dollar and would help to bring about jobs that would eliminate the need for the poverty program. . . .

Sincerely,

B.D.McF. (Memphis, TN)

14

Dear Senator [J. William] Fulbright:

February 12, 1966

. . . I don't pretend to know very much about government affairs—I am only a middle-aged housewife of average intelligence. Usually, I ask my husband's advice and opinion on anything pertaining to government, but on Vietnam I have definite opinions of my own. I don't think we should be there at all—perhaps I am an isolationist. If someone were about to attack our shores (or even *close* to our shores) I would want my husband and son to defend us, but this dirty war in Vietnam, with our men fighting for a people who do not understand our way of life, and who . . . do not especially *want* our help, is a different matter. . . . I feel so sorry for our soldiers, and for the South Vietnamese, whose lives and homes and countryside are being destroyed. . . .

I honestly believe, if the *people* (not the draft-card burning radicals and beatniks) but the people who love their country and humanity, could vote on the issue, we would vote 90 to 1 to get out of Vietnam, even if we have to make some concessions! . . .

Sincerely,

Mrs. J.T.H. (Wynne, AR)

15

Dear Sir [Senator J. William Fulbright]:

February 23, 1966

. . . Our country has no business sending our boys over there to die. If they want to contribute supplies for the beleaguered South V. N., O. K. If the money men want to profit from the misery of others, that too is their business, but not this draining of our youth from our shores, leaving eventually a country of women, old men and babes; a choice plum to pluck by the communist nations. We will be defenseless. Why can't our societie's planners see that? . . .

American is for Americans; England is for Englishmen; Russia is for Russians, etc. There are boundaries around every country. Why should one country enter another country and make it like itself? The same God who created us, created the people in other countries, and He gave them wise men too to govern them and develop them in their own particular way. Let America be for Americans and for everyone else who seeks the wonderful ways and prosperity of the United States. Let them come here and work and develop their talents so that they can truly be one of us. But let us not go and invade another country and disturb their natural way of progress, and evolution. . . .

Very sincerely yours,
B.B. (female, Mountain Home, AR)

16

Dear Senator [Richard B.] Russell [Jr.]:

March 22, 1966

I have noted your comments on the need to expand the war in Vietnam. . . .

From what I have read, it seems that following your suggestions would make a direct confrontation with China and Russia a high possibility. Such a confrontation, if it should occur, would make the possibility of a third world war and a nuclear holocaust likely. Such an event would not be limited to Asia.

People, like myself, who are opposed to our policies in Vietnam are often accused of wanting "peace at any price." I feel this statement applies equally, if not more so, to those who wish the war expanded. Peace at the price of a nuclear holocaust could certainly be had. The earth would be quite tranquil with life nonexistent. Is this the price you are willing to pay for peace?

Statements by the administration have been contradictory. . . . We are told that we wish to see the Geneva Agreement of 1954 implemented and a free election held. If that is true, why did we support Diem in his refusal to hold free elections? And why did we violate the Geneva Agreement by sending in military assistance (before the rise of the NLF and the beginning of the resumption of fighting)?. . . We claim we are fighting for the life of the free world, yet none of the South Vietnamese governments have been free: they have been totalitarian. . . . We say we will go anywhere and talk to anyone in the search for peace, but we refuse to talk with the Viet Cong who are doing the fighting. We claim that the south was invaded by the north, then issue a White Paper that shows the majority of the Viet Cong are from the south. We claim that the Viet Cong are receiving substantial aid from the north and from China, but admit that the vast majority of weapons captured from the Viet Cong are American made. We claim that the people of South Vietnam want to defeat the Viet Cong, then reports come of the large number of deserters from the South Vietnamese army. . . . We claim we are fighting to liberate the villagers from the Viet Cong, but we destroy their villages and the people, civilians, within them if we merely suspect there "might be" Viet Cong within the villages. . . .

Sincerely,

G.B. (Decatur, GA)

17

Dear Sir [Senator Richard B. Russell Jr.]:

March 28, 1966

I consider your position on Viet Nam abhorrent and idiotic. You are executing a neat political maneuver in claiming you were against our initial involvement but now support our efforts completely. Thus you disclaim responsibility for the pine boxes coming home but can still reap the votes a chauvinistic demagogue always will. I would like to suggest that your position is absurd. Are we to pile folly upon folly ad infinitum? If our initial involvement was dubious, why can't we try something other than raising the ante and the casualty figures? All of our previous brilliant escalations (bombing the North, the introduction of U.S. combat troops in huge numbers) have done nothing but exacerbate our dilemma and narrow our options. And if your proposal to blockade Haiphong harbor fails to bring an easy victory (as it most assuredly will) will you then claim some responsibility for the escalation and the casualties that must inevitably follow in order to cover up another mistake? In short Senator, I'm asking you if you will take some responsibility for this war that you are so sedulously promoting. Thank you.

Yours truly,

J.C.H. (Augusta, GA)

18

Dear Senator [Thruston B. Morton]:

December 9, 1966

I am an old man who has observed many events during my eighty-two years. Have never written to my senator telling him how to run our business.

... I am no pacifist in the sense that I do not believe in ample and adequate navy, air, and army protection here at home. The conflict, with its staggering cost and waste, now going on in Corea and Viet Nam, is an uncalled for hideous nightmare. It takes us back into the shadows of the dark ages. It is bleeding the taxpayers white, it is murdering such useful things as road and school construction, industrial expansion which in a way are minor items in comparison to the hell our sons go through, fighting people with [whom] they do not have the least quarrel. ...

In my section the people as a whole and the mothers especially are sick and heart sore with this sorry condition. ... We need a school gym far worse than we need to send boys to be murdered in a hopeless war. If it must go on, give us roads, schools and care for the aged.

Truly,
W.M.W. (Liberty, KY)

19

Dear Senator [Sam J.] Ervin [Jr.]:

February 2, 1967

How can our leaders be so blind as to believe that any nation has the right to brutally inflict suffering, degradation and wholesale murder on another people for its own ends? Are we not in Vietnam namely to maintain the United States as the paramount power in Southeast Asia? For this purpose we are sacrificing the lives of our young men; we are inflicting unspeakable crimes on innocent women and children with our flesh-searing napalm and deadly firepower; we are backing a corrupt puppet government, and losing the respect of most of the nations of the world.

It has not been made generally known to us through our press just how strong the world reaction is against us. When President Johnson claims that most of the free world supports our war in Vietnam, he is *not* telling the truth. The British government has condemned our escalation of the bombing; Sweden refuses to sell us military equipment; France urges us to withdraw our troops; Italians are sending medical aid to North Vietnam; the Swiss are flying to Switzerland a number of children who have been injured by our fire-bombings. Public opinion in Europe is so bitter against us that in several West European nations there are special police guards outside U.S. embassies and consulates.

Only five percent of the Asian population support our Vietnam stand. Even the non-Communist nations of India, Japan, Indonesia, Pakistan, Burma, Cambodia, Ceylon, Malaysia, and Laos oppose us.

Our people could not understand why the Germans stood by and let their leaders perpetrate ghastly mass crimes on innocent people. But is the use of torture, gas, and civilian bombing evil *only* when it is done by Nazis or Communists? Why can we not realize that our present actions are being rightfully condemned throughout the world? . . .

Sincerely yours,
L.S.S. (female) and J.R.S. (Ashville, NC)

20

Dear Senator [Richard B.] Russell [Jr.]:

May 4, 1967

. . . From conversation with missionaries and from reading many reports and books, I firmly believe we should get out of Southeast Asia, including Vietnam. I would like for you to know my reasons for this belief:

IF WE GO ALL OUT TO WIN:

1. There is a risk of involving Russia and China in actual conflict, thus opening up a world war.
2. The more escalation, the more hatred we get from the world community.
3. We will destroy the identity of the Vietnamese people. Any help we give to the people of Vietnam will be to the effect of Westernization. We will thus destroy the Eastern characteristics of a people. The very idea of democracy is Westernization. . . .
4. Our military will destroy the country of both North and South Vietnam. Many will be killed, many injured for life. Buildings destroyed, economy ruined.

5. Never will the Vietcong be defeated. . . . The young men of North Vietnam have known war all of their lives, they are very nationalistic, and they are determined to drive the U.S. off of Vietnamese soil. . . .

IF WE GET OUT OF VIETNAM:

1. Ho Chi Minh would take over all of Vietnam. The country would be united. There would be people killed, but not as many as will be killed if we continue the war.
2. Landlords will lose their property and people will be forced to be loyal to the national government.
3. Slowly, but surely, factories will be rebuilt and new factories started— schools will be started—colleges started. More food will be grown and war-torn land will be reclaimed.
4. China will have little influence, if any at all on Vietnam. Vietnam has a long history of hatred and fear of China.
5. China-US relations will be less tense. . . .
6. I agree with you that the "domino theory" is not real—few, if any, other Southeastern Asian nations will become communist or even be threatened.
7. United States relations with other nations will improve, especially with Russia. . . .
8. Lives will be saved and money can be devoted to fighting poverty and suffering. . . .

Very sincerely,
T.C. (Watkinsville, GA)

21

Dear Honorable [John C.] Stennis:

August 22, 1967

It has disappointed me in your ability as a learned statesman to hear you advocating more bombing in the Vietnam war—especially since this has resulted in two U.S. planes shot down over Red China where they strayed trying to bomb targets so close to the border. We are supposed to learn from past history and the memory haunts me of how MacArthur misjudged the Red Chinese and they entered against us in Korea. Are you absolutely positive that this increased bombing will not cause China to come to the aid of North Vietnam? If you aren't positive, it is comparable to a man trying to drive a car while blindfolded—he doesn't know what his is doing and shouldn't be doing it. You would also be advocating a dangerous war policy for all your fellow countrymen. If we were to enter war with Red China, we would no doubt face the gravest crisis in our history. . . .

In case of a misjudged mission (and I flew in both wars and know how that can happen—do you?) such as a stray bomb load that came too close to the border and fell on China, how can you or anyone be sure that wouldn't trigger China to come in against us? And then can you be sure that wouldn't give Russia the encouragement it would want to join in and wipe us off the earth. The possibilities of something going wrong in the policy that you advocate are unlimited. . . .

But such men as you have led the world to believe that we must police the entire earth and I believe we will bankrupt ourselves shortly if this policy isn't halted.

Sincerely,
W.K. (Jackson, MS)

22

Dear Senator [Harry F.] Byrd [Jr.]:

October 10, 1967

For my own conscience, I have been too long silent on the subject of the unconstitutional, undeclared war in Viet Nam. As I have been delinquent, so has the Congress, for it is the sworn duty of the Congress to uphold the Constitution.

If the President of the United States believes that the vital interests of this country call for the enforced military division of Viet Nam into two countries, it was his duty to call for a declaration of war which the Congress could grant or withhold. This he did not do, and the Congress has contented itself with granting increasing funds and soldiers, meantime perpetuating a peacetime draft and peacetime taxes, and peacetime privileges. And it is now, apparently, going to be the Congress which slashes essential domestic programs to keep this ugly war going at an accelerating rate. . . .

This war has crept up on most of us. Then, one by one, as we began to grasp the enormous evil of it, we kept hoping that the unfailingly misleading promises from the government would come true and that it would end, today, tomorrow, next week, next year.

There are no longer any grounds for such hopes. The whole affair has become a ghastly, bloody nightmare to which there is no end except an awakening, not among the peasantry of South Viet Nam, not among the people of North Viet

Nam—but right here.

I urge you to use your influence to insist that the President stop the bombing of North Viet Nam and press for negotiations for peace directly or through the United Nations.

Sincerely,

C.L.C. (Alexandria, VA)

23

Dear Senator [Harry F.] Byrd [Jr.],

October 20, 1967

I consider it a responsibility as an American to report to you that I have changed from supporting the war in Vietnam to urging that it be stopped as soon as possible.

I no longer think—as I did six months to a year ago—that there is a parallel between stopping Germany and stopping N. Vietnam. N. Vietnam does not threaten to destroy the American way of life and is not a highly educated and highly industrialized nation of great power.

As I see it, we gradually became involved in Vietnam on the assumption that the Communist world is monolithic—I think events of the past ten years now make this an untrue assumption.

We are a most powerful nation. I would like to see us exercise this great power by admitting that the assumptions on which we entered Vietnam have drastically changed and that, therefore, our policy will change. Such a policy change should include: cessation of bombing of N. Vietnam and the creation of a stalemate and a process of negotiation. Our situation in Berlin and Korea has been described as "creative stalemate"—let us bring another one about in Vietnam.

The bombing and escalation do not seem to be effective. . . .

Does anyone firmly believe and do they have strong evidence that we can implant American democracy by force of arms in Vietnam? Are the leaders we have been supporting to date real leaders of the Vietnamese and ones we can support with confidence and pride—or are we involved in a very complex civil war from which we must extricate ourselves? . . .

Sincerely yours,

E.O.D.E. (female, Alexandria, VA)

24

Dear Senator [J. William] Fulbright,

[1968]

My name is K.G. I am 12 years old and in the seventh grade at Ridgemont Junior High School in North Little Rock, Arkansas. I beg of you to listen to my plea and not turn me aside as a "crank" or "junk mail."

I have a question that I feel cannot and never will be answered. My question is, "Is there a good reason for American soldiers to die in Viet Nam?" Or maybe a reason to fight over there at all. I have heard pitifying stories of small Vietnamese orphans all alone in a hostile world but also of American soldiers being shot down unmercifully or led into booby traps by the South Vietnamese people. I need an answer. All America needs an answer. Please write back if you have a reason or not. I know you're very busy but I feel you will not let me down for you are what makes me proud to be an American.

Sincerely,
K.C. (female, North Little Rock, AR)

25

Dear Honorable Senator Sam [J.] Ervin [Jr.]:

February 1, 1968

I am sorrowed by what will probably be the inevitable reaction to this week's Vietcong attacks on American-held cities in Vietnam.[6] I imagine the cry will arise for massive military retaliation. More death and more destruction will be called for.

I urge you, Senator Ervin, to refrain from joining those who want to kill and destroy more rather than less. The attacks were bloody and awful—but they did show that the Vietcong rather than the Americans have the backing of the Vietnamese. The attacks could not have been as impressive, intense, and thorough had the Vietcong not had the support of that nation's people. Sir, I simply ask that

---

6. On January 30, 1968, in what has been called the Tet Offensive the NVA and Vietcong attacked every important urban area and many key military installations in South Vietnam. The NVA and NLF failed to hold any of these cities or to spark a general uprising against the South Vietnamese government, but the offensive demonstrated that the United States and South Vietnam were not winning the war, as the Johnson administration had claimed.

we decrease rather than increase our fruitless and immoral efforts in Vietnam. Please, Senator, no more killing!

Very sincerely yours,
D.H. (Durham, NC)

26

Dear Sir [Senator J. William Fulbright]:

February 12, 1968

From the very first I have been opposed in the strongest terms to my nation's military adventure in Vietnam. I remain adamantly opposed. But I am frustrated almost to hopelessness by the proud and self-righteous blindness with which that policy is so devotedly pursued.

Now I am told that it is necessary for me as a citizen to be taxed with a surcharge on my income in order to finance that very policy. More than that, I am appalled to hear Congress demand economy and reduction of expenditure in almost every other area—some of them vital and crucial—EXCEPT THE WAR!...

Worse, I read rumors that now the military is trying to convince the Administration to permit use of tactical atomic weapons in Vietnam. That is pure insanity! It's high time that our Congress put some brakes on that Gulf of Tonkin blank check that Johnson flaunts in our faces.

... I cannot in good conscience pay a war-tax for this year if it is passed. What am I to do? And thousands like me?...

Sincerely,
D.H.E. (Springdale, AR)

27

Dear Sir [Senator Richard B. Russell Jr.]:

March 12, 1968

For the last several years we have watched in confusion and disbelief as the United States has gotten itself mired deeper and deeper in the horror of Viet Nam. We have stood passively to one side as we first sent "advisors" to Viet Nam, then a "token" military presence, then massive intervention. We have seen over 20,000 American lives tossed away for political gain and personal ego. We have seen our economy seriously overheated as a result of 22 billion dollars a year being thrown away in Asia; we have seen our cities end up in firey ruins at the hands of urban poor whose grievances could be met with only a percentage of the funds being expended in Asia. And now we are told that the Administration is seriously considering a 40% increase in our commitment to the conflict in Viet Nam. In our judgement, such an increase would be an act of total and unrelieved national insanity.

It becomes increasingly clear that we are supporting a puppet government in Viet Nam which has virtually no ties with the people. We are battling nationalism in Viet Nam, not Communism. The simple fact that the Viet Cong and PAVN were able to move in absolute secrecy into and out of staging areas from one end of Viet Nam to the other prior to the Tet Offensive demonstrates that an overwhelming majority of the people either openly helped them or were sympathetic to their aim (the killing of American soldiers). . . . [7]

. . . We need to extract ourselves from Viet Nam before it becomes too late. We need to do this for the Vietnamese people who are witnessing the wholesale destruction of their country and for the American people who do not want to witness the destruction of theirs.

Yours truly,
Mr. and Mrs. D.A.G. (Sandy Springs, GA)

28

Dear Mr. [Dixon] Donnelly [Assistant Secretary of State],

May 25, 1968

Thank you for your letter of April 19 in reply to mine of March 10 to President Johnson concerning why my brother went to Vietnam. I am no longer worried about my brother; after a month in Vietnam he came home dead. My concern now is for those who are still living, for the future of the country for which my brother died, and for myself, that I may someday respect that country again. Your letter did little to reassure me on any of these points.

My conscience forbids me to remain silent in the face of such blatant misrepresentations as your letter contains, and my sense of dignity forces me to respond to such a direct insult to my intelligence. I am appalled that such ignorance, or hypocrisy (I don't know which is worse) is printed on the State Department's official stationery, and paraded about as supreme truth.

---

7. PAVN, the People's Army of Vietnam, was the North Vietnamese Army, also known as the NVA.

You mention the SEATO treaty as the basis for our commitment to the South Vietnamese, and the dangers involved in discrediting "the pledged word of the United States under our mutual security treaties." I suggest that you take a look at that treaty and at the debates of the Senate Foreign Relations Committee and of the Senate concerning its ratification. You will find there nothing which compels our military presence in Vietnam, or in any of the SEATO nations. . . . The provisions of the SEATO treaty, unlike those of NATO, do not specify that an attack on one is an attack on all. . . .

You also assert that Eisenhower, Kennedy and Johnson promised the people of South Vietnam our help. When Eisenhower originally pledged economic support to Diem in 1954, it was with the expectation that our aid would be, in the President's own words, accompanied by the "undertaking [of] needed reforms" by the South Vietnamese government. Obviously, these reforms have not been forthcoming. . . .

You speak of our involvement as part of our policy of "containment." This was a wise policy for the decade following World War II when communism was indeed a monolith, and the world was adjusting itself to the new power structure. . . . Since even the originator of that policy has denounced its applicability in the 1960's, I had assumed that at least the word, if not the idea had gone out of style.[8] . . .

You speak of an "expansion-minded power" controlling Southeast Asia as a threat to all free Asia. Here, I agree with you, only I would add that it is *we* who comprise that threat. And it is a threat not only to Asian, but also to American freedom. We have become an oppressor, a more sophisticated version of the very colonial tyranny which led the men of 1776 to arms. We have meant well, but good intentions do not justify such a compromising of our democratic ideals. . . .

Sincerely,

P.G. (female, Winston-Salem, NC)

8. The reference to the originator of containment was to George F. Kennan, the foreign service officer and member of the State Department Policy Planning Staff in 1946–47, who articulated the strategic doctrine of containing Soviet expansion in Europe and Asia. By the mid-1960s, he had come to oppose the war in Vietnam, declaring the domino theory was not applicable and that South Vietnam was of no strategic importance to the United States.

29

Dear Bill [Senator J. William Fulbright]:

October 7, 1969

... When it comes right up to formulating a plan both Johnson and Nixon administrations and even those who are critics of our war policy still say that we can not pull out and leave (Just like that) WHY NOT? It is what Hanoi has requested all the time and I think we ought to do it (providing that we get our prisoners). ...

We have over the past five decades given more and more power into the hands of a few people and my reading of the constitution of the United States simply doesn't say that it should be. Treaties with foreign countries for instance were to be made with the advice and consent of the Senate. How much has any president since Roosevelt advised with the Senate??

When we have requested the Hanoi government to give us some information about our prisoners there answer has been that we have no prisoners, only War Criminals. Have we ever declared war? No. Then why can't we just do as they request and go home (WITH our War Criminals)? I think one of Mr. Nixon's big errors is that he like Mr. Johnson has listened too much to the MILITARY. ...

To me one of the most neglected of all the folk in this war has been the wives and children of the ... Prisoners of War. ... at the insistence of the Services to which their husbands were attached, [they have lived] a sort of "Hush Hush" existence. You are not to tell that your husband is a prisoner, nor publicise the fact that you have no communication. They were shipped out at once from the military compounds that they had existed in for years ... and told to go home and get along as best you can. No word from the husbands, no knowing whether they are wives or widows, no daily communication with others of the military that has been their life. ...

Get some of those young folks before your committee in these hearings and get their views. If I was a youngster coming up for draft or military service I would look askance at the fact that I was one of the few that would have to go fight a war the majority of the American people don't know much about and seemingly care less until they are personally involved thru a relative close to them being sent over. That I could be sent to die for something that actually has no bearing on my countries safety one way or the other. That I was told that I would be fighting to preserve our independence and to stop Communism in the world. Our youngsters just won't buy that and how can you blame them? . . .

With kindest personal regards,

B.C. (Eudora, AR)

30

Gentlemen [including Senator Sam J. Ervin Jr.]:

October 10, 1969

I write as a constituent who has refrained from public criticism of our Vietnam war involvement, to urge that you use all your efforts to speed our prompt disengagement from that tragic misadventure.

Lay aside what seems to me the essential moral horror of our continued participation in destruction of lives and property in Vietnam. Lay aside the nationally embarrassing spectacle of our military's inability to achieve the military solution whose prediction no amount of post hoc complaints about imposed limitations should be allowed to obscure. . . . Laying these aside, we have to get out simply because this country cannot survive spiritually the prosecution of a military venture which commands no more support than this one does. There is just no way for a President to hide substantial internal dissidence from an enemy in this day and time. . . .

Dissembling with the citizenry comes to seem a virtue when its object is thought to be breaking the will of the enemy. Imputations of lack of patriotism and moral and physical cowardice to citizens of impeccable loyalty and courage, are justified as tragic necessities. The inevitable corruption within the armed forces which accompanies even "good" wars is exacerbated when the war itself seems immoral to great segments of the populace. . . . And while much of youthful "alienation" may be rightly suspect as to its origins, I can testify from my vantage point in the educational system that it is a factor of depressing dimensions. We have to get out simply because we can't stand the spiritual sickness which all of this portends, whether we are "right" or not in being there. . . .

If philosophical justification be sought which will protect the integrity of our commitments, I have no difficulty finding that. We have indeed kept our commitment. It was to go in and provide within the limits of our resources the necessary help for a sovereign allied nation to protect and democratically stabilize itself. We have done that just short of the point of taking over the sovereignty of the country . . . and just short of an all-out declaration and prosecution of unlimited war in that country's behalf. . . .

Only two things then should slow down our extrication: considerations of the safety of our troops *during evacuation*, and logistical problems of equipping the Vietnamese forces. . . .

Respectfully,
D.P. (Chapel Hill, NC)

31

Senator [John G.] Tower:

[written on back of Tower's October 20, 1969, newsletter]

You do not represent the people. Hundreds of thousands of young *people are hating their nation because men like you are more concerned about the vested interests of big industrialists and about U.S. opportunity to get economic control in Asia than you are about democracy within this nation.* You force young men to die or be permanently maimed for this. *The only honorable end to war is to put men in ships and planes and bring them home. . . .*

U.S. is the *war promoter and war perpetuator of the world—has been during this entire century.* If we cannot get into a war ourselves, we provide other warring nations with munitions.

Our economy depends upon *constant* "turnover" of *munitions* and all other war materials. I am ashamed of U.S.A. I have watched our war solicitation for over 50 years.

(Mrs.) E.McN. (Dallas, TX)

32

Dear Senator [Sam J.] Ervin [Jr.],

February 12, 1970

. . . Senator Ervin, there is, I realize a "lunatic fringe" among those who protest against this war. But there are millions of Americans who object to this war for patriotic and responsible reasons. I do so personally because I love America; I believe our own Declaration of Independence is one of the most remarkable documents ever written, and the same holds true for the U.S. Constitution. America stands for freedom, equality, and fair play for all.

And as an American, I am deeply ashamed of what we have done, and are doing, in Viet Nam.

Viet Nam is *one* country. . . . The Vietnamese people were—and are—struggling for their independence from foreign rule—first against the Japanese, then the French now the Americans.

And what have we done? We have killed hundreds of thousands of Vietnamese (mostly civilians), destroyed their crops, burned their villages, dropped more bombs on that poor country than against both Germany and Japan in World War II, to say nothing of the napalm and cluster bomb units, herded the people into detention camps, and earned the hatred of the Vietnamese people (except the military clique of former French collaborators that now rules in Saigon). To say nothing of the 40,000 Americans killed, 300,000 total casualties.

Senator Ervin, I did not come to this position lightly. Originally—to my present shame—I supported President Johnson's policy. . . .

I realize that Vietnamese have committed atrocities against Vietnamese—on both sides. This is tragic; but it is, after all, a *Vietnamese* problem, and in no way excuses what America has done. I am *not* blaming American soldiers for anything that has happened—they are placed in situations in which it is "kill or be killed." I feel that I am responsible, that our leaders are responsible, that we all share responsibility for these things. This is without a doubt the cruelest, most senseless episode of American history. . . .

There is one thing we can do and that is to get out, as soon as it is logistically feasible, consistent with the safety of our troops. Does this mean "abandoning" our "friends" in Viet Nam? After fighting "their" war for them for over 5 years? When the Saigon regime has over a million men under arms, enormous quantities of arms? If, after all this, they lose, then they deserve to.

Would it mean a "blood bath"? In the name of God, what is going on there now but a blood bath! At least Americans wouldn't be getting killed and wounded. But let us offer asylum to those who fear for their lives.

Would it mean an American "surrender"? This is ridiculous! No American troops would surrender to the "enemy," the American army has certainly *not* been defeated, no vital American interests would be sacrificed, our military position would actually be *stronger,* since we would not be bogged down in this morass!. . . .

Sincerely yours,
N.A.C. Jr. (Chapel Hill, NC)

33

Dear Senator [John C.] Stennis:

May 1, 1970

I believe this is the first time I have ever written you with regard to National policy. . . . You know of the high respect and warm friendship which I have for you as person, as a Christian, and as a United States Senator. . . .

I was shocked and amazed at President Nixon's unilateral action in sending United States ground combat forces into another nation and extending the present . . . war, without any authority whatsoever from the Congress.[9] I recognize that his motives are the best. . . . However, good motivation is no substitute for sound judgement and deliberate consultation with other branches of the Government who have direct responsibilities involved.

. . . Naturally, as Chairman of the Senate Armed Services Committee, you possess knowledge of the situation in Southeast Asia which very few people have. However, there is a general knowledge which is causing the rising tide of opposition to the war in Southeast Asia. This opposition is not confined to the young, it is very prevalent in the middleclass and it is increasingly being expressed by people in Mississippi. I was with a group of about forty men last night, representing to a large degree, the leadership of this community. Not a one was in favor of our involvement in Southeast Asia and everyone felt that the sooner we got out, the better. . . .

. . . I respectfully submit that withdrawing from Southeast Asia will have the same permanent effect as a man pulling his leg out of quicksand. In a moment's time, the effect will be lost. . . .

I have a son who will shortly go into active duty with the Army. My secretary has a brother who spent a long time in Vietnam as a Marine and came out without getting hurt. My wife has a nephew who has spent four years in Vietnam and had to be an advisor in the jungle with them. There are many people in New Albany who have gone through hell because of sons or husbands who were there and some of them didn't come back. . . .

Sincerely your friend,
H.N.C. (New Albany, MS)

9. The country in question was Cambodia.

34

Dear Mr. President [Richard M. Nixon],

June 10, 1970

Please find enclosed a list of signatures of those who participated in the June 10, 1970 Peace Vigil in Chapel Hill, North Carolina. The weekly, public Peace Vigil has entered its fourth year of continuing protest against the involvement of the United States in the Vietnam War which now engulfs all of Indochina and threatens to destroy the stability of the cultures in that area. . . .

The present verbosity concerning the constitutionality, legality, morality and domestic sacrifice regarding the Vietnam War is merely symptomatic on the part of the American people of the more fundamental lack of an *ethical justification* for our intervention in the struggle of the Vietnamese people to construct an independent national government. . . .

. . . Lacking a legitimate justification for our military intervention in Vietnam, the American people will *not* support a war that can only bring dishonor and shame on our motives. A dishonorable war cannot be brought to an honorable peace! As a patriotic citizen, and one who loves the traditions of peace, national self-determination, and nonintervention in the foreign domestic political affairs, I implore you, Mr. President, to do the only honorable thing left to do when one is enmeshed in dishonorable activity: Cease the activity and withdraw our presence!

Very sincerely yours,
A.J.K. (female, Chapel Hill, NC)

35

Dear Senator [Herman E.] Talmadge:

June 12, 1970

I approve completely of your stated view that for us to remain in Vietnam serves no useful purpose, and that all of our armed forces should be removed as soon as possible, preferably by the end of this year and of course under direction of the military. . . .

Within the past few months I have talked with many conservative business men on this subject. Everyone with whom I have spoken is now in favor of getting out of Vietnam as soon as possible, although some are reluctant to express their views publicly, apparently in fear of being grouped with certain radicals who automatically oppose anything the government is doing. . . .

Yours sincerely,

T.P.R. (Atlanta, GA)

36

Dear Sir [Senator Russell B. Long]:

Dec. 28, 1970

I am neither a dove nor a hawk, just a mother, who sees our sons still being used as a political football, being sent to a country to be killed, crippled, mentally disturbed or taken prisoners, exposed to prostitution, drugs by our so called allies to get their American dollars.

What good is our false prosperity based on war, when it means our young men's lives must be ruined? . . .

Mrs. C.R. (New Orleans, LA)

37

Senator [Sam J.] Ervin [Jr.]:

February 9, 1971

Once again I write you, my Senator, to ask you to vote in favor of legislation to curb, if not end, our involvement in Southeast Asia. I can not help but feel that I am wasting my time in doing this but I feel that it is my duty to do so. . . .

This hideous war has now spilled into Laos. Have not we wasted enough of our money on this mismanaged stupid civil war? Our cities are decaying, our land is filled with garbage, our water is foul, our schools are poor, some of our people are trapped in the shackles of poverty. How in the name of God can we continue to throw money away when other needs are so pressing?

In conclusion, I beg you to reconsider your previous position and vote for the revised McGovern-Hatfield (Vietnam Disengagement Act). Please. As I earlier stated I feel like I have wasted my time in writing you. Please, please prove me wrong. Will I have to write you in seven months to protest an actual invasion of North Vietnam? I hope not. Mr. Nixon says no, but then look at his record. It speaks for itself!

Sincerely,

E.E.D. Jr. (Raleigh, NC)

38

Dear Senator [Russell B. Long],

February 10, 1971

I wish to inform you of my strict abhorrence of President Nixon's decision to participate in the South Vietnamese invasion of Laos.

The alleged fact that only air support is given by the United States does not in any way blur the fact that this is an act of war, grossly expanding the Indo-China conflict and contrary to the Geneva Accords.

Mr. Nixon pledged an end to this irreconcilable error of U.S. involvement in Southeast Asia and in his warped reasoning expects the American people to believe such a move will help American troop withdrawals. According to his logic it may be assumed nuclear bombing of the entire Asian area surrounding South Vietnam would also help bring U.S. troops home. . . .

Sincerely,

I.M.H. (female, Gretna, LA)

39

Dear Mr. [J. William] Fulbright,

February 22, 1971

I feel that I have just got to talk to Some one up there, and it seems that you are the only one that has any Sence out of the whole Bunch. So please be patient with me, and consider this that I have on my mind. I just want to know what in God's name, is this man Nixon trying to do! Is he determined to Destroy America! I thought it was a Shame Before God for him to continue in V.T.N. But now he has Begin on other nations: how long does this man think he can carrie on such abominations before China and Russia gets tired of his ungodly doings and Stop him: he is getting rid of all our young men. Soon there will be none except cripples in hospitals and prisoners in the Enemy's hands: I am worried sick. All America Should be Scared to Death and yet they are Eating, Drinking and making millionaires out of the Blood of our poor men. God help them Mr. Fulbright, I may not live to see it, as I have passed my four score years. But some of these that are destroying the Earth are going to live to regret it. . . . I know that one man like you can't do very much among a hundred that is against you: But please try to get our men and Poor Boys out of other countrys where they should not have been in the First Place! Thank you for letting me express my mind to you. You are a great man. I'm proud to have one like you from Ark. there in that Bunch of Heathens.

Mrs. F.J. (Little Rock, AR)

40

Dear Senator [John C.] Stennis:

April 13, 1971

This probably will be the most difficult letter I have written in attempting to express my thoughts correctly.

First, a copy will not go to the news media; only my secretary, you and those to whom you might disclose it, will see its contents. My feelings are so strong on the subject that I must convey them to you in order to keep a clear conscience.

I believe I am in a position to have fairly accurate information. I am Chairman of the Selective Service Appeals Board for the Southern District of Mississippi and have been on the Board close to fifteen years. In addition, my type of law practice brings me in contact with many people of different backgrounds and status.

The main point is that the rank and file of your constituents in this State are sick, disgruntled and thoroughly tired of our boys being butchered in Viet Nam. The bankers, business leaders, manufacturing associations, public relations men, etc., in my opinion, are not giving you a true picture of what our common and ordinary people are thinking. These people are beginning to realize that every move now and until the elections next summer, are Washington decisions based solely on political expediency. They shudder to think that our boys will be shot down as a result of a political decision. The real sadness is that most of the middle-of-the-road people hesitate to make their feelings known. They would be subjected to abuse from both extremists' points of view.

Some responsible people with enough knowledge and background to recognize the true situation, must speak for these people but cannot do so through extremist organizations. I hope I can be one of those speakers. . . .

. . . We need a voice such as yours to rise above the political decisions so obviously in the making, and shout loud and clear that the killing of our boys has to stop. Your voice could be heard. . . . I am doing all I can. I hope your conscience is clear after all the smoke clears.

Very sincerely yours,
F.S.B. (Jackson, MS)

41

Dear Senator [John C.] Stennis:

September 15, 1971

I have refrained from writing this letter for many months now—first, because I wanted to be certain that I should write, and secondly because I was and am afraid that I cannot adequately express the hopeless and helpless feeling that I have as an overburdened taxpayer. From every side there is a tax to be paid with the Federal Government, by far, being the government that demands the most. . . .

I suppose if I felt like tax money was being properly handled it would not be so difficult to bear. However, I have never accepted the premise that the defense of South Viet Nam and other Southeast Asian countries is vital to the security of the United States. I am confident that the government of South Viet Nam is corrupt and that our tax money being spent there is being misused or used with less than full efficiency. In the last two or three years I have made a complete turnaround and am now of the opinion that we should withdraw from this part of the world at once and I do not mean a gradual or phased withdrawal. I realize that in this area you have been giving your best.

And, at home, I am opposed to continued abuse in the welfare program. . . .

In short, I am disgusted with the situation that exists today. It is not fair to me or my family that we are prevented from saving for such worthwhile things as education and retirement because of the never-ceasing demands from the Federal Government for taxes to wage war and to give money to those who refuse to help themselves. I, for one, am sick of it.

Very respectfully yours,
J.L.P. (Meridian, MS)

42

Dear Senator [Herman E.] Talmadge:

February 2, 1972

The renewed and intensified bombing of North Vietnam by our air forces is completely outrageous, and I *strongly* urge you to use your senatorial powers to STOP this destruction of land and people!

Surely Indochinese screams in the night can be heard as easily as if they were Georgians? The atrocity of 4,000 pounds/minute of bombs being dropped . . . is impossible for me to live with, and I fervently hope it becomes impossible for you, too!

Yours in hope for peace,
A.B.H. (female, Athens, GA)

43

Dear Senator [Sam J.] Ervin [Jr.]:

March 2, 1972

My wife and I have been increasingly concerned in recent months to see that our winding down the land war in Vietnam has been more than matched by an escalation of the air war. We strongly concur with the general consensus of the American public, borne out by repeated polls, that American involvement in the Vietnam War was a tragic mistake and the sooner we extricate ourselves from that situation, the better. The Administration's arguments that we must carry on the air war in order to protect our ground troops and that we must keep fighting until the POWs are released make no sense at all. It is inconceivable to me that were the shoe on the other foot, that we would release enemy prisoners until we had assurance that a final date for complete withdrawal and cessation of hostilities had been set. President Nixon's recent trip to China has only served to highlight our untenable position in this war: at the same time we are continuing to cause great destruction and inflict many casualties through our bombing in Vietnam, we are making peaceful and needed overtures to the country that has been one of the major suppliers and supporters of the North Vietnamese.

What we have done cannot be undone. I hope, however, that you and your Senate colleagues will do everything possible to urge the Administration to end our military involvement in Vietnam at the earliest possible date, and to be ready to support the provision of generous assistance directed at the reconstruction of that country as soon as hostilities have ceased. . . .

Sincerely yours,
T.L.H. (Chapel Hill, NC)

44

Dear Senator [Herman E.] Talmadge:

April 22, 1972

I am writing to express my deep concern about the recent escalation of the war in Vietnam by the Nixon administration. The destruction by bombing of Laos and North Vietnam in the name of the American people must be stopped.

We have passed the point of considering winning and losing. The vital interests of this nation and the people of Georgia are not inextricably tied to the outcome of the conflict in Vietnam. No one can win this war. The most humane and noble thing we can do is to withdraw as soon as possible and to take our weapons of destruction with us. Destroying North Vietnam will not save South Vietnam for a democratic form of government if her people and institutions do not provide a supporting cultural context for democracy.

We have wasted too many thousands of potentially productive young lives and over 150 billion dollars in this absurd attempt to save our pride and to justify poor decisions from the past. This war, regardless of outcome, cannot benefit the common people of Georgia and the poor of this country. We need our young men, health care, education, and housing instead of more last ditch attempts to save face in Vietnam.

There comes a time when intelligent people must say "Enough." . . .

Sincerely yours,
D.P.B. (La Fayette, GA)

45

Dear President [Richard M.] Nixon:

April 26, 1972

I have never written to a president before; or, for that matter, to anyone other than to my Senator. But the time has come when you *have* to listen to the citizens of this country, like it or not. This letter will probably not be read by anyone more influential than some obscure mail secretary . . , but I have to write to let *someone* know that there are those of us who have had enough.

I am an average American, married, under thirty (but not by much), with a college education. My husband spent five years in the US Army, as a regular Army officer, and two of those five years were spent in Vietnam—one, just a year ago, as an advisor. He was gone on every important occasion of our lives, including the birth of our first child, but I was more willing—then—to make what I considered a reasonable sacrifice. But no more. I have lost friends and relatives, and we as a nation have lost over 20,000 men since you took office four years ago. I voted for you in 1968 because you said then that you had a firm plan to end the war. You must have lied, because the war rages on, with no end in sight. In fact, it appears that our role in the conflict is increasing.

. . . . You may be able to sleep very soundly at night, with no close friends, sons, or even sons-in-law involved, but I cannot.

And now you plan to come on television—in prime time, of course, so you get lots of free exposure in an election year—and tell us more evasions of the truth, more excuses, more tales of the "terrible communist peril" threatening South Vietnam. I don't think I can watch—I have watched you on TV for four years until the sight nauseates me. I will not listen to lies, petty countercharges, more rhetoric. And, I will not cooperate and sacrifice and be a "good American" any longer. You have done in four years what no one else has been able to do in the 28 years I have been an American: you have radicalized me to the point that I will do anything to see that you do not get reelected and have another four years to permit the killing of more men.

We have no business in Vietnam, now or four, or ten years ago. And you have no business deceiving the American people any longer. We are not a nation of gullible dummies, we can read the newspapers and your press releases, and we know now that your "plan" did not exist. Please, have the human decency to tell us the truth now, finally, and to take the necessary steps to get every single American troop, advisor, and pilot out of Vietnam immediately—not next month, or in November, just before the election. Nothing else, nothing less, will be acceptable to the American public.

Yours truly,
J.W.L. (female, East Point, GA)

46

Mr. President [Richard M. Nixon]:

May 9, 1972

I am opposed to your decision to escalate the war by mining the harbors of North Vietnam and taking other drastic measures to cut off the North's war supplies. . . . You have also jeopardized the future of the P.O.W.s—since you have removed them as a bargaining point, why should the North Vietnamese keep them alive any longer? The North Vietnamese have said they will return the prisoners when we withdraw all our military aid. I take them at their word, and believe your toying around is shameful.

You spoke of honor in your speech Monday night, but I am ashamed to be a citizen of a country that is not big enough to admit it has made a terrible mistake.

You are forcing each American to be responsible for the continued killing and maiming of Vietnamese people and the ruination of their country. The "bloodbath" following a communist takeover of South Vietnam could certainly be no worse than what the people of that country have had to endure while we have been securing their "peace." . . .

Please display the courage and leadership expected of a President, and help us to undo the horrible wrongs we have done to an innocent people. It would be far better to be the first President to do such a great humanitarian act, than to attempt to win this immoral war.

Sincerely,
L.M. (female, Atlanta, GA)

47

Dear Senator [Herman E.] Talmadge:

May 9, 1972

I find myself reacting to President Nixon's recent Vietnam initiatives with mixed emotions, but mainly with a sense of *déjà vu*.

The president's latest decision concerning Vietnam was based, according to his televised address, upon four considerations: first, the insulting recalcitrance of North Vietnam at public and private negotiating tables; second, the protection of those American troops still in Vietnam; third, the protection of South Vietnam; and fourth, the repatriation of U.S. prisoners of war.

Allow me to comment briefly on each of these elements.

1. The President's anger at the enemy's "negotiating" posture is understandable, to say the least. Venting that anger in the way he has chosen, however, is immature and not worth the probable cost.

2. As the President effectively acknowledged in his address, the removal of the threat to American troops can best be brought about by the removal of the troops.

3. The announced escalation as a means of protecting South Vietnam, or the government of South Vietnam, is a matter of throwing good money after bad. The sacrifice of more American lives cannot redeem the lives already lost. . . .

4. That we must bring home soon our imprisoned soldiers is undeniable. Yet instead of the mining of Haiphong harbor, there must some-

where be a better bet—one that will not require additional ante of *more* POWs and *more* American lives.

In short, we have again been presented with the sort of short-run wishful thinking, superficially reasonable, that carries with it very undesirable consequences. Again and again we have been asked to buy a risky, escalating game plan because it will shorten the war.

Watching last night's televised production of "The President on Vietnam," I realized that

I had first seen this show in 1964, and that I had sat through annual reruns for eight long years. That's as long a period as the duration of World War II and the Korean conflict put together.

I'm tired, and I want to go home.

Sincerely,
D.T.B. (Athens, GA)

48

Dear Bill [Senator J. William Fulbright]:

January 2, 1973

We have been waiting four years for President Nixon to make peace in Vietnam. He seemed on the verge of making a peace the last two months, on about the terms he could have gotten four years earlier, and thus saved thousands of American lives, untold dollars, as well as all the native lives and devastation to Indo-China. He has muffed peace efforts again. He seems to be clinging to the idea of a military victory, or at least some face saving formula that will make it seem we have won.

It is past time for Congress to withhold funds for any further action in Indo-China. The President is not in the midst of a battle, but in the middle of negotiation. Our men are out of Vietnam—they are not in danger. He is using bombing to force terms on the North that he has not made clear to the public or anyone else, and that he will not get. He is using extermination and terror as a political device.

Congress should at once pass a resolution withholding all funds for this war effective immediately, and Nixon will then have to accept terms that will get our prisoners released. Why give him more time? He's had four years!

We have just seen the spectacle of the President attempting to bomb a small nation out of existence at a cost in two weeks of half a billion dollars and 100 pilots, besides untold deaths of local civilians. All without any results. Since the President won't end this war, it is the definite responsibility of Congress to end it now. . . .

Cut off the money now. He can still negotiate a settlement that will bring our prisoners home. Regardless of the present situation, Congress should limit the President's right to involve the country in other Vietnams.

Sincerely yours,
G.M.R. (Morrilton, AR)

49

Dear Senator [J. William] Fulbright:

January 6, 1973

The time has come for the Viet Nam war to end, and from all indications the legislative branch is going to have to do it. The atrocities now being perpetrated in the name of national "honor" must stop: Simple morality will allow for no other course. President Nixon has repeatedly shown himself to be irrational on the subject, and will undoubtedly merrily bomb North Viet Nam back to the Stone Age out of nothing more than personal pique and an aborted concept of what our "national honor" is and demands—this must not be allowed to happen.

. . . If there was ever any rational reason for our presence in Viet Nam it has long since ceased to exist, and our country is now in the position of bombing another country into a lunar landscape in order to "save" it. This is, put simply, madness and insanity.

It is now the duty of the legislative branch to reassert itself, to emerge once again from the ossification and inertness which have characterized it since Roosevelt, and, by whatever means necessary end this war at once.[10]

This war is at present a moral cancer on our nation, from which many if not most of the grave problems presently facing us derive, most notably an apathy and deadness of moral spirit. Moreover, none of the problems now facing us can be solved until the war is ended, even those not directly attributable to the war. . . .

Sincerely,
D.A. (Fort Smith, AR)

10. President Franklin Delano Roosevelt (1933–1945).

3. Black Southerners

Gallup polls revealed that African Americans were much less supportive of the Vietnam War than whites. As early as 1966, 35 percent of Blacks opposed the war; by 1969, the figure had increased to 56 percent. African Americans were consistently more supportive of U.S. withdrawal from Vietnam and more opposed to the war's escalation than their white neighbors. In 1966 16 percent favored withdrawal versus 11 percent of whites, and 33 percent of African Americans advocated escalation compared to 48 percent of whites. In April 1967 a *Chicago Defender* survey found that 57 percent of Blacks queried approved the United States withdrawing its troops. The next year, Black responses on withdrawal and escalation were 37 and 20 percent; white preferences were 23 and 39. And in 1970 Black support for withdrawal had grown to 57 percent and those backing escalation had dwindled to 10 percent, as opposed to 37 and 29 for whites.[1]

Multiple factors prompted a decided majority of Black southerners to oppose the war. The conflict diverted attention and resources from African Americans' longstanding primary concentration on domestic issues—especially the Civil Rights Movement and the Black quest for equal political, economic, and social rights. The newer, more aggressive Civil Rights organizations, such as the Student Nonviolent Coordinating Committee, the Congress for Racial Equality, the Mississippi Freedom Democratic Party, and the Southern Christian Leadership Conference were more outspokenly antiwar before 1969 than the National Association for the Advancement of Colored People and the Urban League. Still, Blacks generally recognized the war's diversion of focus and resources needed for progress at home. The war's injurious, domestic impact reinforced African Americans' objection to the United States fighting wars abroad in the name of freedom and human rights while oppressing minority groups on the home

---

1. Plummer, *Rising Wind,* 318; Lunch and Sperlich, "Public Opinion and the War in Vietnam," 36. These are national figures. For the *Chicago Defender,* see Simon Hall, *Rethinking the American Anti-War Movement,* (New York: Routledge, 2012), 95.

front. Black activists and newspapers often asserted that African Americans were fighting a "two-front war" in defense of freedom at home and abroad.[2]

Blacks were also more likely than their white counterparts to be drafted, to serve in combat, and to be wounded or killed. From 1965 through 1970, African Americans comprised just over 11 percent of the nation's draft-eligible men. Over these years, the Black percentage of total draftees ranged from 13.4 percent in 1966 to 16 percent in 1967 and 1970. At the height of the war in 1967, 64 percent of eligible African Americans were drafted, compared to 31 percent of eligible whites. In a glaring example, Blacks made up 32.7 percent of the population of Shreveport, Louisiana, and 41.3 percent of the town's draftees.[3]

Once drafted, African Americans were more frequently assigned to combat units where they were wounded or killed in disproportionate numbers. *Ebony*, a Black magazine, contended in 1968 that African Americans comprised 60–70 percent of some combat units—although that figure would not have applied across all Army and Marine detachments. From 1961 through 1965, 18.3 percent of U.S. Army casualties were Black. In 1966 Black combat deaths rose to 22 percent of all U.S. casualties; and for the entire span of U.S. involvement (January 1, 1961–April 30, 1975), 12.6 percent of the 58,022 U.S. deaths were African American.[4]

These draft, combat, and casualty figures were not accidental, given the poverty of southern Blacks and the region's racial climate. Like the South's poor whites, few southern African Americans could take advantage of the options that enabled middle- and upper-class whites to avoid the draft. Nationally, only 5 percent of Blacks went to college during the Vietnam War, and the numbers were even lower in the South. Race reinforced the likelihood of poor Blacks going to Vietnam. African Americans were dramatically underrepresented on U.S. draft boards. In 1966 only 1.3 percent of board members nationally were Black, and

2. For Blacks, the Civil Rights Movement, and the Vietnam War, see Daniel S. Lucks, *Selma to Saigon: The Civil Rights Movement and the Vietnam War* (Lexington: University Press of Kentucky, 2014); and Simon Hall, *Peace and Freedom: The Civil Rights and Antiwar Movements in the 1960s* (Philadelphia: University of Pennsylvania Press, 2006).

3. James E. Westheider, *The African American Experience in Vietnam: Brothers in Arms* (Lanham, MD: Rowman & Littlefield, 2008), 23; Herbert Shapiro, "The Vietnam War and the American Civil Rights Movement," *Journal of Ethnic Studies* 16 (Winter 1989): 136; Peter B. Levy, "Blacks and the Vietnam War," in *Legacy: The Vietnam War in the American Imagination*, ed. D. Michael Shafer (Boston: Beacon Press, 1990), 211; Herman Graham III, *The Brothers' Vietnam War: Black Power, Manhood, and the Military Experience* (Gainesville: University Press of Florida, 2003), 16–17.

4. Westheider, *African American Experience in Vietnam*, 44–45, 47–49.

six southern states (Alabama, Arkansas, Georgia, Louisiana, Mississippi, and South Carolina) had no Blacks on their draft boards. This distorted institutional structure had changed only marginally by 1970 when South Carolina had only six black board members and Mississippi still had none.[5]

Nor were southern Blacks able to avoid the draft and service in Vietnam by joining the reserves or National Guard—both of which served as safe alternatives for middle-class whites. Like the striking racial imbalance on draft boards, this form of discrimination prevailed across the country but was especially blatant in the South. For example, in 1965, Alabama's population was 30 percent Black, but only fourteen African Americans were members of the state's National Guard. That same year, Georgia had three Black guardsmen. Four years later, Mississippi with a population that was 42 percent Black, had one African American among the state's 10,365 guards.[6]

Given these oppressive realities of class and race, many young Black men viewed the military as their best economic and professional alternative—as one man declared, a good way to escape Selma. Moreover, African Americans were not immune to the nation's appeals to manhood and patriotism. Draftees and enlistees often admitted to succumbing to the "John Wayne complex," while Black commissioned and noncommissioned military careerists subscribed to the domino theory and often viewed the war as a "good cause."[7]

Letters from Black southerners reflected and elucidated these racial and class realities and polling data. The great bulk of the letters in this chapter were written to the *Louisville Defender,* which had a far more consistent "Letters to the Editor" section and included many more Vietnam-related letters than any of the other southern African American papers consulted. The *Journal and Guide* (Norfolk) yielded nine viable letters, the *Post Tribune* (Dallas) four, and the *Atlanta Daily World* two. No home front letters addressing Vietnam were found in the *Forward Times* (Houston), the *Jackson Advocate,* or the *Tri-State Defender* (Memphis).

To assess this relative dearth of Vietnam letters in the other six southern papers, I conducted digital searches for 1966–January 1973 in five important, northern Black papers: the *Afro-American* (Baltimore), *Amsterdam News* (New

---

5. Westheider, *African American Experience in Vietnam,* 27–29, and *Fighting on Two Fronts: African Americans and the Vietnam War* (New York: New York University Press, 1997), 24–25, 28.

6. Westheider, *African American Experience in Vietnam,* 34–35, and *Fighting on Two Fronts,* 28.

7. Fry, *American South and the Vietnam War,* 155–57.

York), *Call & Post* (Cleveland), *Chicago Defender,* and *Pittsburgh Courier.* The average number of useful home front letters in these papers was 10–12 or essentially the same as Norfolk's *Journal and Guide,* and the arguments presented in those letters were consistent with those found in the *Louisville Defender, Post Tribune, Journal and Guide,* and *Atlanta Daily World.* This examination of major northern papers leads to the conclusion that the four southern ones were representative of the Black perspective and that the *Louisville Defender* was a most welcome outlier in the volume of Vietnam letters it published.[8]

I have assumed that persons writing to these African American papers were Black, and I have included three letters written from outside the South on the assumption that these authors had moved from the South and were writing back to their local papers. I have also included four letters from African American soldiers, since they spoke to the Black burden that accompanied fighting to protect liberty abroad while confronting discrimination at home and in the U.S. military.

Like white southerners, the South's African Americans voiced both pro- and antiwar arguments. Prowar Blacks cited a worldwide communist threat, endorsed containment, warned against appeasing Russia and China, favored military control of the war's prosecution, charged that a biased media and antiwar protestors were encouraging the enemy and prolonging the war, and asserted that patriotic service by African American soldiers would cultivate white goodwill and domestic equality.

In contrast to the standing of prowar southern whites, Black supporters of the war represented a decidedly minority perspective in their community. While speaking for the African American majority, antiwar Blacks voiced many familiar criticisms of the Vietnam War. Their letters to the editors of southern Black newspapers rejected the geopolitical rationale for U.S. intervention. This civil war in a small, relatively insignificant Southeast Asian country bore no resemblance to the threat to U.S. security posed by the Axis powers in World War II, thereby rendering the containment doctrine inapplicable. Moreover, if the United States

---

8. The letters included from Baltimore's *Afro-American* and the *Pittsburgh Courier* were written from the South; the writers to the *Atlanta Constitution* self-identified as African American. For the period of 1969 to 1972, the *Jackson Advocate* published only three letters to the editor, two from government agencies and one on a local burial; for 1964, 1972, and 1973, the *Tri-State Defender* published no letters to the editor; and for the 1969–August 1970 period, the *Forward Times* only occasionally published a "Sounding Board" section that included one letter from a soldier in Vietnam. For the Black press more generally, see Eldridge, *Chronicles of a Two-Front War.*

were to suppress the Vietcong and North Vietnamese, a prolonged and costly, Korea-like occupation would follow. Black antiwar critics also raised moral objections. President Johnson had rejected opportunities for negotiating an end to the war; Nixon had prolonged the conflict for domestic political gain; and the United States had inflicted genocidal force upon the Vietnamese.

To these rather standard antiwar contentions, Black southerners added a persistent and informative racial perspective. Most fundamentally, they emphasized the blatant U.S. hypocrisy of claiming to fight a war to promote freedom in Vietnam while simultaneously oppressing nonwhite minorities in the United States. The war, they stressed, diverted badly needed attention and resources from efforts to address domestic racial and economic inequality. Fully conscious of this discrimination within the United States, Black letter writers described and castigated the racial and class inequalities of the draft. These African American authors also noted the discrimination against African Americans in the military where they served in combat and were wounded and killed in numbers disproportionate to their percentage of the U.S. population. Many considered Vietnam a white man's war in which Blacks were being forced to confront other nonwhites and to fight and die for white America's foreign policy objectives.

Blacks provided other telling racial observations. While debating whether opposing the war would advance or hinder the Civil Rights Movement, they noted that Julian Bond and Mohammad Ali elicited very different, more hostile responses while opposing the war than did prominent white antiwar figures such as Senators J. William Fulbright and Wayne Morse. Freedom of speech in America was much more accessible for whites than for Blacks. Moreover, Fulbright was willing to break with his prowar constituents on the war but not to support civil rights legislation. Nor was it an accident that the Vietnamese villagers murdered at My Lai were nonwhites or that the strongest support for Lieutenant William Calley came from office holders, media, and residents of the South.

In two final, provocative commentaries, African American authors objected to legislators such as Congressman L. Mendel Rivers from South Carolina seeking to make flag burning a crime. This symbolic act was much less a desecration of the flag, which stood for equal opportunity, than the draft that discriminated against poor and nonwhite citizens. In an equally arresting insight, one writer suggested that the frustration and impatience Americans felt over the lack of progress in Vietnam was the closest white Americans could come to experiencing Black responses to long-term bias, prejudice, and mistreatment.

1

To the Editor of the *Journal and Guide* (Norfolk):

May 22, 1965

Please find enclosed an open letter to Uncle Sam, which was written by the sister of Pfc. D.O.L., son of Mr. and Mrs. G.L. of Woodsdale, N.C., who was killed in action in Viet Nam.

The original copy was sent to her congressman, Ralph J. Scott. She is an honor student at Person County High School. Please print it in your newspaper. . . . I think that it might lift the spirits of others who have lost loved ones in Viet Nam.

Mrs. E.W.E. (Roxboro, NC)

Dear Uncle Sam:

I am 14 years old and in my second year in high school. Today I returned to my school after attending the funeral of my brother on yesterday. I am not able to concentrate on my lesson because my heart is so heavy with grief. Only four years ago he was at the same place preparing for his future. He had achieved his goal of becoming an aircraft mechanic, but he only had a chance to enjoy it for a short length of time.

He was killed on Feb. 10, in a hotel blast at Qui Nhon, South Viet Nam, as a result of a sneak attack by the Communist forces. Uncle Sam, I cannot tell you how sad this incident has made my family and me even though he did die a hero's death.

Uncle Sam, is it worth the price that these young boys are paying? How many more young men will be cut short of their goals because of Viet Nam? How many more young ladies like my sister-in-law will be made widows in their late teens and early twenties by this war? How many children will not remember or know their fathers because they have been taken away from them by this war?

Although I am young, I believe my country can prevent the spread of Communism in South Viet Nam in a much better way than it is doing. Uncle Sam, I have seen in the news where Russia is sending ground-to-air missiles to North Viet Nam. I believe that the United

States is the strongest nation in the world, military wise, and that it can protect its interests in South Viet Nam in the same way the Russians are now doing.

When the first issue of our school paper came out, my heart swelled with pride when I read the alumni news—Former Student Assigned Viet Nam Duty. This headline had referred to O., my 21-year-old brother. Imagine my feeling as we are editing this issue's alumni news—Former Student Killed in Viet Nam. . . .

I shall like to close, Uncle Sam, by saying please fight like the nation we are if we must fight, or bring our loved ones home.

A grief-stricken young girl,
V.C. (Woodsdale, NC)

2

To the Editor of the *Louisville Defender*:

July 22, 1965

The Viet Cong and the government of North Vietnam and Red China must be baffled and engaged by the stupidity of the Johnson Administration.

President Johnson's willingness to engage in a land war on the Asian mainland with all the strategical and tactical advantages on the opposing side, is incredible. It reminds me of Adolph Hitler's order to the German armies around Stalingrad, although German Generals told him that Russians were ready to spring the trap.

Hitler believed his armies would win because they were Germans. President Johnson thinks American troops can defeat Asian troops in their own backyard simply because they are Americans.

J.A.

3

To the Editor of the *Atlanta Constitution*:

January 13, 1966

At this point, it is more with profound regret and pity than anger that we repudiate as senseless and uncalled-for the remarks made by John Lewis and SNCC about the war in Viet Nam and the clumsy remarks made about avoiding the draft. It was a weird kind of intellectual sophistry to mix so flagrantly the issues of the civil rights struggle in America with the conduct of the war in

Southeast Asia. The whole civil rights movement, we submit, has been damaged by these remarks.[9]

It is too bad that SNCC forgot its high identification with the civil rights movement even for an instant and allowed itself to become so bluntly and antagonistically involved in a kind of ambiguous but dangerous defiance of the laws of the United States. These people forgot that Negroes in this country have mainly won and achieved only hard-fought legal and legislative victories, and that now, in this hard and complex society, we have a piece of the real world to win. With the whole civil rights movement churning up to consolidate beachheads so sorely won, this was no time for blind acts or oblique utterances on highly sensitive and complex foreign policy issues that touch all Americans in perhaps a raw, sensitive way, regardless of how these Americans feel about civil rights. This is no time to be undone by our friends or persons in the front rank of the Negro protest.

Long we have labored for the precise purpose of making all America see that protesting and demonstrating against racial injustices is not treason. Long have we labored to keep the Negro cause from being branded as a protest outside of the American tradition. Longer yet have we had to resist ideologies and values from being foisted upon us by those who do not necessarily share in the dangers involved in the civil rights struggle. And saying that makes us ponder the possibility that perhaps somewhere in some way, a deliberate attempt is being made to capture some politically naïve minds in some segments of the civil rights struggle for ideals and purposes not necessarily in the best interests of the struggle.

A.C.B. Jr and F.C.C. (Atlanta, GA)

4

To the Editor of the *Afro-American* (Baltimore):

January 15, 1966

I wish something happens quickly with this war in Vietnam It seems like such a waste of blood and money for the United States and a burden too, for other countries and people are looking and saying—"get out you don't belong

9. John Lewis was the chairman of the Student Nonviolent Coordinating Committee from 1963 to May 1966. In January 1966 Lewis and SNCC released a statement sympathizing with Americans unwilling to submit to the draft or commit aggression in Vietnam. When Julian Bond, the SNCC information director, endorsed the statement, he was denied the seat in the Georgia legislature to which he had been elected. Bond was ultimately seated in the legislature in 1967.

there." And I am in all agreement. How can they expect our sons, in particular to go over there and fight for the Vietnamese, when we still have so much more fighting to do over here? What do our sons have to look forward to, how can they be motivated? Let's do something about it.

L.C. (Richmond, VA)

5

To the Editor of the *Louisville Defender*:

February 3, 1966

In my opinion the war in Viet Nam will end only when the United States Armed Forces get out.

This will come to pass when U.S. casualties become so big that jingoist chauvinists and ruffians in Congress either change their minds or they are swept out of office by the people. Do these neurotic Congressmen who see Communist under every bed and are suffering from a lack of inhibitions . . . ever ask themselves why the Japanese democratic institutions and the representatives of Japanese capitalism do not share their fear of Asiatic communism?

Japan is much closer geographically to Communist China and North Viet Nam than we are.

Why are the Japanese not asking for nuclear weapons and U.S. troops? Why are there no Japanese troops in Viet Nam?

L.B.

6

To the Editor of the *Louisville Defender*:

March 17, 1966

I have watched with growing disgust the furor raised by Cassius Clay's disinclination to risk his life in the Vietnam jungles. . . . [10]

---

10. Cassius Clay (who changed his name to Muhammad Ali in June 1967) was an African American boxer and the nation's most prominent draft resister. Ali originally failed the mental aptitude portion of pre-draft testing in 1964 but was later drafted in 1966. He denounced the war, objected to being sent to kill other nonwhite people, appealed his draft call, and requested a deferment as a conscientious objector. When this appeal was denied, he refused induction and was convicted in June 1967 of draft evasion. He remained free while the case worked its way through the courts. In June 1971 the U.S. Supreme Court upheld his CO status and his appeal.

The very nature of the fight in Vietnam—a fight for freedom—should entitle him to say just what he wants to about not wanting to be drafted. After all, the right of free speech is one of the basic rights of this country. Those people who would deny him the right to pursue his profession—the art of fisticuffs—are far more un-American than he can ever be.

I was disappointed that the Negro press didn't rally to his support. After all, Julian Bond went on record as supporting the same type of thing stated by Cassius and he was not personally involved. Yet when the Georgia House denied Bond his seat, civil rights organizations and the Negro press gave him their wholehearted support. This support was not given because they agreed with what he said—most of them emphatically disagreed—but because as an American citizen, he had a right to an unpopular opinion and a right to express this unpopular opinion.

Senators Wayne Morse and Fulbright (members of the President's party) are most vocal in their opposition to the situation in Vietnam. Senator Robert F. Kennedy has advanced some unpleasant (to the "Hawks") suggestions on how to achieve a settlement in Vietnam. Yet no one has sought to tag them with "Un-American" labels and boycott their attempts to earn a living.

Perhaps we should consider what Cassius said and the situation in this country more closely. An Army officer was shot and killed in Georgia last year for no reason at all except that he happened to be a Negro. Last week, a Negro officer was shot and seriously wounded while making a telephone call in Mississippi. Again the sole reason for the assault was the dark skin of the soldier.

At the same time, Negro soldiers were fighting and dying in Vietnam in the name of freedom and justice. If these very soldiers had been in the same spot at the same time as these officers, they would have been shot in the name of bigotry and prejudice. Cassius sees no reason to risk his life in the Vietnam rice paddies to die in Mississippi, Alabama, or Georgia just because he is a Negro.

Furthermore, Cassius has a legitimate complaint about the change in his classification. At the time he was scheduled to go into the service (and do the six months like all other athletes over the country) he was ruled unfit and held to ridicule. Now, however, because there is a need for cannon fodder, he suddenly has become a desirable candidate for military service. I agree with him utterly. He has no quarrel with the Viet Cong. Just because our blunders (failure to hold elections despite a promise) have gotten us in an impossible situation is no reason for Cassius (or anyone else) to be eager to die in Vietnam.

I happen to know professional soldiers (with 20 years service) who are getting out of the service because of the threat of serving in Vietnam in a war without rhyme or reason. While these men have served in two wars (Big II and Korea) with a sense of "What will be will be," they draw the line at this muddled-up affair. Surely Cassius Clay has the right to express his displeasure at the same affair.

If drafted, Cassius, like some other Americans, in all probability, will pull his service and try to get out as soon as possible. Until he breaks the selective service law by refusing to serve, we have no right to censure him. Rather, we should be censuring those who have gotten us in this predicament in the first place.

A Negro American with misgivings.

7

To the Editor of the *Louisville Defender:*

March 31, 1966

I don't know why there should be a big hue and cry about whether or Cassius Clay will be called into the service. In my opinion that's just where the loud mouth belongs.

After all, he lives in these United States and enjoys its privileges. If doctors, lawyers and other professional men can go to service, why not the champ?

M.D.

8

To the Editor of the *Louisville Defender:*

April 7, 1966

Georgia's State Representative Julian Bond is right about what he said about Vietnam.

Every voter in the State of Missouri should write to United States Senator, the Hon. Stuart Symington and request the . . . "Memorandum of Law of Lawyers' Committee on American Policy Toward Vietnam" and read for themselves, . . . Why Senator Symington? Because he has been to Vietnam and is not telling his constituents the truth about Vietnam. Every voter should know the truth. The Memorandum tells the truth as bitter as the truth is.

There has never been a just war nor an honorable one, all wars are morally wrong, they are caused by wicked and greedy men who put the wrong above the right. Why should parents bring their children into the world, feed, clothe, care for them and try to educate them and then have the child snatched from them and sent thousands of miles away to die protecting our borders? There must be a better way to run a government.

It would seem that the time is now, that the people should be given the choice for voting for or against those who want peace and those who want war. . . . It would seem that the time has come when the candidates should declare themselves.

Peace Lover.

9

To the Editor of the *Louisville Defender*:

May 5, 1966

The magazine writers and newspaper writers are having a "field day" in giving Cassius Clay a ride about his trouble with the Draft Board.

Well, how about the "longhair boys" we see dancing and singing on TV.

They must have relatives on their Draft Boards. But kids just out of high school get the "business" from the Draft officials.

So why should Mr. Clay be the "Goat" for the so-called feature writers.

J.DeL.

10

To the Editor of the *Louisville Defender*:

May 12, 1966

One wonders why there are anti-Vietnam demonstrations in this country today. Can Americans so quickly forget that world war II started when the Western powers decided it was better to get out than to fight? We pulled out of Austria and Czechoslovakia in 1938. We appeased the Nazis in the hope a small morsel would keep them happy. That didn't so we gave them another. . . . But that is history.

The Communist powers have openly declared that their goal is complete world domination. . . . Can we afford to give up Vietnam knowing that morsel will not satisfy the Chinese dragon?

To surrender Vietnam to the Communists in hopes aggression will stop is to ignore the lessons of history. The free world cannot afford to make the same mistake. Remember, one can live with demonstrators but cannot live with Communists.

D.C. (freshman, U. of Colorado)

11

To the Editor of the *Louisville Defender*:

June 16, 1966

I am at loss at the United States total involvement in the war in Viet Nam.

How did we ever get there in the first place, it seems like all at once somebody said Viet Nam, and the war was on. Then the government started talking about all the money it was costing us to stay there, and how we had a moral obligation to stay there.

It seems to me that this is a matter of these people to settle themselves, since it is one nation of people, and since they can't seem to make up their minds or get together on what they want to do, the United States in my opinion should get out of Vietnam.

I would also like to know if the 5.8 billion dollars that we spent last year in Viet Nam, will be increased and if so how much.

Another problem that arises in my mind is, if we have to be in Viet Nam to fight a war, why don't we fight with everything we have, win the war and come home. We have atomic and hydrogen bombs, missiles of all description, all of which the tax payers paid for, so why pay more taxes, when we could drop a few atomic bombs over there and be through with it.

Mrs. J.B.

12

To the Editor of the *Journal and Guide* (Norfolk):

June 18, 1966

The incipient liberal coalition which perceives a symmetrical congruence in the moral perverseness of the United States' action in Viet Nam and the nation's internal drive for minority rights cannot look to Sen. J. William Fulbright, D-Ark, as a leader in their cause.

While he has been among the vanguard in expounding the former, he has been conspicuously nonvocal in the latter. I cannot see how he can reconcile his actions in the two.

Sen. Fulbright does not appear to be the least bit concerned with "bucking" the national populace and his Arkansas constituents while presenting his views on Viet Nam, yet he has demonstrated a surprising reluctance to speak in favor of the civil rights movement. . . .

Admittedly, Sen. Fulbright is an authority on the Viet Nam controversy; and while his arguments in some instances are theoretically sound, his actions on behalf of the other moral crisis in our country, the fight for equal rights, have been totally lacking. . . .

W.M.F. (Seaboard, NC)

13

To the Editor of the *Post Tribune* (Dallas):

June 18, 1966

Fighting Soul

I'm a Soul Brother

Born of a Negro mother

Fighting to keep man free,

But who fights for me.

I'm a southern Soul.

And I'm rather bold,

To do the things I can,

To aid my fellow man.

This freedom you speak of,

In a land so full of love—

Is there freedom for me?

Can I enjoy this liberty?

Is this too much to ask?

Since I share the task,

Of fighting day and night,

To maintain freedom's light.

If in Viet Nam I die,

Can you tell me why?

I'm a Soul; I'd rather like to know,

Why I'm discriminated so.

Give me the right to vote.

Show me the laws you quote.

Give us our equal rights.

We'll fight the wars you fight.

True, there's war in Viet Nam,

And we keep you from harm,

Though you, so far away,

Don't see Souls die each day.

Is it so hard to see

How helpful we can be?

Even in this tiny war,

Souls earn The Silver Star.

American, we strive to be,

But the task is hard, you see.

If things weren't so rough,

We'd make you proud of us.

Yes, we honor the flag,

So take off that white rag.

For it's time to be a man,

Let's forget the Ku Klux Klan.

Then we can band together,

Like all birds of a feather.

We'll show each other land,

In America, a man's a man.

Then America will be

What you want others to see;

A place where every man is free,

Even Brown Souls like me.

N.M. (Terrell, TX)

14

To the Editor of the *Post Tribune* (Dallas) (via a local pastor):

July 9, 1966

Please accept this belated and small gift, but from the heart upon the new addition of our house of worship. . . . Upon closing I would like to ask that everyone utter in their hearts a prayer. Not just for members such as D.R., R.S. or myself, but for every red blooded Americans, that are giving their lives and blood for a cause that is just. That we someday overcome and return to our loved ones from this bitter, dirty and wicked war; and that we may be led to see a new light in our Lord. For if we permit communist aggression to rule South Viet Nam today, then it will be in our backyard tomorrow. That is why we are here. And if we as a Negro Race think that we are going through hardships today to gain our full freedom, it's a small thing, a very small thing of the hardships, troubles, and pain that not only we will suffer, but the whole free world if we permit these people to rule. . . .

P.F.C. C.C.M. ([Dallas,] TX)

15

To the Editor of the *Louisville Defender:*

July 21, 1966

Each time the United States intensifies the military conflict in Vietnam, President Johnson and those supporting his policies in this war repeat a curious credo: that it is impossible to negotiate with an enemy that refuses to negotiate.

As early as the fall of 1963, at a press conference right after Diem's assassination, Secretary Rusk turned down a French proposal for a neutral, independent South Vietnam. Hanoi, at this time, expressed willingness to discuss the establishment of a coalition, neutralist government in South Vietnam.

In July 1964, the United States rejected a suggestion by U Thant for reconvening the Geneva Conference of nine nations that had negotiated the original settlement of the Indochina War in 1954.

In December 1964, Ho Chi Minh notified France of his desire to discuss an accommodation with the United States; and in early February 1965, President De Gaulle, at the urging of the Geneva Conference to discuss the future of Southeast Asia and the United Nations. . . .

The Administration's reaction was to say that we had given France no mandate to act as a mediator and were not interested in a return to the conference table at this time. . . .

One cannot but be amazed, in view of these . . . documented missed opportunities for exploring the sincerity of North Vietnam's offers for negotiation, that President Johnson declared . . . in July, "I must say . . . that there has not been the slightest indication that the other side is interested in negotiation or in unconditional discussion, although the United States has made some dozen separate attempts to bring this about."

In efforts to make this melancholy war seem reasonable to the American public, the Johnson Administration is steadily overlooking and underpublicizing these chances for an early peace that have been offered by the other side.

A.S. (Cleveland, OH)

16

To the Editor of the *Louisville Defender*:

August 4, 1966

The President's tragic decision to escalate the war in Vietnam once again shows that the world is moving in one direction, and U.S. foreign policy in another. The use of naked force against a tiny land in Asia is a reckless military provocation against the peace of the world, a flagrant action that has alienated even our traditional allies. It shames America in the eyes of the world. . . .

At the end of World War II, the people were fired with a vision of freedom and fulfillment; . . . America, which gave the world the Declaration of Independence, the Bill of Rights, and the concept of the Four Freedoms, was uniquely endowed to inspire the global search for freedom and independence. But the men in Washington, abandoning the interests of the people, are seeking to seize, instead, control and domination of the whole world.

This madness has now resulted in a full scale massacre of the helpless Viet Nam people. . . . The bombing of Haiphong has led us one step closer to total war. There are not too many steps left. This disastrous policy must be changed, soon, before it destroys us all.

A Citizen.

17

To the Editor of the *Louisville Defender:*

September 8, 1966

The storm of protest in the United States over the alleged threat that captured U.S. airmen in North Vietnam might be tried and executed as war criminals may have influenced the treatment of war prisoners by the Hanoi regime. But there is no evidence that the treatment of Viet Cong or North Vietnamese war prisoners by the U.S. has altered in the slightest degree. United States spokesmen insist that U.S. military forces in Vietnam rigorously observe the 1959 Geneva Convention relative to the Treatment of Prisoners of War. But when newsmen ask to see a prisoner-of-war camp to see for themselves they are laughed at. The reason—there are no U.S. POW camps. When U.S. forces take prisoners they are turned over to ARVN (the South Vietnamese Army).

For one Army to turn prisoners of war over to another Army is in itself a violation of the Geneva Convention. Moreover, the fate of such POW's in the hands of the ARVN is well known. . . .

Many are tortured to death. Indeed, photographs of torturing are frequently published in the press. . . .

On July 28, 1965, the New York Times reported that the Administration in Washington "is taking steps toward insuring that both sides in the Vietnam conflict abide by the principles of the Geneva Convention in treating prisoners of war." The report stated that American prisoners in the hands of the Viet Cong "get better treatment than most South Vietnamese combatants." . . .

. . . a letter widely published in the United States press from Pfc. Charles C. Hobbs, in Vietnam . . . said in part: " . . . I was in on that deal where we threw four VC out of a helicopter 800 feet up just because they wouldn't give the information we wanted. At the time I thought it was fun, but now that I think about it, it was animalistic and inhuman * * * * * * *." . . .

Pfc. Hobbs wasn't punished. And the U.S. spokesmen who were outraged over the prospect of war crimes trials for U.S. airmen did not blush in calling the North Vietnamese "monsters."

Unsigned.

18

To the Editor of the *Louisville Defender:*

October 13, 1966

I was piqued when I learned that the percentage of Negroes serving in Viet Nam is higher than the ratio of Negroes to the total population because this is not the black man's war.

As more and more money is poured into this quagmire, less and less money becomes available for fighting poverty and racial inequalities in America.

The whole idea of war is absurd. For society to condone and perpetuate this evil slaughtering of innocent people over something that should be settled intelligently over a conference table is frightening. . . .

The U.S. has reached an all-time low in decadence with the present draft law. It is unfair to the poor who can not avoid it in college as the well-to-do and to those who are not Quakers or divinity students, homosexual, George Hamilton, et cetera.[11] I find it most unfair to the Negro, many of who are poor and pounced upon by draft boards. How many ghetto-reared [pass the] deferment test which is clearly oriented toward the middle class white student? Few.

The high Negro ratio in Viet Nam has been attributed to huge Negro enlistments and reenlistments. This is evidently due to their sad lot in civilian life which reflects our "Great Society." This imbalance should seemingly be leveled off by reducing the amount of Negro draftees.

G.W.G. (Louisville, KY)

19

To the Editor of the *Louisville Defender:*

November 17, 1966

The U.S. government and newspapers say that the Viet Cong terrorize the peasants into submission, but the peasants obviously don't hate the Viet Cong.

If they did, the Viet Cong could not operate in the countryside or recruit men for their army.

The French had to crush many uprisings during their rule in Indo-China. The Viet Nam people finally revolted and kicked them out.

---

11. George Hamilton, an actor, received a hardship deferment to look after his mother who lived in a Hollywood mansion.

After the French left the peasants still lived in poverty and misery, and the Viet Cong promised them a better life if they helped overthrow the Saigon regime.

The Viet Cong had the government beaten until Saigon called in American troops.

Now the peasants hate the Americans more than they hate the French.

I wonder how long it will be before the American government realizes we can't win the war in Viet Nam and should get out.

No amount of anticommunist propaganda or schizophrenic thinking by the military can win it.

J.A.

20

To the Editor of the *Louisville Defender:*

January 12, 1967

Back in 1964, I supported Lyndon Johnson in his bid for the Presidency, because of two things: (1) I believed he would not escalate the war in Viet Nam, (2) I believed he would promote a far reaching "war on poverty" here in the U.S. to raise the lot of Americans poor, especially poor Negroes.

He was elected and since that time Johnson has proceeded to escalate the war in Viet Nam to a point five times greater than when he took office, and to cut his "war on poverty" funds depriving our poor of absolutely necessary money. Now we are told that as long as we are involved in Viet Nam, the battle against poverty, against slums, against hunger and all the nightmarish things with which the poor are so acquainted, will have to wait until the end of the war. . . .

R.C. (Providence, KY)

21

To the Editor of the *Louisville Defender:*

February 23, 1967

I have read of the lynchings and castration of American Negroes by white animals in this country, and have pledged not only to fight for the freedom of these defenseless black people, but to destroy these animals if we have to. . . .

There is no difference between the white racist Gestapo women of Germany and Lurleen Wallace of Alabama. Twenty five years does not make a pig any different from the sow.

There are fifteen states in the U.S. where black and white cannot marry because the former is considered to be inferior. Still, there are thousands of these black boys fighting and dying in Vietnam for democracy. The only time I have found the black people of America or any other country equal to the white man is when he, the black, is asked to die in defense of what the white man wants. . . .

I saw the black women of the U.S. working on the plantations in the South-lands, those cleaning floors in the North, the welfare recipients living in inhuman tenements with their children, and now these black kids must die fighting the white man's war! If tomorrow morning these Negroes should say, "I shall not fight in Vietnam until I am accorded the same freedom as the white man in this country," the war would be over in 24 hours, and why? The white men of the United States would rather lose a war in Asia than accord the black American the same status as his fellow whites have!

R.T.P.

22

To the Editor of the *Louisville Defender:*

March 30, 1967

I am at a loss for words to adequately express my indignation and horror of the needless slaughter of our youth and the War Department's deliberate psychological minimizing of our casualties in Vietnam.

In my opinion, the many American mothers cannot take any consolation in this preponderance of the murder of their sons, and insult on top of injury to themselves by our government.

What in Heaven's name do we gain in minimizing our dead? . . .

Our government is guilty of deliberate genocide in Vietnam. As I see it, even if we win the military war in Vietnam, and we extend our influence into all of Asia—what then? What are we going to do with it?

We will have to keep two or three million soldiers in all of Asia, to police the Asian people for many decades to come. We will also have to feed them, provide them with shelter and medical needs. I do not believe the American people and taxpayers will want to assume the financial burden of such a military adventure.

If we wish to convince the world that we Americans are humanitarians in principle and that we seek no military, economic or political gain, then we should withdraw our soldiers from around the world, including Vietnam.

By such a move, we would be accepted as the guardians and keepers of world peace. In my opinion, our adversaries would then follow suit.

M.B.

23

To the Editor of the *Journal and Guide* (Norfolk):

April 1, 1967

If student deferments are discontinued on the undergraduate level, for the first time all classes of American society will be involved directly in the steadily deteriorating Vietnam struggle.

. . . To date few American families have felt the direct impact of the war in Vietnam. Unaffected Americans have tended to sit back passively and instinctively accept their government's policy for Southeast Asia.

Elimination of student deferments would undoubtedly being more people into direct contact with an irrationally stalemated war. Perhaps more direct impact for those more or less unaffected by Vietnam to date, would awaken the American conscience and humanitarian spirit to the brutalities practiced by both sides in the Vietnamese stalemate. . . .

Should we follow the horrible footsteps of men marching to battle if there are alternatives to war in Vietnam and the underdeveloped nations throughout the world. I should think that if more families were hit by the war . . . , Americans might begin to think more seriously in terms of alternatives to sanctioned murder.

It is time for all of us to examine the role of America as leader of the Free World and propagator of the foreign policy of communist containment. Through constructive foreign aid, our country might well find a realistic vehicle for the avoidance of future foreign policy headaches. . . .

United support of such an effort in the highest spirit of American humanitarianism will at the same time bring the totalitarian menace to its knees.

O.W.W. (Portsmouth, VA)

24

To the Editor of the *Louisville Defender*:

April 13, 1967

Dr. Martin Luther King has joined the Communist and Pacific groups opposing the war in Viet Nam on the grounds that the war there is a major obstacle to gains in civil rights and to the war on poverty here.

The cost of the war in Viet Nam is being used by reactionaries to oppose further expansion of the war on poverty, but reactionaries would oppose such expenditures anyway. Our economy is sufficiently strong . . . to finance both the Viet Nam war and a greatly expanded war on poverty. Dr. King is not enough of an economist to know this.

. . . Clearly we could easily expand the war on poverty and pay for more vigorous enforcement of civil rights without cutting down on the war in Viet Nam, where we are protecting some dark skinned people.

Negroes in the armed forces in Viet Nam have made an outstanding record of heroism. Many white soldiers or marines will come back owing their lives to a Negro buddy and vice versa. In the long run this greatly helps the civil rights movement, more so I believe than Dr. King's marches by Negroes into white areas, which stir to a boil white antagonism to civil rights which had hitherto been dormant, and thus intensify the white backlash.

A.B.L.

25

To the Editor of the *Journal and Guide* (Norfolk):

May 13, 1967

Sir, here is hoping that this letter will help to allay the fears of so many of our spokesmen that Dr. Martin Luther King has gotten off on the wrong track when he speaks out against that terrible war that is raging in Vietnam. It is inconceivable . . . to expect a person who has won a peace award for his effort to obtain peace, to take any other position.

And as far as being afraid that civil rights will be less inclined to be achieved, well, that would be comical if it was not so misleading. In the first place, civil rights is not something that sprang up overnight. People have struggled for civil rights since the days of Reconstruction. . . .

Dr. King as a world citizen, which is what we all should try to be, cannot do anything else but oppose violence at home and abroad and that includes Vietnam. . . .

(Madam) W.E.P. (New York, NY)

26

To the Editor of the *Pittsburgh Courier:*

July 22, 1967

Articles and editorials appearing in the press here in Atlanta concerning Dr. Martin Luther King and his opposition to the war in Vietnam have disturbed me greatly.

I respect the press's right to disagree with Dr. King's position and mine. I wonder, however, if the press ought to align dissent with disloyalty, as it has done.

. . . suggesting that American Negroes have a special responsibility to support this country's foreign policy or that dissenting from that policy equals disloyalty is simply not true.

Neither Negroes nor Jews nor Italian-Americans or any other group of Americans has any special responsibility to support any policy—domestic or foreign—of the American government.

It is rather the highest duty of a citizen to seek to correct his government when he thinks it mistaken.

If anything, the callous treatment Negroes have received from this country for the past 400 years indicates our first concern ought to be with making democracy work here instead of in the rice-paddies of Southeast Asia.

If Negroes seek the same treatment accorded other Americans, then can we not be allowed the equal right of dissent? If Senators Wayne Morse and William Fulbright can suggest that this country is wrong in Vietnam, then cannot Dr. King be given the same right?

Those who criticize the war are now being told that we are somehow responsible for American deaths in Southeast Asia, when in fact if we had our way, not another American boy would die there.

J.B. (Atlanta, GA)

27

To the Editor of the *Louisville Defender:*

July 27, 1967

. . . I find it morbidly fascinating that many of the United States congressmen (L. Mendel Rivers of South Carolina, Maston O'Neal of Georgia, James Quillen of Tennessee, and others) who are passionately seeking severe laws to punish the handful who desecrate the American flag are among those who have been most notably silent or resistant to the passage of laws intended to remove inequities which have desecrated the lives of millions of Americans through the centuries.

Flag-Burning, though it cannot be condoned, still must be recognized as a symbolic act; whereas acts of a far more significant and profound character which dishonor the American flag, such as the harsh and unjust treatment of minorities beginning with the American Indian and continuing down to the present day of American Negroes, Mexican-Americans, and Nisei (Japanese-Americans) are tolerated by the vast majority of self-righteous, flag-conscious Americans. . . .

Let Those Congressmen and others who are outraged at the flag burners spend more of their precious time and energy toward working in positive fashion on the very real problems which undermine American freedom and liberty and justice.

O.W.W. (Portsmouth, VA)

28

To the Editor of the *Louisville Defender:*

October 5, 1967
Now we are finding out why bombing of North Vietnam has not succeeded in destroying the Viet Cong's ability to wage war. The Senate Committee on Military Preparedness reports that only 22 of 242 targets on the Joint Chiefs of Staff's list were struck and less than 1% of the sorties were flown against these targets! What the devil have our planes been bombing then?—Rice paddies?

Let's turn this war over to our military men, win it, then get out.

Very truly yours,
W.R.K.

29

To the Editor of the *Louisville Defender:*

October 5, 1967
The war in Vietnam recently took the life of our son, T. His death, and those of over 10,000 other boys like him have resulted, we feel, from the common people not expressing their true feelings about the war. If the public would speak out, the politicians would react.

Any person who feels that this war is not to our national interest and does not speak out is betraying his conscience.

A.T. and V.T. (female, Helmet, CA)

30

To the Editor of the *Louisville Defender:*

December 11, 1967

I am a Marine serving in Vietnam. I have been troubled by my presence here as a Negro soldier. I believe I'm serving the wrong cause and should be with my people at home who are trying to gain complete freedom and equality.

I believe I am fighting in a war which I don't belong or believe in. I, like other Negro soldiers, was ignorant of how great our struggle was here when I joined.

I have been labeled a "white dog" because I am here helping the white man in his efforts to help a country free itself from Communism.

I regret to say that I have found that racial prejudice exists in the military service even though I'm here helping him to gain another victory to boast of.

What will I gain?

I will return to the Southside of Chicago that is full of racial tension and unrest. I will not feel victorious, but ashamed, because I didn't take part in the march toward freedom and equality in my own country.

Where do I belong? Should I quit the white man's struggle or remain and feel that I am guilty of being an "Uncle Tom?"

Pvt. M.A.E.

31

To the Editor of the *Louisville Defender:*

January 11, 1968

Throughout history, it has been a point of honor for great leaders to march into battle at the head of their armies in support of a cause they felt just. . . .

Our current leaders excuse themselves from combat duty saying this is a "young man's war." Assuming this to be true, those who are requiring other men's sons to die in Vietnam should consider it a point of honor to be represented by either a son or a close relative on the field of battle.

Will you please tell us which, if any, of these leaders have during the six years of our Vietnam involvement ever been represented in actual combat by some blood relative. . . .

President Johnson, Vice President Humphrey, General Wheeler, General Maxwell Taylor, Walt Rostow, Barry Goldwater, Senator Dirksen, Dean Rusk, Ronald Reagan, General Lewis Hershey, Richard Nixon, J. Edgar Hoover, General Eisenhower, William F. Buckley, Elsworth Bunker.

Mrs. J.C.M. (FL)

32

To the Editor of the *Louisville Defender*:

February 8, 1968

I agree with Eartha Kitt.[12] We would not have the unrest in our cities if it were not for the knowledge that the war in Vietnam is draining away our resources so that there is no money for improving conditions in the ghettos.

In some way the bombing of North Vietnam must be stopped. An American policy should be to let people of other countries choose their own form of government.

All that the average citizen can do is make his opinions known. This, Miss Kitt has done for many, many Americans.

May she continue to be blessed with wisdom and courage.

Mrs. L.S.

33

To the Editor of the *Louisville Defender*:

February 23, 1968

AN OPEN LETTER TO ALL AMERICANS

. . . In Vietnam we have made a mistake and history will prove it. The people of Vietnam are being interfered with by our country as a nation over an internal problem that they can be the only ones to solve. Surely during the time this great country was having the civil war, we would not have allowed another country to have solved that problem. . . . The Vietnamese North are the same as in the South.

Vietnam has known exploiters raiding their country for centuries. Today they both and I repeat both, resent Americans on their soil, and they have resented the French, the Dutch, the English and last but by no means least, the Chinese. They have hated the War Lords of China for centuries, . . .

Now let's look at our side of this conflict. I can understand a young American, who makes noises of resentment to being drafted into the army and swiftly trained to kill or be killed. Can you imagine a young, healthy American being sent over, only to return in several weeks with an arm or leg torn from his body along with the memories of dead friends he has experienced? He will find it hard to explain to his son in history lessons that this involvement of our government was only a mistake.

12. Eartha Kitt was an African American entertainer who publicly confronted Lady Bird Johnson about the injurious effects of the Vietnam War during a White House luncheon in January 1968.

I am earnestly asking and hoping to appeal to the American woman to stop our involvement in this great conflict. If our leaders won't withdraw, then the mothers of this country should flood and appeal, by any method to the Congress to withdraw our forces from Vietnam.

. . . If we stop our great war producing machinery, we would find ourselves in a financial depression that would take 3 to 5 years to right itself. But isn't this better than fighting war for possibly 10 at an expense of 1 million dollars per minute. That is the present rate and it will double in a few years. . . .

With the great election that is up this year we need a leader to arrive on the American scene and announce that we will deescalate this war, and return our forces. The Vietnamese people, both North and South will resolve their differences and insure us with the best South East Asian buffer against China that we could have. . . .

J.B.C. (Miami, FL)

34

To the Editor of the *Louisville Defender*:

April 18, 1968

A plausible rumor has it that General Wheeler will ask for another 100,000 men to be sent to Vietnam.

This is a war we should never have got into. No wickedness in Washington but misconceptions shared by the American people got us into it. . . .

Over the years (and several administrations) Washington has allowed itself to be funneled into a situation that has brought it at last to intellectual bankruptcy. Continuing failure in Vietnam drives it constantly to compound the military commitment because it can think of nothing else to do.

Up to now I have limited my public comment on this wrong and calamitous war because it has been (and still is) so hard to see how we can get out of it without disaster. But this must be our entire aim, and in pursuit of that aim it is essential that we get in no deeper than we already are.

If the American people and the Congress refuse to allow the Administration to go any further in increasing the size of our commitment, it may be compelled to face the need of some alternative to the impracticable military way out—as the French Government was compelled to do in 1954, when the attitude of the French people prevented it from sending any conscripts at all to Indochina.

L.G.H.

35

To the Editor of the *Louisville Defender*:

April 25, 1968

As a teacher, with several promising graduate students, I, too, am dismayed by our Government's new draft policy. But I cannot join in the shock and surprise. We see all around us the spreading disruption of our society, as one endeavor after another is made hostage to our Vietnam adventure.

Why not our graduate schools now, along with help for our cities, resolution of our racial strife, salvage of the poor, care of our natural resources, and virtually every other source of domestic hope for a better nation?

If the same university leaders who now are beseeching the Government to revise the draft policy would speak out as loud and clear about the cause of their problem—about the disease of the war itself instead of the mere symptom of broken-up graduate programs—then they would sound a good deal more appropriately broad in their perception of the matter. . . .

T.N.

36

To the Editor of the *Journal and Guide* (Norfolk):

May 25, 1968

Since my return from South Vietnam, I have been very much concerned about the amount of protest over so many things in America. The one I was concerned with most was the draft. . . .

According to figures I have gathered, the State of Virginia has 129 Selective Service Boards. Out of this number there are only 25 Negroes serving on such boards and this is supposed to be an all-time high. . . .

According to his [General Lewis B. Hershey's] office, the State of Mississippi didn't have any. General Hershey said that some people did not like to work for nothing but that was not the reason Negroes were not appointed. He stated that the governor of each state has the power to appoint Negroes to such boards but they just did not do so.

. . . I am sure of this—Negroes are not satisfied with the present system. I am sure that Negroes feel they should have some say as to who in their community should be drafted and who should not.

In reference to the draft bill, I know of no law that Congress has ever passed which gives the governor so much authority. . . .

I have often wondered how so many good Americans in my state could let things like this go on without speaking out. . . .

Let's take Southside, Virginia. Could you believe that Negroes in some of the counties bought their own school buses and also paid the drivers of such buses. The students then had to pay by the month to ride to school. If you didn't pay, you couldn't ride to school. . . .

At the same time, every able-bodied person was drafted—whether you were Negro or white.

I have served in the last three so-called wars as a draftee and enlistee. My two brothers were also drafted. I am quite sure we were by far more eligible for deferment than many of those who were actually deferred.

All I have said can be put into one sentence. "Do unto others as you would have them do unto you." . . .

M/Sgt. D.F.H. (Washington, DC)

37

To the Editor of the *Journal and Guide* (Norfolk):

June 8, 1968

. . . this year finds poor, hungry and hurt Negroes camping in the shadow of the Washington Lincoln Memorial begging for a freedom which should be the gift of every man through birth.

More than a hundred years ago an internecine war was fought from which this freedom, supposedly was a byproduct. . . .

Fourteen years have passed since the historic Supreme Court decision outlawing public school desegregation. Five years have passed since the lamented Martin Luther King, Jr. expressed his dream, "that slaves and the sons of slaveowners will sit down together at the table of brotherhood." . . .

So little has been done in these intervening years to keep these dreams alive. This is especially true for the large masses of Negroes. . . .

Do we wonder why black power? This is a cry of anguish, a cry of desperation. Let us not sloganize it to death! Do not allow others to define it. This is a call for economic and political solidarity. . . .

The question of violence is irrelevant. Certainly the white man has forfeited the right to raise the question of violence. Those who come into the courts of equity must come with clean hands. The relevant question is, will there be change? . . .

The pressing immediacy of bread, jobs, housing and dignity will not allow us the luxury of engaging in ultimate questions. Truly, man does not live by bread alone. Nor does he live without it.

The following are the reported words of a Negro father to his son in Vietnam: "Dear Son, I'm proud that you're defending the freedom we are trying to get here."

L.M.T. (Atlanta, GA)

38

To the Editor of the *Louisville Defender*:

September 26, 1968

The news media covering the Chicago convention should hang its collective head in shame for the most biased national coverage ever perpetuated upon a nation and the world in the saga of "The news media, hippies and leftists vs. those entrusted with maintaining law and order."[13]

The gullible were led to believe that these were sweet innocent children and young people with high motives and good intent being brutally attacked and clubbed by the Chicago police with no provocation.

. . . I personally did not see one film showing the rabble charge the police line thus initiating the fray or one picture of a wounded police officer—thanks to the biased coverage.

Let me tell the news media and the world here and now that if I ever . . . see my 6 foot, 170 lb. 17-year-old son shout "I don't give a damn about America," tear down the American flag and attempt to raise a North Vietnamese flag or charge a police line doing their duty—I shall personally club him . . . and if the dogooders—leftists—the press etc. want to charge me with cruel and in-human treatment—cruelty to children . . . so be it—but you'd better believe I'd CLUB HIM!

HIS 100 LB. 5' MOTHER

39

To the Editor of the *Louisville Defender*:

December 26, 1968

13. The reference is to the Democratic National Convention, August 26–29, 1968, during which antiwar protestors clashed in the streets and Grant Park with Chicago Police and the National Guard.

Newspapers today are carrying big headlines of Negro students attempting to take over predominantly white schools as well as those under Negro supervision.

Just what is wrong with Negro students in institutions of higher learning? It is that their main purpose in attending these schools is to foment and disrupt the program of these institutions?

Black power seems to have gotten complete control of a large segment of Negro students. The actions of Negro students in colleges throughout the country is utterly disgraceful.

There is no doubt in the minds of many that students have grievances of various kinds and a right to be heard. These grievances should be presented in an intelligent manner and with dignity. . . .

It should be remembered that great strides and advancements have been made by our forefathers through the years, not through rioting or civil disorders and the like, but by fighting intelligently and by convincing the powers that be that Negroes are human beings. . . .

. . . It should be remembered by university students that there is justification in presenting bonafide grievances to proper authorities . . . if no consideration is given to said grievances, there are many avenues of recourse.

Boards of regents, alumni associations, civic organizations and other groups are always glad to support grievances of the proper nature.

Respect can never be gained through rioting and taking over institutions of learning. It should be remembered . . . that large contributions have been made to the Negro college fund by many large corporations in recent years. . . .

Negro students are to be commended for their black power attitudes. But apparently they are using it in the wrong manner. No better way can be thought of to use black power than to use it intellectually, economically and politically. . . .

A.C.M.

40

To the Editor of the *Louisville Defender*:

January 2, 1969

Well, here I am—another proud black member of the Marine Corps ready to die for his lily, white country and WHY? Don't get me wrong. I realize that there's a threat to our freedom overseas, and I intend to do my best to put it down; but while I'M over there, what about the bigger problem here? After injustices my race has suffered in the past, is still suffering and shall continue to suffer; why does any black man continue to work for the good of the U.S.? . . .

. . . What do we have to do to prove our worth? We breathe, we eat, we even have guts enough to die fighting Charlie.

Yeah, they tell us there are only perverted minds who voice their dislike of Negroes, but as I grow up I find more and more of these "perverted minds." KKK and John Birch Society say, "Send us back to Africa"; but where will they send the Indians?

We were born here, too. I am an American, proud of my country, ready to lay my life down for it but when and if I come back I want a clean country to live in. I want the freedom to live where I want within my economical range.

Don't get me wrong—things are changing at a faster rate than ever before, but not fast enough. . . .

Pvt. J.B. Jr.

41

To the Editor of the *Louisville Defender*:

April 3, 1969

A short time ago I met a young man all bedecked with ribbons and stripes. He told me that he had just returned from 18 months in Vietnam.

During our conversation he said, ". . . if I had known then what I know now, I never, never would have gone to Vietnam. No American should be forced to fight and kill under the conditions that exist there. Long years of tragic and barbaric warfare have brought almost indescribable devastation and suffering."

He also said, "There appears to be a continuously growing dislike and distrust among orientals for Americans. They like our candy and our cigarettes, and above all our money, but they don't like us."

"This feeling of dislike and distrust is much stronger than most folks at home realize. These people seem to feel that we are there not so much to help them as we are to protect and advance our own interests."

"I feel strongly that if the white man at long, long last would pull right out of Vietnam, the people there would work out their problems and be infinitely better off."

In the years to come, I predict that history will record that one of the most inexcusable blunders that any country ever made was our becoming involved in the horrible and outrageous mess that now exists in Vietnam.

We are dissipating our very life's blood financing this blood adventure and our children and children's children will inherit the burden and obligation to pay and pay and pay.

C.C.L.

42

To the Editor of the *Journal and Guide* (Norfolk):

May 29, 1969

While hundreds of thousands are living in wall-to-wall poverty, we continue to waste millions in lunar gymnastics.[14] We continue to squander billions in an apparently futile war, eight thousand miles away, under the pretense of bringing self-rule and democracy to the benighted Vietnamese. We have no exportable democracy. It is all needed for home consumption.

It is reported that since the start of the Paris talks, U.S. casualties have topped 60,000 (nearly 9,000 dead). Black unrest continues to explode on white and black campuses. Conferences are convened to hear scholarly papers dealing with our common malaise. . . .

Perhaps we need to try walking on this earth in dignity before walking in space in pride. . . .

L.M.T. (Atlanta, GA)

43

To the Editor of the *Louisville Defender*:

June 12, 1969

Unjust, inhumane and cruel actions are taking place in S. Vietnam directed mainly towards the black soldiers fighting there.

My brother has been wounded twice in Vietnam, both times in the leg. In this same leg, he has had two infections of cellulitis as a result of being returned to the bush too soon. He has been the recipient of two Purple Hearts.

Still, the Marine Corps refuses to return him to the base until his tour of duty is up in August. This is their policy and black soldiers are being treated like dogs by "the beast," as the white officers are called by black soldiers.

---

14. "Lunar gymnastics" refers to the U.S. space program that would land two men on the moon in July 1969.

... Well, he has learned the truth and it hurts, but all nonwhite people must accept the bitter pill of rejection from the people of this country.

All black women and fathers and those who have brothers should know what is happening to them thousands of miles away in the hell hole of S. Vietnam.

How many more black soldiers must suffer this before our black politicians demand human and equal rights just as the white soldiers are receiving?

Mrs. D.J.

44

To the Editor of the *Journal and Guide* (Norfolk):

June 21, 1969

I am a product of Norfolk and I am serving in Vietnam. I have been receiving the Guide while in the Army.

In the May 24th Home Edition ..., a young man expressed his opinion of how the whites have treated him. He said, "We pray, eat and fight together as one."

I am also a black man serving in Vietnam, and yes, it's true we do "pray, eat and fight together." But the Honkies are getting all the rank. On the last day of the month, when the payroll comes around, then you can see how together things really are.

We work side by side the whole month, doing the same job. And on payday, who's getting the money? I'll give you a very limited one guess....

Brother K.

45

To the Editor of the *Louisville Defender:*

July 31, 1969

... After 100,000 American deaths in Korea and Viet Nam from combat, disease and wounds, plus an expenditure of 100,000 millions of dollars, the majority of American still feel they are "containing communism."

Like incompetent gardeners, we hack at the branches of the problem and exhaust ourselves making war on little Asiatics who present no military threat whatever to our country.

Meanwhile, the root of the challenge to our freedoms and security, communist Russia, grows apace and gleefully supplies the weapons to kill our men.

K.D.T.

46

To the Editor of the *Louisville Defender*:

August 28, 1969

It is extremely doubtful if in the entire history of the world there has been conflict as universally unpopular, as totally unprincipled and as completely hopeless of any manner of victory, as the tragic holocaust now going on in the tiny country of Vietnam.

The American people were not in any manner consulted about our involvement in this unholy and outrageous affair. But 18 and 19-year old boys can be compelled to go to Vietnam to do the fighting and the dying—so the war has dragged on and on.

Not many Americans seem aware of just how freighting conditions have become in this country. Our vast resources and revenues are not going to improve the living condition of our people. Instead, they are being dissipated on a weird profit-saturated war and space program.

Mark my words, unless somehow we come to our senses and entirely change our course and sense of values and priorities, we are going to witness ever increasing inflation, ever increasing private, and public debt and ever increasing crime and violence. . . .

C.C.

47

To the Editor of the *Louisville Defender*:

September 11, 1969

It is difficult, virtually impossible to project upon the white American the feeling of racial prejudice. But the Vietnam War, it ironically seems, has given the white man a chance to gain some semblance of what it feels like to be the object of prejudice. That "frustration," "demoralization," "hopelessness," "mental agony," and "impatience" with the war which most of us now bear is precisely the kind of feeling the black man has felt in this country for so many years.

I would go further in paralleling the Vietnam war with the civil rights movement. Both began in significance at the beginning of this decade. Both started with the highest ideals, one maturing into massive manpower and firepower, the other maturing into massive legislation and litigation. Now both are in limbo, mellowing in the summer of 1969, awaiting final judgments that both death and paper could not bring.

It must be the supreme irony that the man so mesmerized with civil rights and the conscience of the Vietnam war—Lyndon Baines Johnson—is the very man who gave us the ultimate and everlasting method of ending our problems, his greatest gift—"reasoning together."

J.S.D.

48

To the Editor of the *Louisville Defender:*

October 16, 1969

"The streets of our country are in turmoil. The universities are filled with students rebelling and rioting. Communists are seeking to destroy our country. Russia is threatening us with her might and the republic is in danger. Yes, danger from within and without. We need law and order." (Statement of Adolf Hitler, 1932)

Secretary of Housing and Urban Development George Romney deserves the thanks of all Americans for his recent statement that American intervention in the civil war in Vietnam was "the most tragic foreign policy and military mistake in our history."

... Romney stated that the United States has three basic choices of decisions to make on the Vietnam conflict: "Admit our mistakes and pull out, negotiate a camouflage surrender, or do what is necessary in our bargaining and fighting to prevent our past mistakes from becoming an even greater mistake for those we intended to help as well as for ourselves.

The news we are in is so complex and pervasive that our national survival is at stake."

E.T.S.

49

To the Editor of the *Louisville Defender:*

November 13, 1969

America has just suffered another disaster, this time in the attitude revealed by President Nixon in his "plea" to the silent majority of the nation ... millions of Americans are hoping and praying that the president would finally and at last promise them victory in the war in Vietnam, but instead being fed a confusing and disillusioning false dilemma.

Mr. Nixon presents this false dilemma ... : 1) either give in to the war demonstrators and pull out of Vietnam forthwith, or 2) back him in some kind of secret deal for some kind of withdrawal in some indefinite period of time.

At least one other striking and forceful possible course of action exists; namely, we may choose to win, to secure victory, and then get out!

Where in Mr. Nixon's speech is the word "victory" and the word "win"? . . .

While it is commendable that the various organizations of the silent majority declare for backing Mr. Nixon, these organizations and the whole of the silent majority should realize that they have been dealt a false dilemma, and that it is tragically futile simply to back Mr. Nixon.

R.O.H.

50

To the Editor of the *Louisville Defender:*

November 20, 1969

While all Americans must in humility give thanks to God for a land of plenty, Americans of conscience cannot celebrate this Thanksgiving while millions starve and the Vietnam war continues.

There can be no thanks for the deaths of over 750,000 men, including more than 45,000 Americans, on the battlefields of Vietnam. There can be no Thanksgiving celebration in a nation that spends over half of its national budget on war and the military. There can be no Thanksgiving in a nation whose government lends economic and military support to the Saigon government, a corrupt dictatorship which continues to violate basic human rights and democratic principles and imprisons thousands of its citizens . . . for calling for peace and reconciliation.

Americans of all religious faiths will observe this Thanksgiving with a fast beginning Wednesday noon, November 26, and continuing through Thanksgiving Day. . . . Our fast will give us renewed spiritual strength in our struggle to bring peace to the people of Vietnam and to end militarism and injustice at home.

W.J.M.

51

To the Editor of the *Louisville Defender:*

December 11, 1969

This incident constitutes the irony of ironies.

We have thousands of young America men dying to save the Vietnamese people and a fiendish white American captain, apparently with premeditation and malice, shoots and kills 109 Vietnamese people. . . .

He and many other racists in this country especially those from his section of the country . . . do not go along with the idea of risking their lives for people whose skins are not lily white.

A leopard does not change his spots. Uncle Sam got this fiend out of North Carolina and the U.S., but did not get the racist, biased, and stupid attitude concerning people of dark skin out of him.[15]

T.F.

52

To the Editor of the *Louisville Defender:*

December 25, 1969

A Nov. 12 letter stating that it was fortunate that the generation who fought World War II "did not quit and refuse to fight," was unfair. World War II cannot be compared to the war in Vietnam.

World War II was against a "mad man" Hitler. This war in Vietnam is a civil war. It has nothing really to do with us, except that we were asked by their government long ago to advise.

The Korean part of World War II was somewhat like the Vietnam war in that we fought communism. The Korean situation is still not settled. I fear Vietnam will end like Korea—endless.

Mrs. M.B.M.

53

To the Editor of the *Louisville Defender:*

February 12, 1970

Matter of choice? Hardly. Whatever color people are, it does not give them the right to deny the flag they were born under. Isn't it rather that the dissenters really are confused about what is right?

Should they refuse to salute the flag, it is our personal opinion these

---

15. The author is referring to the massacre of Vietnamese civilians at My Lai in January 1968. The "fiendish white" officer was USA Lt. William L. Calley Jr. from Florida. See chapter 5 for a description of this incident and the response of the white southern politicians and pubic.

people are not entitled to the privilege or protection the stars and stripes offer to them.

Let's invite them to sojourn in a country—any country—that makes it mandatory to be a "qualified citizen by right of bearing arms" and see how fast they pledge allegiance to Old Glory.

R.E.N.

54

To the Editor of the *Louisville Defender:*

March 5, 1970

Some years ago, the commander of the U.S. Marine Corps made this statement: "The function of the Marine Corps is to act as a police force to protect the investments of American big business, no matter in what part of the world those investments are located."

Today, hundreds of military bases have been established at enormous expense and every single day vast amounts of deadly and destructive military supplies are leaving our ports. . . . More than four million tons of napalm fire bombs have been sent to Vietnam alone. Just think what that means.

Many smaller countries are now hard at work to produce the most devastating and horrifying nuclear weapons. A tinder box is being created. This simply can't go on. . . .

C.C.L.

55

To the Editor of the *Post Tribune* (Dallas):

May 9, 1970

The American public has grown tired of the seemingly endless war in Vietnam and now the President of the United States has taken a giant step to end it with the effort to eliminate the supply bases of the North Vietnamese in Cambodia.

In talking to several G.I.'s just recently returned from duty in S. Vietnam and who are concerned about their buddies still there, they stated: (1) "That unless the supply bases of North Vietnam in Cambodia are disposed of, there is no way to end the Vietnam conflict. Also needed, was the resumption of bombing of North Vietnam where the supplies originate. . . . (2) It is possible that if the American action is successful, any American prisoners of war (POW's) held by the North Vietnamese in Cambodian prison camps, may be liberated."

President Nixon has stepped forth to fulfill his warnings to the North Vietnamese upon their escalation of the conflict. He well need the support of the Americans for his decision.

Mrs. E.G.K.

56

To the Editor of the *Atlanta Daily World:*

May 17, 1970

Dear Sir:

I am appalled by the knowledge that some members of our Senate would ever consider withholding funds which support our men in our effort in Indo-China. It appears to me there are too many interested in placating the minority whose actions are deplorable and whose guidance is questionable. What better impetus is given to the communists than to know they have only to bide their time and we will withdraw, no longer interested in fighting to defend freedom at home or abroad. . . . I believe far too many Americans have been quiet while known communists backed organizations are spreading dissent, fear, and anarchy across our nation. . . .

Our youth say they "want it told like it is." Why not tell them the following which I believe to be truths. Freedom is not a God-given privilege: it demands serious responsibilities. . . . We are fighting to contain communism abroad so freedom will be preserved. We must also fight communism at home. Much of our news media has practiced negative reporting for so many years that our youth have grown up reading and hearing negative things about our country and now mistakenly believe we are an all-wrong nation. . . . The forces of Vietnam and the United States did not invade Cambodia but answered a plea for help in routing the communists from Cambodian land which they held. The Vietnamization program is paying dividends. . . . Our negative news reporting dwells on the dissenter, rarely on those who support our government, for the dissenter is believed to be the more sensational story. . . . I believe if the communists knew we supported our government, this struggle would be shorter. I believe a positive news media would, dishearten the communists whereas the negative media gives them hope and comfort. . . .

I commend President Nixon for his actions regarding Cambodia and will back him in any measure he must take in our effort to contain communism and build world peace. . . .

R.E.Mc. (female)

57

To the Editor of the *Atlanta Daily World:*

July 30, 1970

I find this paper's editorial statement concerning . . . testimony before the Presidential Commission investigating campus disorders reactionary and absurd. Certainly no one can blame Nixon entirely for United States military presence in Vietnam. But he is highly responsible for the anguish of many young people today. President Nixon has toyed with the futures of these people much too long with his deceiving promises of troop withdrawals and "Vietnamization" policies.

You mentioned the fewer American fatalities in Vietnam. Would not many more American and Vietnamese lives be saved if we immediately pull out?

In repressive and trying times such as these, we especially as blacks, cannot afford to concern ourselves with the jingo, hardhat philosophies. We must adhere to doctrines of self-pride and self-determination.

G.R.B. (female)

58

To the Editor of the *Louisville Defender:*

December 10, 1970

It seems the networks . . . have taken to making all the characters in their programs doves.

On "Medical Center" the doctors can't pass each other without the customary sign and saying "peace." On the "Interns" operations can't be performed without doctors giving the sign to the patients, and "peace" officially replaced "see you later" as a farewell. . . .

The peace sign is the symbol of an ideological position which makes Neville Chamberlain a hawk by comparison. It is no innocent gesture. It is placed in these programs for the purpose of propagandizing the American public.

D.J.S.

59

To the Editor of the *Post Tribune* (Dallas):

December 19, 1970

The Dallas "Another Mother for Peace" group is suggesting that people send Christmas or New Year cards to Conscientious Objectors in more than thirty U.S. Prisons and army post stockades. Government rules do not permit written messages but the sender can write his name and address on the card in the six cent sealed envelope.

Mrs. Sue Murray of the "Peace Mothers" can supply names and addresses of C.O. prisoners in the USA. . . . While many good hearted people are sending cards in the spirit of Christmas to young men in our military service, the young men who choose to serve their country by refusing to fight in an unjust and illegal war should not be forgotten.

C.B.

60

To the Editor of the *Louisville Defender:*

March 4, 1971

During the drive into Cambodia to clean out the communist sanctuaries, the cry went up that President Nixon is prolonging the war. History proved them wrong. Our boys are continuing to come home.

Now the same liberal crowd among the politicians and news media are spreading their gloom and doom again, that President Nixon is prolonging the war by supporting South Viet Nam troops in destroying the Ho Chi Min trail in Laos.

When will that certain minority of our population stop aping the propaganda line of the communist party and stop spreading their philosophy of gloom and doom?

W.G.B.

61

To the Editor of the *Louisville Defender:*

April 8, 1971

The verdict is a national disgrace. There is no doubt in my mind that Lt. Calley is a scapegoat on the military sacrificial altar.

K.Z. (female)

62

To the Editor of the *Louisville Defender*:

April 8, 1971

Just who is the Army kidding? I am a World War I veteran, and we had quite a few officers we called 90-day wonders. But they were instructed to do what they did by higher ups. How in God's name did they convict Calley? Why doesn't the Army go after the generals, all the way down to the majors? Just who is the Army protecting? If this keeps up, you will have no one in the Army.

F.C.W.

63

To the Editor of the *Louisville Defender*:

April 8, 1971

As a veteran of World War II I was indeed surprised and amazed at the Calley guilty verdict. In basic training, I was instructed to protect and defend myself at all times; in fact, once I was gigged for being too far away from my fire arm. Now all of a sudden you are a premediated murderer. It sure doesn't make sense.

As a 20 year plus service officer I have seen and heard many cases. Most of these youngsters still in their teens are still very much confused.

P.C.G.

64

To the Editor of the *Journal and Guide* (Norfolk):

April 24, 1971

Lt. William L. Calley Jr. was tried, convicted and sentenced to life imprisonment by a military jury. . . .

I think the men of the U.S. military did a fine job under the law and under our present system. But there are some things beyond the law and our system and this is one of the things I am talking about. . . .

Lt. Calley is a white man, but I'd say the same thing if he was a black man under the same conditions. I know it was wrong to kill and I don't condone killing in any form, but let's face up to our responsibility and speak.

I, TOO SERVED in the U.S. Army with the 92nd Division in World War II where soldiers died every day from many different causes, and I can say once you undergo the strict training they put you through, you will never be the same. So I must raise this question. Who is without sin?

We kill more people here in America in one day than Lt. Calley could kill in a life time. . . . Just think about the mercy killing, the decision that a person is dead even though his heart is still beating, and I don't have to mention our abortion system for that is legal and is the law in some states, killing babies before they are born and children dying of malnutrition. We are more guilty than Lt. Calley.

The Bible says thou shall not kill. . . . So now, if one man is guilty, what about the system and law? Free Lt. Calley or else issue some warrants. Write your president, your congressmen, or governors and representatives and let them know how you stand on this issue.

J.H.J. (Norfolk, VA)

65

To the Editor of the *Louisville Defender*:

May 20, 1971

Did I read somewhere among the articles being written re the Calley trial that there is a member of the U.S. Congress sponsoring a bill giving soldiers immunity from killing civilians? As a Black American and an ex-soldier, images of the West side in 1968 flash in mind.[16]

Army "elite" troops camped in Grant Park, pictures of a youth being shot in the back and killed for running off with a sixpack in Newark. I recall reading what happened in the Warsaw ghetto 30 years ago and that the U.S. has "detention" centers scattered about this country.

It is significant to me, that most of the outcry over Lt. Calley's sentence comes from the deep south; that he was visited by known racists and that the people who were slaughtered in that ditch were not Caucasians.

Lt. Calley was duly tried and convicted and sentenced under the system of law and order which is being questioned in his case but on the other hand, Angela Davis sits in a California jail, although we have no eyewitnesses that saw her pull a trigger.[17]

Wake up America, we are on a collision course to hell.

R.E.M.

16. The "West Side" refers to the week-long riot in Louisville in May 1968 in response to the arrest of two Black men. Over seven hundred persons were arrested.

17. Angela Davis was a Black activist and member of the U.S. Communist Party. She was arrested and charged with murder in an attack on a Marin County, California, courthouse in 1970. She was acquitted of all charges in 1972.

66

To the Editor of the *Louisville Defender:*

June 10, 1971

I am appalled by the unsophisticated, deceptive and biased leadership that President Nixon and Mr. Agnew have shown to Blacks and poor whites.

Mr. Nixon used very poor judgement during the Kent and Jackson State campus murders. He and Agnew called the kids bums instead of being remorseful and giving the mothers and fathers of the kids that were maliciously murdered heartfelt condolences.

I can say that Mr. Nixon and Mr. Agnew are cut from the same cloth of goods of Strom Thurmond and George Wallace. . . .

R.C.

67

To the Editor of the *Louisville Defender:*

July 22, 1971

I am a private first class in the United States's Marine Corps. The brothers in the First Marine Brigade are in serious trouble. A few weeks ago "the higher ups" passed a law saying we (the Blacks) cannot give the Soul Brother's handshake nor the power sign while in the military. If we do military action will be taken. And, it has been done.

The Soul Brother's handshake and power sign is nothing more than a physical greeting between brothers, but "the higher ups" are saying the shaking of hands is not military and it may cause a racial problem.

Some Blacks have already gone up for office hours, a little less than a court-martial. A person receiving office hours will go before a major or higher. The major has authority to fine, take rank and/or send a person to jail. Thus the Blacks who have been caught shaking hands have lost their rank or been fined.

. . . The First Marine Brigade is in Hawaii.

The cry of the Brotherhood now is: "Save the brother in the Pacific." Because if we must go to jail for shaking hands we will go. . . . If we are criminals for shaking hands let us be criminals.

PFC E.G.

68

To the Editor of the *Louisville Defender*:

August 19, 1971

It's a mockery to call America "free." First its young men are enslaved, then they are sent to Vietnam where they are maimed, mutilated and killed.

And no one gives a _____. Least of all the news media.

They only get hysterical when they think their worthless "Freedom" is threatened.

I invite young men not to succumb to conscription. Not to commit murder for bloodthirsty, power mad tyrants. Not to commit suicide for a monstrous lie.

B.B. (female)

69

To the Editor of the *Journal and Guide* (Norfolk):

February 12, 1972

The hostile reactions of white Americans and the opposition of a few Americans of color to Judge Merhige's Richmond school decree are but the fruits of frustration and despair America is reaping nationally because it failed to act promptly and fairly on its racial problems.[18]

The American propensity for putting off today what should have been done days and years ago has finally caught up with us and all Americans, whites and nonwhites or Americans of different colors, are reaping the whirlwinds of confusion, frustration, disorder, disruption of education, congressional failures, nationally disunity and the inability of President Nixon to terminate the Vietnam War.

Americans always look for a scapegoat or someone to blame for their failures. . . .

Yet none blames himself as the real culprit, who never intended to obey laws which condemned his prejudiced attitude and behavior. . . .

Even of late, President Nixon is blaming Hanoi for the nontermination of

18. Judge Robert R. Merhige Jr. was a U.S. District Judge for the Eastern District of Virginia who ordered the integration of multiple Virginia schools systems. These decisions elicited intensely hostile reactions and led some to describe him as the most hated man in Richmond.

the Vietnam War, not his administration's failure to end the war. Politically the Nixon administration blames Daniel Ellsberg and correspondent Jack Anderson for making known to the American public the mistakes and errors of their secret-dealings. . . . [19]

The major problems of race, war, poverty and population explosion that face America and the world today cannot be solved by waiting to see what happens or placing the blame on some judge, on Hanoi, on welfare recipients, or women who don't take the pill.

America has only to find the cause of its race problems, solve it, and its other major problems of war, poverty, and population will quickly be solved. All of the antibusing, anti-integration, clever political maneuvering, economic manipulation or outright legal defiance must be destroyed. The many truths that have long been suppressed and hidden must be known about America's citizens of color. . . . The truth must be told.

J.R. (Norfolk, VA)

70

To the Editor of the *Louisville Defender:*

February 17, 1972

Having served in Germany in the U.S. Army for several months, I know that Black servicemen are constantly discriminated against in rank, promotions, job assignments and housing facilities. . . .

In my opinion, and that of many other Blacks serving overseas, Blacks shouldn't have to serve in the U.S. military. This country hasn't done anything for Blacks since we've been on earth. . . .

So the only solution is to pull Black GI's out of western Europe and Vietnam too.

H.J.

19. Daniel Ellsberg was a defense analyst working for the RAND Corporation in 1971 when he released a classified Defense Department study of U.S. decision making relative to Vietnam through 1968. The study, which came to be known as the *Pentagon Papers,* was originally published in the *New York Times* and *Washington Post.*

71

To the Editor of the *Louisville Defender*:

April 20, 1972

As veterans we are appalled by the hypocrisy of President Nixon in declaring the last week of March a week of concern for our Indochina prisoners.

His devastating lack of concern for our men held prisoner is shown by:

1. Calling off the Paris Peace talks.
2. Escalating the bombing of Indochina.
3. Insisting on the maintenance of the Thieu puppet regime in Saigon.

This man promised the American people four years ago he had a plan to end the war. As veterans we know that prisoners come home only when a war is ended. The vast majority of Americans agree with the position of Veterans for Peace on ending the war—immediate withdrawal.

If Nixon had any concern at all for our prisoners, that's what he's doing.

L.W.

72

To the Editor of the *Louisville Defender*:

December 7, 1972

I recently sent the following advice to our recently reelected President. Perhaps now, with his landslide victory and no new worlds to conquer, he can listen to the advice of an old friend.

Dear President Nixon:

Your good friend, Dwight Eisenhower, admonished you not to let the military get too strong. Remember?

Your alliance with the powers of fear, hate and violence which depend on bombs, guns, B-52's, defoliants, napalm, atomic and nuclear weapons, and physical strength (as you say) will not in the long run persevere.

If you would remember Eisenhower's advice and your Quaker background and espouse human dignity, nonviolence and decency, then mankind would be forever grateful. Why have enemies? We are all human beings on planet earth to aid, support, protect, and love each other. These principals in the long run will persevere because in them lies true strength. Won't you please be truly strong?

E.F.S.

4. Southern Families

More than 2.9 million U.S. military personnel served in the Vietnam War zone. Although the eleven states of the Confederacy plus Kentucky were home to only 22 percent of the nation's population, they provided 30 percent or 884,000 of the U.S. soldiers. Southerners also died in disproportionate numbers. Twenty-seven percent, or 16,437 of the 58,220 military deaths, hailed from Dixie.[1]

Southern devotion to honor, manhood, patriotism, and the military ethic and tradition helps explain these numbers. A Tennessee army officer viewed "this type of service as a duty and obligation"; a Texan sought "to prove to myself that I was a man"; and a third-generation southerner "went because my father had gone, and his father before him, and before that, my great grandfather, who'd fought for the Confederacy." Young southerners also generally subscribed to the domino theory and the official Cold War explanation that the United States was fighting to block North Vietnamese and Vietcong communist expansion and to preserve a free, democratic South Vietnam.[2]

The influence of class and race reinforced these ideological and cultural considerations. In his excellent book *Working Class War*, Christian G. Appy contends that class was the primary predictor of who went to Vietnam and served in combat. He estimates that the nonofficer segment of U.S. forces in Vietnam was "25 percent poor, 55 percent working class, and 20 percent middle class, with a statistically negligible number of wealthy." These predominately poor and

1. Wilson, *Landing Zones*, xi–xii; "Data on Vietnam Era Veterans . . . Veterans Administration . . . September 1981," p. 7, Government Document Call No.: VA 1.2:V 672/2/981; "Statistical Information about Fatal Casualties of the Vietnam War," pp. 3–5, https://www.Archives.gov/research/military/Vietnam-war/casualty-statistics.html (accessed May 27, 2014).

2. Brinker, *Time for Looking Back*, 59; Marshall Paul interview, Feb. 3, 1990, pp. 3–4, 9, Oral History Project, Sam Johnson Vietnam Archive, Texas Tech University, Lubbock, TX; Larry Gwin, *Baptism: A Vietnam Memoir* (New York: Presidio Press, 1999), 11–12; Fry, *American South and the Vietnam War*, 149–50; Dixon, "Vietnam War and the U.S. South," 12, 16, 115–16, 125–37.

working-class soldiers usually had no more than a high school education and lacked the means or inclination to attend college and with that attendance secure a deferment from the draft or a more favorable combat assignment. As residents of the nation's poorest section during the 1960s and early 1970s, southern youth not only were more likely to be drafted but also often perceived the military as a possible vocation. Given these economic realities and viewing the conflict through the regional lens noted above, southerners were more likely than other Americans to fight and die in Vietnam. As explained in the introduction to the previous chapter, this fate was even more pronounced for southern African Americans.[3]

Letters from the families and friends of these southern soldiers provided vivid insight into the burdens, apprehensions, agony, despair, pride, loss, and bitterness experienced and expressed by Americans on the home front. Parents complained that the draft, denounced by one as "forced labor," dramatically restricted their sons' life choices and hung ominously over the young men and their families; as one young wife protested, her husband's induction forced them to put their life together on hold. Mothers noted that they had spent the previous two decades, the best years of their lives, raising these young men to be honorable, loving Christians, only to have them drafted into the military and taught to hate and kill. One of the most alienated mothers charged that by compelling young Americans to serve and die in Vietnam the nation was committing "murder." Numerous southern letter writers stressed that the draft hit the poor and working-class hardest. These southern Americans fully understood and bitterly denounced the fact that their more prosperous neighbors and countrymen had greater access to college deferments and often to the safe haven of the guards or reserves.

Once their sons had been deployed to Vietnam, parents worried about the conditions their children endured—the rain and heat; the lack of food, sleep, equipment, reinforcements, and bombing support; the search-and-destroy missions that employed U.S. soldiers as bait; the unseen enemy; and the ungrateful, unhelpful South Vietnamese. One mother agonized over her response to the war, over the state of her patriotism as she sought to support the soldiers while opposing the war. Other parents expressed pride in their sons' service, opposed bombing halts, and endorsed the war and its anticommunist objectives. Family and friends also

---

3. Appy, *Working Class War,* 14–15, 25, 27; Fry, *American South and the Vietnam War,* 148–49; Dixon, "Vietnam and the U.S. South," 73, 79–80.

emphasized the constant fear that their soldiers would be injured or killed, that the dreaded telegram or official U.S. military vehicle would arrive at their home.

When the horrible news of a son's death was received, southern correspondents described the devastating grief, the unimaginable loss and void in their lives, the ongoing despair and nightmarish burden of living without the lost child, and the personal wound that never seemed to heal. These parents searched for some explanation for their loss. Some blamed the divisions at home and failure to provide U.S. soldiers united, unconditional support or the decision to fight a limited war and refusal to employ all U.S. weapons and power. Those responding in this fashion usually argued that the United States needed to win the war so that the lost American soldiers would not have died in vain. More antiwar southerners found their explanation in the unwise U.S. decision to intervene in Vietnam and to fight an unnecessary, immoral war. Their sons had been the victims of these tragically misguided decisions, and they prescribed immediate U.S. withdrawal from Vietnam as the best way to avoid more loss of American and Vietnamese lives.

1

Dear President [Lyndon B. Johnson]:

June 11, 1965

. . . our only son is a Marine in Viet Nam. You won't know what that means since you only have two girls, which you can keep home with you and not have to worry about. You don't know about going for thirty-seven days without hearing from your child, about lying in bed at night and wondering if he is sleeping in the rain or has enough to eat. From his letters we learn that this is just what he is doing—eating B-Rations, never seeing fresh fruit or milk, sleeping in the rain and on snakes.

Maybe you can explain to me and all the other mothers what this is for. You're worrying about people seven thousand miles away, and never thinking about the lives you are ruining and the hearts you are breaking here at home. . . .

The boys who are in the service are just poor boys who can't afford to go to college, which would keep them out of the clutches of the draft. I think that you want to have these wars to keep these boys killed out so that they won't have families. Then, you'll have more room and more jobs to bring in people from every other Country that want to come in. . . .

All the people who agree with your sending our sons into Viet Nam are people like you who have no boys over there. In the last war, my husband spent three years in Europe, with a twenty month old son at home he had never seen. The big shots in Washington told them they were fighting so their sons would never have to go—Yet, twenty years later, where is that twenty-month old boy? Yes, a Marine in Viet Nam. That's your great, peaceful society! . . .

Yours truly,

Mrs. J.F.G. (New Market, AL)

2

Dear Sir [Senator Albert Gore Sr.]:

January 19, 1966
. . . I have given considerable thought before writing you, but this problem has weighed heavily on my heart, and I felt I had to write. It concerns our boys in Viet-Nam. I think it is imperative that we rotate our fighting men, so that after six months in Viet-Nam they could return home as originally planned and have other units from the states replace them.

As you know the majority of the boys over there are in their late teens and as in the case of my son in law not married very long. My daughter 17, and son in law 19, were married 26 days when he left for Viet-Nam. They spent the first Christmas of their married life 10,000 miles apart, but because of their love for God and their country, they both knew it was right for him to be there. . . .

They can tell us all they want to about the high morale of the boys over there, but we at home who get the letters know different. Each letter now gets more depressing. My daughter has received two letters in the past six weeks, when they are on a long range patrol it is impossible for them to write, so the morale of the ones left at home can be pretty low also. I am afraid if our young people are separated for more than six months at a time, we will have not only the wounded to deal with, but many with mental breakdowns. As a Major just returned from Viet-Nam stated in the newspaper this week, "I would like to serve another six months, but I have my family to think of." I think we have the enlisted mens families to think of too.

I think these boys have done their part, and I think it is time we sent these healthy 19-? year olds who join the National Guard to keep from being drafted. They take a few months training, return to normal life, and laugh up their sleeves at the boys doing their fighting and protecting their country.

I have three sons in college, the draft board now tells us they might have to take them before they finish their education. This is fine with us. We want them to do their part, and let the ones who have done their share come home, but if they take them and not the ones in the National Guard I am going to fight it all I can. . . .

Respectfully yours,
G.B.O. (female, Paris, TN)

3

Dear Senator [John C.] Stennis:

January 26, 1966

I am writing you because your TV reports of late have been very gloomy; and, because I respect you as a genuine Christian man. In addition, I have a son 19 years of age. He is now a Freshman in college and is deferred until October 1, 1966; but, if the war in Viet Nam gets worse, as you predict, it is very likely that he and thousands of others like him will be called up.

With all my heart I believe in freedom, as our forefathers believed in it. I believe in the great Godfearing principles upon which our nation was founded. I would not want to live anywhere else in the world, but at the same time I am heartsick over the sad state of affairs in our nation. I do not condone "draft card burning," but at the same time I tell you frankly that I am not willing to see my son and other dad's sons go to Viet Nam to be shot at and suffer and die for NOTHING.

Lyndon Johnson very piously speaks about our defense of freedom, and yet he will not let us win the war. We made the same mistake in Korea. . . . If we are going to be in Viet Nam and our boys are going to die over there, why don't we go over there to *win* instead of dillydallying around with the communists? They are all atheists and liars. . . . Truth will never be able to negotiate with lies; evil cannot find a common ground with good. . . .

I hate to feel as I do. I would love to be able to give wholehearted allegiance to everything our country is trying to do, but we are so far removed from the principles our forefathers fought and died for, and so far from good, honest government that I can't help but feel sick over the whole thing.

It seems that there's nothing anybody can or will do. Therefore, it is just my prayer every day that God Himself will step into this mess and bring us to our knees before it is too late.

Yours sincerely,
W.G.W. (Jackson, MS)

4

Dear Bill [Senator J. William Fulbright]:

January 28, 1966

I read with a great deal of interest the stand you have taken on the WAR IN VIETNAM that appeared in the mornings [Arkansas] Gazette. All power to you my friend and the sooner we get our boys out of that damnable mess—the better it will suit me. . . .

If you want to see a heart breaking scene Visit the Little Rock Airport any afternoon and see the dozens of boys there—away from home for the first time—on their way to the West Coast. A lot of them so young they have been nicknamed CRADLE FRUIT. Some have tears streaming down their face. They are under orders—YOU KNOW—AGAINST THEIR WILL—TOO YOUNG TO BE MAD AT ANYONE—ON THEIR WAY TO VIET NAM—"I ASK YOU FOR WHAT?" THE GENERAL IMPRESSION SEEMS THE CRADLE ROBBED OF ITS FRUIT— SHIPPED TO FOREIGN SHORES—AND THE SLAUGHTER PENS OPENED— COULD IT BE TO SOLVE AN UMEMPLOYMENT PROBLEM—OR JUST KEEP PROSPERITY GOING. . . .

My kindest regards to you always,
Sincerely,
F.G.B. (Little Rock, AR)

5

Dear Senator [J. William] Fulbright:

February 20, 1966

This letter is prompted by the hearings held by the Senate Foreign Relations Committee. . . . Senator Fulbright, you have performed a great service for this nation. Permit me to say that I am in full accord with your stand on the Vietnam conflict. . . . You have exposed the Administration's stand for what it is—rigid, unbending, unrealistic, and dangerous. . . .

Our twenty year old son—our one child—is a rifleman in the Marine Corps. Last August 30th he passed the Selective Service examination and en-listed in the Marine Corps rather than be drafted. He will be shipped to the Far East in the very near future. This means that he will soon be in Vietnam and in combat. I can and will give all of my support to those who are sent to Vietnam. Our troops are marvelous soldiers and again prove the excellent quality of the American fighting man. Yet I find myself in a quandary because

I cannot and shall not support the policy that ordered our soldiers to Vietnam and keeps them there.

Respectfully and sincerely yours,
M.G.D. (female, Fayetteville, AR)

6

Dear Senator [Albert Gore Sr.],

[March 1966]

I don't have any idea that you will even see this letter but, at least, I will have eased my mind a little. . . .

During the beginning of a *legitimate* war I volunteered my services and I'm sure my son would feel the same way. Since that war I've worked at hard labor and raised a son and daughter that any, and every citizen that knows them, can be and is proud of.

We are poor, proud, & devoted to our community & fellow man and up until now I have felt that I was very patriotic. Let me put it this way.

I don't see why we have any more right to go into a country anywhere to guarantee them a so called freedom and ward off a so called oppressor, than Russia or any other country would have to come to the rescue of one or all of our states such as our southern states who have had laws pushed down their throat, I'm not a hell raiser normally, but I'm not only mad, I'm bitter. My son was drafted this week & I'm sick at my stomach of the Johnson Administration. During the war in 1943 I thought Johnson was an able & intelligent, forceful man, but I see now that prosperity in his reign is his foremost desire even if it costs the lives of our sons so long as his son-in-law to be is safe in reach of home.

Surely you know all of this so I won't go on, I'll go to the polls as every one I've talked to will do. I've voted for 3 Democrat presidents & one Republican. I'll vote for you but no more prosperity hunter Son Killers.

T.H. (Knoxville, TN)

7

Dear President [Lyndon B.] Johnson:

May 17, 1966

Over fifteen years ago, you sent me the attached telegram * * * my first word that my husband . . . was missing in action, to be declared dead at the end of 1953.

Now my husband, S/Sgt. G.N.M., . . . is on orders for Viet Nam July 1 and suddenly war is a very personal thing again. It's a little boy who doesn't play war any more because his daddy is going off to a very real one. It's having to tell your mother *again* that your husband is off to war in a country she never heard of before * * * only this time she is older and you just don't know quite how to break the news.

It's the daily possibility of facing a lifetime of loneliness, because I am older, wiser and know that such things happen because it has already happened to me *before* * * * in Korea.

Whether we are right or wrong to be in Viet Nam, I cannot say. It seems like walking into a stranger's house and trying to settle a fight between husband and wife. It seems that we are trying to defend the rights of people who have no responsibilities themselves.

And it also seems that we are not doing our best to defend the ¼ million Americans who are already there. Why respect Hanoi and Haiphong? I pray every night to wake up in the morning and hear that you have lifted your ban on those two cities. . . .

I realize that I feel very strongly about this war. I also feel very strongly about the Buddhists and black-marketing, the profiteering there and the peace-marching here by people, in all probability, subsidized by welfare checks from our Great Society * * * and even your $10 million subsidy to the HemisFair when our men are fighting and dying in a war they did not create, facing reported bomb shortages. I feel so strongly about it, having lost one husband under Truman and facing that possibility again under this administration, that I hope the country is still here in 1968 so that I may vote to protect my son.

Sincerely,
Mrs. G.M. (San Antonio, TX)

8

Dear Senator [Albert] Gore [Sr.]:

August 16, 1966

I have been intending to write you since the Senate Foreign Relations Committee Hearings on U.S. Policy in Vietnam and Southeast Asia were televised. The Hearings were most helpful and it was good to see Tennessee represented by a Senator who raised basic questions and did not simply "go along" with current Congressional thinking. . . .

Now I write you shortly after a young nephew, ... of Murfreesboro, has been killed in Operation Hastings in Vietnam. The whole family, his mother and brothers, his young wife and both families have just gone through the shock, the painful waiting for the body to arrive, and the final hours of the funeral and burial, filled with memories of a gay, mischievous boy grown to a bright and outgoing young man, about to be reunited with his wife and baby daughter for a furlough when he was killed.

But even as we thought of him, we were aware of the many others, who have gone through, who are going through, who will go through a similar tragedy. And for what? For what glorious cause? To carry on a war in the midst of a war-weary people who are divided among themselves; who desert the battle because twenty years has been enough; who feel no gratefulness, most of them, but only a deep desire for the bombs to stop falling, for life to go on in their little villages.

We ask you, in the name of one young Tennessee Corporal's family, and all of the other families we do not know, Americans and Asians, to make every effort in your power, as a Senator, as a national Democratic leader, to help bring this war to some sort of settlement, not a Pyrrhic victory.

Sincerely,
A.I.H. (female, Knoxville, TN)

9

Dear Sir [Senator J. William Fulbright]:

September 19, 1966

Oh, Mr. Fulbright, if there is anything you fellows up there in Washington can do to help stop this senseless war in Viet Nam, please set about doing it. How can you sit idly by and watch our young men being sent to give their lives for political reasons? Seems most of this administration believe that by escalating this terrible war, which in turn makes for prosperity, they will be elected back to office. Mr. Fulbright, who wants prosperity bought by the blood of our sons in some far away land whose people resent their very presence and would kill them as readily as they would a Viet Cong. ...

Yes, as you may have guessed, we have a son there in Viet Nam. Only last week we watched him board a plane in Memphis Tenn. and fly off to war. If you fellows who have the power to do something about these things could see the heartbreak, I think surely you would be more concerned.

I saw where Linda Johnson[4] landed in Hawaii, our son also landed in Hawaii the same day. But what a vast difference. Who does Mr. Johnson think he is? Is he the great white Father who says, your son & yours & yours etc. must go give his life while me & mine are secure in our wealth and position. If the situation were reversed surely he would be trying to stop this hideous war.

Mr. Fulbright, on behalf of the hundreds of thousands of young men in Viet Nam and those of us who love them, won't you talk to McNamara and everyone else who has any power to do so and try to help bring this war to an end.

You know what goes on in Washington, we don't, but surely there must be something someone can do to bring this thing to an end.

I only wish it was possible for me to sit across the desk from Lyndon B. Johnson and tell him just what he is doing.

This is not impossible for you Mr. Fulbright so have compassion upon us and see what you can do.

May God bless your every effort to bring about a peace.
Yours sincerely,
Mrs. I.H. (Rector, AR)

10

Dear Senator [Richard B.] Russell [Jr.]:

February 10, 1967

Yesterday the war in Viet Nam was brought to reality to me. I told my young brother goodbye and he left in tears. . . .

Until yesterday I thought we were doing the right thing by fighting communism in Viet Nam. Now I'm not so sure. It seems that no one wants to be there. They're not fighting for the safety of our homeland, are they? If my brother was fighting for the safety of his home and family I'm sure he would gladly give his all. But it seems to me that all we're doing is asking the finest young men in our country to give their lives for a country and people who don't seem to want to help themselves. It seems like a horrible waste. My brother has spent all of his life up until now preparing to live—now will he have that chance?

Can't something be done? I respect and admire you and your opinion. I realize that we can't sit back and let communism take the world. But isn't there another alternative to war? Can't we use the millions we give to wars in building up the

---

4. The reference is to Lynda Bird Johnson, the older of Lyndon and Lady Bird Johnson's two daughters.

standard of living in these countries so that the promises of communists won't be so appealing to the poor and ignorant of these countries? . . .

Sincerely,
B.L.B. (female, Monticello, TN)

11

Dear Senator [Richard B.] Russell [Jr.],

March 15, 1967

Please take the time to read my letter. Since you have no sons of your own I know you cannot possibly know the grief that one suffers when she sends her only son away probably never to return.

I suppose with a whole country to be concerned with it seems one boy's life is nothing to waste. With us mothers it is very different. We used the best years of our lives to rear and train our sons in an honorable manner to love others and to try to support themselves but no where along the way did we have dreams that our efforts would be wasted and that our sons would be counted with the worthless thousands of other lives lost in a mudhole in a strange land.

We know we need to defend our country but do we need to avenge another country's loss?

If there be volunteers let them fight but when we have nothing more to gain than another country of hungry, unappreciative mouths to feed, let us have a choice.

God be with you and our other lawmakers as you choose to end this bloody conflict.

Sincerely,
Mrs. C.E.W. (Canton, GA)

12

Dear Senator [John C.] Stennis:

April 26, 1967

As the mother of a Marine Infantryman serving in Vietnam, I stand behind your Vietnam policy. My son is proud of the job that he is doing for our country and our God. I know that he may not return, but am proud of him.

I hope that more troops will be sent soon. From my son's letters recently, they had lost many men and I know there are not enough Marines up there to hold back three Divisions of V.C.'s.

Many Marines died as a result of the last truce. We do not need any more.

Our boys are sent thousands of miles away and are fighting so bravely while nothing is being done here at home to clean up the antiwar demonstrations, communists, draft-card burners, American flag burners, and other dirt. I would like to know who is protecting them and why this is allowed to go on in our country. We should not let our fighting men down nor our country.

I have my American flag out now and am proud to see it waving. I only hope that our congress will stand together and come to the aid of our wonderful America.

Sincerely,

Mrs. R.E.E. (Hattiesburg, MS)

13

Dear Senator [John G.] Tower:

April 29, 1967

Today Cassius Clay refused to be inducted in the army and walked out a free man. If the government doesn't throw him in jail for this, every white person should refuse to serve, and every draft board in the United States should resign. If the federal government is to follow a double standard on who is to serve and who is not, then this country is dead—it is not worth fighting for.

I have a son who is 18 years old and will soon face the draft, and I'll guarantee you that if Clay isn't thrown in jail my son will not serve either. Every person I have talked to feels the same way I do, and I think it is a rotten disgrace that he can refuse to serve and walk out a free man and drive off in his cadillac while the rest of the inductees are off to training camps.

Sincerely yours,

J.S.B. (Waskom, TX)

14

Dear Senator [Richard B.] Russell [Jr.]:

[May 1967]

On April 9, 1967, my nephew, 2nd Lt. K.A.C. was killed by hostile small arms fire in Viet Nam. K., like so many of his colleagues, was a fine young man with a zest for life. . . .

The question most often asked by friends and relatives since K.'s untimely death has been—"Why?" The question was not prompted by the unpatriotic and treasonable sentiment of the bearded and longhaired "peaceniks" and draft-card burners. It was prompted by the strong feeling of patriotic Americans that our country should do whatever is necessary to *win* the war in Viet Nam. The almost universal feeling is that our young men are dying in vain.

My nephew was an intensely dedicated and idealistic youngster. He had volunteered first for active duty, then for paratrooper training, and finally, for service in Viet Nam. Since his arrival in that country in early January, he had been almost constantly engaged in fierce fighting. . . . K. realized before he left his home the danger he faced. He loved life, but he was not afraid of the tremendous odds against survival as a platoon leader in ground combat. His only expression of concern was that WE were not willing to do enough to lend the probability of success to THEIR efforts and sacrifices.

It is my firm belief that the great majority of Americans concur in K.'s expression of concern. Indeed, the will of the American people is that we get on with this business of war. The sooner the better. . . . We are gradually dissipating not only our valuable material resources but, our most precious asset, our young men. We can never *win*, in the true sense of the word, a limited ground action in Asia. We can only bleed ourselves with no apparent beneficial result. . . .

Very truly yours,
L.E.S. (Decatur, GA)

15

Dear Sir [Senator Richard B. Russell Jr.]:

January 5, 1968

. . . . I am a *very bitter man,* and I feel I must tell someone how I feel. . . .

I was a share cropper and finished school just in time to get in World War II. I spent several years in the U.S. Navy and upon discharge came back to Barron County, my home.

In 1948, our only child, a son was born. We worked very hard to give this boy a home and an education. He finished high school in 1966 and at nineteen years old was drafted into the army. He was all his Mother and I had and now all we have to look forward to is worry and heartbreak. If he had been a man's son with money he could have gone on to school and stayed out of the army, and that's one of the things that has made us so very bitter. Why must it always be the poor man that has to fight wars? And these bearded people that burn their draft cards and cause so much trouble, why aren't they in the army? We raised a good boy, and now he is being taken from us to be slaughtered in some Godforsaken Country because our President and some others got us into a war that we have no business at all in being in. . . .

If this country was in danger I would not say a word, and would gladly go to fight myself. But to give our only child to a cause such as this is enough to drive us mad, and it has almost done just that. I hope you can understand why we are so bitter and heartbroken. We have nothing to work for or look forward to.

I'm not asking for anything except an answer as to why we are there and what to do to keep from going crazy. Im sorry to take your time, but as I said I feel I must tell someone how we feel and if you could find time would like very much some kind of answer.

Thank you for your time.

Yours truly,
W.L.W. (Bethlehem, GA)

16

Dear Sir [Senator Richard B. Russell Jr.]:

February 9, 1968

. . . We have just put our only child on a plane headed for Vietnam, and Sir it's something that will be on my mind for the rest of my life, watching him say Goodbye to a young wife and Mother, heading for somewhere 7000 miles away that he had No Part in starting and for the simple reason our President says we should be there.

He has had very little life of his own. He was called into the Army at 19 years of age just out of high school. A young man has no chance at all, he can't even get a job until he has been to the Army. This is suppose to be a free country, but there is certainly nothing free about it for our young men. The sad part of it is, if there was danger to this country no one would be bitter about it, we should get out of Vietnam and stay out. Our president says we should be there, so our best young men are sent there to be slaughtered for a country that doesn't even want to fight for themselves. . . . Our government can't police the world and should not try. . . . This thing is a Civil War and should be up to that country to solve it. The whole country is not worth a single life of one of the young men our President is sending over there by the thousands. We have terrible problems here at home and we need every bit of that manpower & money that's being wasted over there to fight this battle. . . .

I have always tried to be a good citizen and do the right thing, but Sir, I'm just about fed up. Whats the use of trying, our son was our very life, all we have worked for has been taken from us, so now all we have left is a life of worry, anguish and despair, and a life of this is just not worth living. Can't something be done about taking an only child from his Parents? . . .

One other gripe, this thing about exempting college students is about the most unfair thing I've ever heard of. Also exempting men for National Guard duty . . . why should the poor who are unable to go to college fight our war while the better class of people stay home and enjoy themselves? I'm sorry for this long rambling letter Sir, but I feel I must tell someone how I feel and hope and pray that something can be done to stop this mess. We certainly cannot support our President in the coming election unless some changes are made.

Thank you sir.
Sincerely,
W.L.W. (Bethlehem, GA)

17

To the Editor of the *Atlanta Constitution*:

February 29, 1968

Can I say my two-cents worth? I'm so sick and tired of these people blaming everything on the "Johnson Administration." Honestly, can't we see that the President, be he Democrat or Republican, must do what he feels is right for our country? I have a son in college. He has one more year before he graduates. We hope that he can finish before going into the service, but if he can't, he can't.

God forbid, but if he has to serve and die, it is for his country. He won't be doing anything new. Young men, and always our finest young men, have been serving and dying for their country for quite a few years. What makes our sons any better?

Some people may say that I don't love my son. That isn't true. I do love him, but I love my country too. I'm sick and tired also of mothers being very content for "Johnnie down the street" going into the service, but "leave my son alone" attitude. Our son wanted to get his masters. Now he can't, but he has many years in which to finish.

I doubt seriously if any young man has looked forward to dying, but plenty have done so. Why not get behind our country and what must be done, and if we change our attitudes, maybe our young men won't try everything in the book to "keep from going."

Mrs. R.J. H. (East Point, GA)

18

Senator [John J.] Sparkman:

April 1, 1968

    First of all may I say that I do not pretend to know politics or how the war should be run in Vietnam. I'm just an American and a Mother with a son in Vietnam, my only son. I would be very happy to see my son brought home to his family, and out of danger, from war, but not at the risk of sacrificing everything that I believe in, the principles of our great country, with freedom and justice for all peoples in all countries. As an American I can not understand how any one can say they are an American, and still do things or even say them that may jeopardize the lives of our courageous men, regardless if they are relatives of some of them or not. How our great men, learned men and our representatives can say bring our men home and leave the South Vietnamese to fight for their own country, is beyond my comprehension.

    I have no idea if this can accomplish anything or you as our spokesman can help, in anyway. But I feel that if the American Mothers, Fathers and Friends of our men in Vietnam would speak out on or ask for publication of some of the mail we receive from Vietnam, on how the men there feel about what they are doing, and how they believe in it, so that we could be heard, that it would help a great deal. Otherwise, if we just keep quiet and say nothing, we may be helping to jepordize our sons, or helping to prolong the time for victory for a worthy people that have had to bear so much, with out accomplishment of anything except the prolonging of our mens stay in Vietnam, and many lives lost for no purpose.

    My concern for our men there and such things as the TV broadcast of the Senate Foreign Relations Committee and the attitude of Chairman Fulbright and some of the others, prompted me to write this, also the fact that Our President has halted the bombings, as I fear what could or may happen during this pause. I realize the President has so much pressure placed upon him, and we the meek have not protested, so this is a or rather the only form of protest, that I would recognize, as being in accord with the American principles.

Sincerely,

Mrs. L.J.T. (Albertville, AL)

19

Dear Mr. [J. William] Fulbright:

May 20, 1968

I have been a long time admirer of the things you stood for in Washington. I heard your speeches on T.V. You asked Sec. Rusk was it worth the price we are paying in Vietnam. I feel the same way. I recently lost my son, P.F.C. T.H.B. near Saigon. He had only 4 months training before going over there, and hadn't been there three weeks. I, too, wonder if it is worth it over there. Our boys getting slaughtered over there. I know my son was no better than any other mother's son, but it seems he didn't have enough training before going. So many older ones more experienced in the army. He was barely 20 years old.

I heard Mr. Johnson ask a labor group if they had ever had it so good. Maybe times are better than they have ever been, but to me the price of one boy is not worth all the riches in this world.

Will you write and tell me just why are the boys over in Vietnam?

With all regards,

Mrs. M.B. (Stephens, AR)

20

Dear Senator [Russell B.] Long:

May 29, 1968

. . . Let me preface my remarks by saying that I consider myself to be a loyal, red-blooded, flag waving, patriotic, sober, clear-thinking American. I am a graduate of Louisiana State University, class of 1941, a veteran of World War II with about two years service in the Mediterranean. As a matter of fact, I believe I had the dubious pleasure of locating your L.C.T., along with several others that managed to get past, and get headed into the proper beachhead at Anzio.[5]

---

5. L.C.T. is a reference to the Landing Craft Tank, an amphibious assault craft used during World War II to transport tanks onto a beachhead.

With regard to Vietnam, I consider myself a "hawk" and I rather suspect most veterans would classify themselves as "hawks."

Today, I am middleaged, the father of draft age children and very much concerned about the future of America and our way of life.

I have a twenty year old son who is a PFC in the United States Marines. He volunteered for service because the marines attracted him. Today, he is in the Hawaiian Islands. According to scuttlebutt, he is part of a brigade being "formed up" for subsequent duty in Vietnam.

I am sure I am no different from many other fathers with a son in the service . . . that is, I am apprehensive, concerned, troubled, reluctant and proud. I wish he was enrolled in some college here in the U.S.A., preparing himself for a future I consider better than the one he appears to have. At the same time, I firmly believe that every generation has the responsibility of defending its freedom at whatever far-flung point on this troubled globe that defense is necessary. Make no mistake, my son, along with all the other sons involved is defending freedom in these United States. He is not, in my analysis, preserving the freedom of the South Vietnamese, and the President would do the cause a great service if he would cease referring to our effort in Vietnam as an action to preserve freedom for the Vietnamese. If Vietnam goes, so will Laos, Cambodia, Thailand, Maylasia and all of that part of the world. After that, Australia and other nations will be threatened, and finally this nation.

While I dislike my son having to serve in Vietnam, I think I recognize the necessity of that country's defense. The thing I object to and consider downright treason and criminal is the action of our government to deny my son the full military support and protection my government is really capable of giving. If we must fight in Vietnam, why must our men be denied every tactical and logistic support this country is capable of providing. . . .

If my son must help defend freedom in Vietnam, why, in the name of God, must he do it with one hand tied behind his back. I am aware of all the arguments about the effect our greater involvement might have on our image abroad, about world opinion, the effect on our friends. Who's kidding whom? What friends, what image, what allies? The way to get friends, allies and a good public image is to gain the respect of the world. You don't obtain respect letting some two-bit nation like North Vietnam have you dance to their music. I am also aware of the danger of Red China and/or the Soviet Union becoming involved. My answer to that is this—if we are going to get the stew hacked out of us without Red China or the Soviet Union being directly involved, we might as well get the stew hacked out of us with them being involved.

Frankly, Senator Long, I have a strong urge to advise my son to do whatever is necessary to avoid combat in Vietnam unless and until my country is prepared to back him to the hilt. Why should he fight and possibly die while his bearded, long haired contemporaries are burning our institutions of higher learning and their draft cards, or escaping to Canada and Sweden (two of our friends) to avoid military service. Why should he bleed, and possibly die in some far away land for a cause so few of our people support and one which has divided this nation as never before.

Why must he experience active full time military service while others escape this service by making college attendance a career until they have either exceeded draft age or have acquired a wife and one or two children, thereby escaping military service forever. For those not wanting to take the college option, they can join a National Guard or Reserve Unit, put in six months of "yard bird" duty at some camp, then return home with complete immunity from active duty and an opportunity to preserve freedom in America. Oh, I know several units have been called to active duty and some may even go overseas but most of the fighting is and will be done by enlistees and draftees. . . .

Of course I am not going to advise my son to do anything except his duty. He wouldn't listen to me anyway. He's a marine and one thing this country could use is something a marine has—pride. The least we can do is our duty—either decide to pull out of Vietnam or resume unlimited bombing of the north and mount an offensive that will win the war, including an invasion of North Vietnam if necessary. . . .

Very sincerely yours,
H.D.E. (Franklinton, LA)

21

Dear Senator John [G.] Tower:

March 16, 1969

. . . I will begin by saying that I am a woman of thirty-three years of age and the mother [of] two children; a daughter age nine, and a son age six. I have no sisters and only one brother who is at this time serving his country in Vietnam. He is only twenty three years of age, so you can see I feel more like a mother to him than a sister. By now you have guessed why I am writing. VIETNAM!!!!!!!

I am not a Democrat and I am beginning to wonder if I am a Republican since there seems to be such a fine line between the two these days. I do not feel that my brother is any better than any of the other boys (or should I say young men) in Vietnam, but I do believe that it has to strike home for the average person to wake up to the fact that we are at war whether we call it that or not. I must admit that I do not fully understand this "war," especially when I think of what has happened to Cuba, just off the shores of Florida. What can be done to wake the people up?

. . . I have come to the conclusion that this is definitely a political war. I am now beginning to wonder if President Nixon is going to be a complete disappointment as President Johnson was. Don't you think the life of just ONE of our boys is a high price to pay not to mention the THOUSANDS. You will notice I live in Manvel and you no doubt don't know where that is because it is just a wide place in the road about 10 miles from Alvin. Since 1967 Alvin has lost four boys in Vietnam and I am not sure about the number wounded. We feel that our little town of Alvin has already paid a high price for this war.

Three weeks ago we received a copy of the orders of my brother's "Award of the Army Commendation Medal with 'V' Device." Naturally we are proud of him, as it mentioned his gallantry in action, his courage, and if he had not done what he did, the results would have been tragic. Most of all we are thankful to God that he came through it. Do you know what it is like to live with the constant fear that next time someone you love dearly might not come through it? Friday we received a letter from my brother and enclosed was a copy of the Memorial Service held for two of his friends who did not come through it. My heart goes out to their families and I do not even know them. Please, stop, just for a minute and think of all of the boys we have lost.

Is this going to go on and on until my six year old son is fighting in Vietnam? What are we going to do? Have these thousands died in vain? Do you *really know* why we are there? Do you people in Washington really care and are you really trying to do a job for the people who have elected you to office? No, I don't want to carry a sign or start a riot and I am not a "crackpot." BUT, I am definitely fed up. I don't know what an individual can do, we vote but then what? I am thankful that my brother was not one who wanted to burn his draft card, but if he and all of the others are there to fight, then why don't you let them fight? I mean fight to win! . . .

I will close now with the prayer and hope that you, and the others who are in a position to do something about the awful situation in Vietnam, WILL do something. . . .

Sincerely,
J.B. (Manvel, TX)

22

Mr. [Herman E.] Talmadge,

[April 1969]

Please help to end the war in Viet Nam. We both voted for you. We thought Mr. Nixon would have already ended this thing. Why do so many people have to die?

My husband & I were married Dec. 1, 1968. He got his notice to take his physical 4-24-69. We have to stop living now for two years. We don't go to college we just work. Please don't take my husband & send him back to us in a box, he is only nineteen. We live in a great & powerful nation.

Please end the war. Thank you for reading this. Please help us.

Thank you,
Mrs. G.W. (Donnelly, GA)

23

My dear Mr. President [Richard M. Nixon]:

[April 1969]

This was my son. [Obituary with picture attached]

Now he is no more. He has died in vain (as have all the boys who died and are dying in Vietnam) unless through his death I am able to be of some influence, however small, in bringing this immoral war to an end, and helping to prevent further useless, mass deaths.

As the Flag of the U.S. is an outward symbol of an inward feeling, I am returning the Flag presented to me at my son's funeral for this reason: I do not want a Flag which represents a country which is sacrificing her young men as this one is doing.

I cannot help comparing this situation to that of the Biblical baby Moses, ordered killed, with all the young males, by the dishonorable king. If a young man goes out to defend his country because he believed in it and what it stands for, this is his decision, but when he is *forced* to give his life, is this not murder? A difference between the baby Moses and the sons of American mothers is that we are allowed to give them a few more years loving care before they are so brutally taken. Who can wonder at the rebellion of our youth? What goals are they allowed to have?

From personal interviews with the men who returned, I discovered it must be a hell-hole. Do you underestimate the American people's intelligence? Personally, I am deeply humiliated over our world-wide reputation, as well as crumpled and crushed over the loss of my son. Our flag is one of the most despised in the world, and now it is being hated at home.

I might bring out that I was the mother of five until my recent loss. They are citizens their country can be proud of. It was my thinking first to teach them to love and serve their home, then they would in turn grow up to love and serve their country. Now, mothers seek to protect their sons *from* their country. . . .

As you can see from W.'s portrait, he was tall, good-looking, intelligent, with high ideals. He was studying to be an attorney and would have been an honest, good one, an asset to his country. But you have him killed. WHAT A LOSS. Can you imagine the agony of packing up his youthful camping equipment, his clothes, his toothbrush? You should be so ashamed. I would appreciate it very much if you would retract that "form condolence" you sent. . . .

I do extend my thanks to those who were in charge of the burial of my son. They were patient, understanding, and very sympathetic, denying no request on my part as far as was in their power.

I add that I resent paying the taxes that took my son, buried him, and help continue to kill and maim our fine young men. . . . For a real cause, I would have been proud that I had a son to give for his country. As it now stands, the loss of my respect for my country is surpassed only by the grief over his murder. . . .

Sincerely,
Mrs. M.S. (Warner Robins, GA)

24

Dear Sir [Senator Sam J. Ervin Jr.]:

April 28, 1969

While college students riot, protest, make outrageous demands, destroy buildings and records, every effort is made to make sure none of their rights and freedoms are tampered with. They can't be thrown out of college, and most certainly not drafted.

This is allowed while the decent young men are being slaughtered like animals in Vietnam. THIS IS ENOUGH TO MAKE THE BLOOD OF ANY PARENT BOIL.

We bitterly resent the fact that our only child (son) is given no choice as to his future. The United States Government has already made that choice for him. It is his obligation to serve his country. Just what are these boys being forced to fight for?

Corrupt, power hungry, greedy politicians have allowed this war to drag on too long. President Johnson and Robert S. McNamara was given too much authority, and this should be corrected. The people voted for a change, but this was just the promise of another corrupt politician.

We want and expect our son to have every consideration every other young man is given, and believe any government is headed for destruction when this promise becomes vain.

As concerned parents, we urge you to work diligently toward bringing this war to an early end. . . .

Yours truly,
Mr. & Mrs. R.B.S. (Morganton, NC)

25

Dear Senator [Richard B.] Russell [Jr.]:

August 6, 1969

This letter is written to plead with you men who have the power to stop this killing. My son is dead and nothing can bring him back but I have a seventeen year old also a son in Korea and another in the National Guards. We have been a poor family but so happy and these sons were our treasures. We expect to be taxed to death and I know we are in the sucker class where you only should be intelligent enough to accept the increased tax digs but when it comes to sons Sir these cannot be replaced. Can you possibly imagine how it feels to lose a beloved son? Every morning I awake from a fitful sleep and feel as though I must ward off a crushing blow but the night mare is ever present. No more will my son come in with a "Whats to eat Mom?" No more will he join our family get togethers, he cannot marry the good Christian girl who loved him nor will I have the grandchildren I looked forward to. Sir it seems so plain to us who have to sacrifice our sons that it's a politicians war, that Ky and Thieu are only little two bit dictators who never had it so good before. . . . While we struggled to raise our sons politicians weren't very interested in them but as soon as they get old enough to serve power mad mens purposes they draw on them at will. The draft is wrong too. It just isn't fair for every male to be subject to [the] draft no more than it would be fair to force all into the same occupation. . . . The average law abiding citizen sees the labor leaders and black militants get away with most anything while the average citizen is taken for granted and their rights trampled. . . . If you Senators had to lose a son, I'll bet this silly travesty of justice, this futile empty war, would stop soon.

Mrs. W.P.G. (Winston Salem, NC)

26

Dear Senator [John J.] Sparkman:

August 18, 1969

As I sit here unable to sleep at 2:30 AM shedding tears I must share my sorrow with you. My little brother, Sp. 4 P.R. a poor man's son is leaving for Vietnam to fly missions on a helicopter. My heart is so heavy and fear keeps me awake at this hour and I pray till I am weak that he will make it back home. I never hear of any Senator's sons being killed and it all seems so unfair and useless. Why can't we win this war? Why is the draft so unfair? With the draft laws we have today you might as well say, "Son if your father earns so much per year you can stay home, but if your father is poor you go to war." Why is anyone any better than my little brother? When we were small we starved together and I love him so. Heaven help you for you may take advantage of the poor now but in the real end you will have to answer. We are children of a coal miner but we are just as good as anybody. I have seen so much, "Big I little you" junk all my life I am sick.

I have heard poor boys who are lucky enough to make it back from Vietnam say that the South Vietnamese do not know what they want. They do not even know what is going on. It is my belief that we are getting no where over there. I am beginning to think this is a political war. Please, I beg of you do what you can to end this awful war and please tell me what my little brother's chances are of coming back. I must also ask you to do what you can to get more fair draft laws so that war will not be a rich man's profit and a poor man's fight. Please pray for my little brother.

Mrs. F.B. (Morris, AL)

27

Senator J. William Fulbright,

Oct. 4, 1969

A few months ago I wrote to you concerning my son who was about to go overseas then. Well he finally did go to Vietnam on July 23 and on Aug. 10th he was killed in action at Quang Tri Province. We didn't even get to see his body when we finally did get him back home, the telegram said "Remains not viewable."

I wonder how Mr. Nixon and Mrs. Nixon would feel if it were a Son of theirs? They couldn't possibly know what a great loss we have suffered, he had just turned 19 on the 29th of July, he hadn't even become a man yet. To us he was just a young boy and we never got to finish raising him. It hurts to see all of his clothes and things that he has kept since he was a small boy in school, and now we must put every thing away, as though we never had a Son.

I know you are trying still to end this war, and even if it is too late for our Son, maybe you can still try before to many more Sons are killed. I wish some day you could tell Mr. Nixon to lose a Son is one of the most heartbreaking things we have ever had to do in our life. The wound is so deep it well never heal, and he was our only Son. I'm sorry if I sound so bitter, but I am. Please keep trying to do all you can, and maybe some day we won't have any war.

Thanking you, I remain,
Mrs. H.C. (East Point, AR)

28

My dear Senator [Richard B.] Russell [Jr.]:

November 6, 1969

I am an ordinary American with a high school education. I have always stopped short of writing you because I feel inadequate to express myself. However, I feel that I must speak up in defense of my belief about the Viet Nam War.

I am 47 years old, have worked since I was in high school and still work in an office of 175 to 200 people. I am not a hippie, a dropout from society, a Communist or any other of the things Mr. Agnew has called us. I do read the newspapers and all the columnists in the Atlanta Journal. I also read any article I find in the magazines in my home and take advantage of TV documentaries, etc.

I feel Mr. Nixon has incorrectly labeled his silent majority. From my contacts in the business world with mothers of sons in the Army, in Viet Nam, facing Viet Nam and facing the draft they *all* are against this war. Certainly the young people don't want it. The silent majority is made up of people like me who never make themselves heard and who depend on you people in Washington to make the wise decision and look after our country.

We have listened for years to ideas and plans for being victorious in Viet Nam. None have worked. And now, Mr. Nixon has just tried to placate us a little longer.

What have we been doing? Maintaining a holding action, not allowed to win. Just slowly draining the lives of our young men and maiming many thousands for the rest of their lives. Fighting for a country whose own people refuse to defend, supporting a corrupt government, black marketeering. Even our own army is in a mess. . . .

I am sure I sound bitter and perhaps immature but I haven't struggled for 19 years to raise my only son to die in the jungles of Viet Nam. What future generation is Mr. Nixon speaking of? The sons of young men in the National Guard, the Reserve, the highly intelligent ones who can pick their branch of the service and never see overseas duty or the ones whose fathers have enough influence to keep them out of the draft?

My son will do what he must do and will acquit himself well. He is now in his second year of military college but the whole war is rotten and I am against it. . . .

Sincerely yours,

E.S.C. (female, Atlanta, GA)

29

Dear Senator [Russell B.] Long:

November 18, 1969

We are writing you and sending you a copy of another addressed to the Commanding Officer of the unit our son was assigned to when he was killed in action with the enemy in Vietnam on 19 Oct. 69. We both feel very strongly that you as our elected government official serving in the US Senate should know of our thoughts and feelings after having our son killed in such an impossible, useless and terrible war. The attached letter speaks for itself so we will not go further into detail, but we do wish to make a statement to you concerning the death of our son. We firmly believe at this time that the only results and accomplishments which have been derived from his sacrifice is that it gives the right to the draft dodgers, communists, longhairs, non-voters, non-taxpayers and the 4-F's to parade and destroy, burn, loot, burn our flag, carry and raise the North Vietnam flag in our nation's capitol, burn draft cards and take over cities and towns. That is what we think our son gave his life for on the battle field on a foreign soil. Will our President and other elected officials let this continue to happen? We hope and pray that you as our elected representative serving in the

Senate do all that you possibly can to see to it that our son did not die in vain, and that this terrible mess in Washington will cease. . . .

Respectfully yours,
Mr. and Mrs. H.G. (Ville Platte, LA)

30

Dear CPT [William H.] Edmondson:

November 18, 1969

Thank you kindly for your letter of 10 Nov 69 concerning the loss of our son, G.J.G., in Vietnam on 19 Oct. 69. It was very thoughtful of you to take the time to write us and we certainly appreciate it. You mentioned . . . in closing that if you could be of further assistance to please write you. The purpose of this letter is to accept your offer requesting answers to several question and to ask a favor of you. We crave more information and we assure you that even though our questions may seem immaterial or impertinent to the cause and reasons of his death, the answers and knowledge thereof would be of much help to us. . . .

How many other of the PC crew were killed in this action besides our son?

How many other APC's were in this action? . . .

How long did he stay alive and was it an instant death?

Was there a Chaplin available in the immediate and did he get the last rites? . . .

Why did the command put him in combat actions when he was so inexperienced? . . .

What was his assignment on the APC [Armored Personnel Carrier]? . . .

If there were any survivors . . . on the same APC my son was on, will you ask one of them to write us and give us his version of the whole incident?

. . . I do not think that the United States is fair to our soldiers; they send them or assign them on Search and Destroy missions and that makes them sitting ducks for the Viet Cong. . . . We sincerely feel that our men and boys are suffering and dying in vain. When and if this mess ever gets over with, all this country's politicians will do is to go over there and rebuild the whole area, North and South Vietnam. That's been our history. The only actual results of this war would be that the industries will make millions and we have lost our loved ones, and others have suffered untold miseries. . . .

. . . You know as well as we if not better, that we could have done away with the Viet Cong and North Vietnam in a matter of hours if our own politicians would not have fought so much among themselves. Yes, we would have destroyed many innocent people, including women and children, but what have we lost and now loosing, the cream of our manhood, is what. The politicians say, "to save South Vietnam from communism and stop them over there rather than over here!" You know and we know that in the end we'll get out and they will move in. All we'll have to show for it is our dead sons, our injured and wounded, and richer industries. . . . We cannot make our selves believe that G. died for the freedom of his country. He died for the power hungry politicians and so that the rich can become richer, and not for America safe from communism. . . .

We will remember you in our prayers, CPT Edmondson, that God speed you and your men, and all of the others who are on duty in Vietnam, back home to their loved ones. We will especially pray that God will reward our son and all other sons who died in this terrible conflict, in life hereafter.

Very sincerely,
Mr. and Mrs. H.G. (Ville Platte, LA)

31

An open letter to the President of the United States of America
[Richard M. Nixon]:

[February 1970]

It took the editors of Look magazine to finally arouse all of my hostility when in their January 17, 1970 issue on page 18, they displayed a photograph of a moratorium marcher placing a poster with the name of my dead son printed on it into a coffin during the September demonstrations.

My son demanded the opportunity to serve his country and his God feeling that by going when he did it might prevent someone else from being separated from his wife and children. His letters from Viet Nam provided constant evidence that he grew more convinced of the necessity for our forces to aid the South Vietnamese and that it was God's will that inspired him to fulfill his mission. I think anyone who so nobly lays down his life in defense of his country and his fellow man deserves the affection and respect of those who benefit from his supreme sacrifice.

Now I would never be in favor of suppressing freedom of speech or press, but I wish there was some way to protect our dead heroes from degradation at the hands of fools like those who support these moratoriums and our news media who could have spared me a near nervous breakdown by not using my son's name to sell their magazines.

In other words, since good taste and professional ethics are so rare, I wish there was some way to defend other Gold Star mothers from this harassment at the hands of people or organizations who seek publicity and profit at our expense. Above all, though, I wish there was a way to preserve the honor and dignity accorded to our dead sons that they so richly deserve for having gallantly laid down their lives in our defense. They recognized, as you do, Mr. President, that communist aggression must be checked wherever it occurs to assure the liberties all of us enjoy and only some of us are willing to defend.

Very truly yours,
Mrs. D.G.B. (Greenville, SC)

32

Dear Senator [Albert] Gore [Sr.];

February 28, 1970

I wrote you some time ago to protest the war in Vietnam. The member of my family was killed in action on Jan. 29, 1970. At the present time we have no boys of age, but this does not change my feelings about this unjust war. It is impossible for me to understand why these young inexperienced kids are sent to that mosquito, disease infested country. I'd much rather go myself for I feel I'm better equipped to face the enemy. I feel sorry for all young American boys. I feel he doesn't have much to look forward to in this terrible unjust world. I don't think too many people care; as a young man only becomes a number, and you often hear the news broadcasts. American casualties were light, only 75 or 80 etc. This is wrong there are no light casualties. B. (my nephew) was not a light casualty. It was a great loss to our family. Seeing him brought back in a casket—no one can know how it hurts except those that have experienced the same thing. I think it's over 40,000 at this writing. He was only a kid but how five months in that whole had aged him. He did not go dirty, wear long hair or Roman Sandals. I'm sure if he had done those things he would not have been drafted. He graduated from high school and was on his first job. His mother is a widow and he had no father to advise him. Maby had he known he could have gone into Naval Reserve or something else and be alive today. I'm sorry he had to wade the swamps and fight on the front for those ungrateful people. . . . I do hope you in Congress will see that the same thing will not happen in Laos. . . . I don't think a president should be given the authority to send our young to those foreign places with out the approval of Congress. I hope you and Mr. Fulbright will keep up your good work.

Sincerely,

M.D. (female, LaFollette, TN)

33

Dear Senator [Ralph W.] Yarborough:

April 3, 1970

Another neighborhood boy stepped on a land mine in Viet Nam. It blew him into a thousand pieces.

His parents invested nineteen years of love and care and sacrifice into him. He grew bright and clean, strong of limb and body. He feared God and respected his elders and his country, seeing for himself a clear and golden future. Now bits of his flesh are rotting in the jungle. Splinters of his once-strong bones are imbedded in the dirt beside some trail.

His mother grieves, asking herself if justice can ever exist again; asking herself if her two other sons, now aged eighteen and sixteen, will also be nothing but flesh fodder of the "government" of a land she has grown to despise.

You, Sir, are the government. . . .

. . . Look at what you slaughtered. . . . Look at him as if he were *your* son, Mr. Government. Remember all the nights you sat up with him, making sure he was well. Remember the first steps he took, and the bugs he collected. And remember the freshness of his young smile.

He was not my son, but I remember him and I puke at the thought that my own three sons could end up in the same jungle being eaten by the same ants by the same trail. . . .

I avow this day, my esteemed politician, that you will not have the bodies of my sons. . . .

. . . The next time one of your constituent's children is slaughtered, YOU deliver the message to his parents. YOU tell a grief-blinded father that it was all for a good cause. YOU tell the mother that her nineteen years of building this golden child were not in vain. . . .

R.D. (Houston, TX)

34

Dear Sir [Senator Sam J. Ervin Jr.]:

May 18, 1970

Amid all the antiwar protests and demonstrations, we feel that we must speak out and openly support our country and our president in these troubled times.

On May 19, 1967, our oldest son was killed in Vietnam, before he even reached his 21st birthday. He felt so strongly about our obligation to ourselves and to the people of South Vietnam and the world, that he volunteered for duty with the U.S. Marines and then for duty in Vietnam. We have another son, just 18 years old, who is presently in the Marines and in all probability will be required to serve in Vietnam. This could make it very easy for us to join the protesting students, as this would be the easy way out. However, we feel that time has not altered our obligations and a just peace is just as necessary now as it was in May of 1967.

Many of the young people who are demonstrating, and we feel they are a small minority, say that we of the older generation have nothing to lose as we will not be called upon to serve in this war. But we know all too well that the most difficult task of all is waiting for a son or brother to return from the war.

Our son gave his life for this country. We support the cause for which he and so many more of our fine young men have given their lives. How can we do less? How can anyone?

Sincerely,

Mr. and Mrs. J.G. Jr. (Goldsboro, NC)

35

Dear Sen. [Albert] Gore [Sr.],

June 22, 1970

I have written to you on previous dates. Today, my son left for Viet Nam. I can't describe how I feel. For my son to serve his country would be fine and patriotic. But to see him go away, not knowing if I will ever see him again, to serve in Viet Nam, just to keep that dirty, low down, rotten, crummy little dictator Thieu and Ky in power goes against everything I stand for. I have often wondered how Pres. Nixon, or any of you politicians can sleep or have any peace of mind knowing that this war is just a farce and only to make rich men richer is a mystery to me. Surely, surely, there will be a day of judgement . . . [for] the men who are just keeping this war going to fatten their pocket books. . . . May history not record what we have done and are doing to the youth of our land. . . . Sen. Gore I appreciate what you have done in trying to end the war. . . . If you ever see the

(King) Pres. Nixon, would you please tell him that I never talk to anyone, (and I talk to a lot of people,) who say they have any confidence or believe anything that he says. He has misrepresented (lied if you please) to the American people until they have completely lost all hope in anything he says. . . .

Sincerely,
Mrs. C.G. (Knoxville, TN)

36

Dear Mr. President [Richard M. Nixon]:

June 23, 1970

. . . In late March Pfc. T.S. sat in our living room, visiting his former scout-master and wife before going to the Vietnam area for Army duty. His young wife was with him and they spoke of his plans to attend college on the G.I. bill and study forestry * * * after completing his military service. Since he was the first of seven children of a factory worker his family had been unable to send or even help him attend college. He loved the outdoors and wanted to help preserve the beauty of nature which we have in abundance in this area. . . .

We bade T. goodby and told him we would be glad to help him apply for college entrance when he finished the Vietnam tour. We never saw T. again. They said all that remained of his body after a direct shell hit in Cambodia was in a flag-draped box in the living room of his parents home where they received friends and relatives prior to a full military funeral.

For years I have pondered and agonized over the reasons the U.S. is in Vietnam and Southeast Asia, and I can think of none to justify the death of Pfc. T.S., let alone thousands and thousands of Americans and Asians. . . .

Is the blood of T. on my hands? I did not write a letter specifically asking you not to go into Cambodia, although we have written both you and former President Johnson saying we couldn't understand why our country was doing this. Yes, I feel the blood is on my hands and on the hands of all Americans in varying degrees because this thing is done in our names. But you can do some-thing we cannot. Order immediate and final withdrawal from Cambodia and Vietnam and quit forever this policy of war. The world needs an army of Peace Corps workers to teach people skills they need for living—not dying. . . .

May I somehow be forgiven for not taking a more active stand against this war several years ago, and may fate decree some mercy for you and every citizen of this country for letting T.S. and so many, many promising, young and gentle Americans and Asians die for nothing.

Sincerely,

Mrs. E.P. (Stone Mountain, TN)

37

Dear Sir [Senator Herman E. Talmadge]:

July 17, 1970

. . . I would like to know how you Senators can let the Army draft our young boys, train them for four months and ship them over to Vietnam in the thick of battle. You are taking the cream of the crop and killing them out and leaving the criminals and hippies here to run our country in the future. How can you turn a boy into a man over night. Don't tell me I am wrong about training our boys for only four months. I have no children but I do have a nephew that I dearly love. He was drafted out of his fourth year in college and is married and was sent to Fort Campbell for nine weeks and then sent to Fort Polk for nine weeks and now is on his way to Vietnam in a Mortar Battalion. How I can be patriotic and wave the Big Flag after my country leaves the Reserves and National Guards and Regular Army sitting here on their fannies and sends draftees with four months training to Vietnam. No wonder so many boys (45,000) have been killed. They do not have enough training. Why take our taxpayers money and pay the Reserves, National Guard, and Regular Army if they are exempt from war. Also if Congress has no say so why pay you. Do away with Congress. I am fed up with Senators getting up in public and talking about ending this war and doing nothing to bring it to an end.

I wonder how you and President Nixon would feel if David [Nixon's son-in-law] or a son of yours had only four months training and was sent into battle. No, Nixon has his little family all under his protective wing so this war doesn't tear his family apart. If you are not from a political family, then you are a nobody. But remember it is us little people who put you where you are today. . . .

I am,

Mrs. B.M.W. Jr. (East Point, GA)

38

Dear Senator [Harry F.] Byrd [Jr.],

September 1, 1970

I am a concerned mother with a question important to my family. . . .

Our son C. was drafted into the Army on June 4; completed his basic training at Ft. Campbell, Kentucky and was sent immediately to Ft. Polk, Louisiana where he is receiving advanced infantry training. Because of this training I am fearful that he will be he sent to Vietnam as an infantryman. We are not an unpatriotic family. We are most willing to have our son serve his country in any positive way, however, we do not see the corrupt political *situation* in Southeast Asia as a threat to our great nation or our national security. When the Vietnam war comes as close to affecting family unity as this war appears to us, it is a frightening and very unpleasant experience. This is the third time that I, along with *many* other women, have been touched by war; my husband served with the U.S. Marines during World War II and again during the Korean conflict—now it is my son.

My question is whether it is government policy to send an only son into the combat zone? I know that the sole surviving son—where the father or brothers have been killed in combat—is not sent into the combat zone. Does this policy apply to an only son? C. is our only child and he alone is left to carry on our family name. Frankly, Senator Byrd, I am most reluctant to have my son exposed to the dangers of combat in southeastern Asia when there appears to be little justification for such action. Three years ago my husband was severely afflicted with rheumatoid arthritis and although he is able to work, the stress of concern over his son does not benefit his arthritic condition.

C. is not unwilling to serve his country; we are proud to have him serve, yet under the circumstances, combat duty appears to be a maximum risk.

I do not know what you can do to help me but, as a mother, I had to write hopeful that you will understand. I would appreciate your advice on this question of our only son being sent into a combat zone. . . .

Sincerely yours,
N.B.McG. (Blacksburg, VA)

39

Dear Senator [John C. Stennis]:

January 16, 1971

. . . The column starts out: "How about Mississippi's Sen. John Stennis switching from Hawk to Dove!" It goes on telling how you have changed your opinion and mentioning your name in the same sentence with Senator Fulbright. Personally, I think I'd rather be categorized with Benedict Arnold than Fulbright!

Don't misunderstand me. I have always been in the Hawk category, but I too have changed my opinion, not because of Peacenik propaganda, but because of the deteriorated condition of the war. I have long believed that if it had not been for the Fulbrights and the Gores, we'd have won the war and far fewer lives would have been lost. . . .

Incidentally I have a son who will graduate from Ole Miss in a very few days, and of course the army is waiting for him. His attitude, thankfully, is that distasteful as it is, it is his duty to serve his country. But you know it wouldn't be half as difficult a situation if the Peacenik element had not cut the ground out from under our fighting men. It is fully understandable that morale has dropped so low when men living in danger are not willing to take risks knowing that their government is not backing them up, knowing that Cassius Clay and others are able to dodge the draft. Frankly if I was a member of a draft board, I'd refuse to vote to draft another young man until steps are taken in Washington to see that draft dodgers are treated like everyone else. In my own family the son of a cousin of mine, living up North has been allowed to dodge the draft because of Quaker upbringing. He's a member of the SDS and has hair down to his shoulders. This jerk should be treated like everyone else, not allowed special privileges because he has what could be accurately called "traitor's rights."

My point is that while I now have come to the realization that staying in Vietnam under the present circumstances is futile, I don't think that the Fulbrights should be allowed to say smugly, "I told you so." I sincerely feel that the monkey should be placed squarely on their backs. The nation should know that their perfidy has caused us to lose the first war in the nation's history. . . .

Cordially,

C.R.J. (Brookhaven, MS)

40

My dear Senator [John C.] Stennis:

February 24, 1971

I am a mother of a member of the United States Air Force and wish to seek your assistance. Like so many others, I do *not* wish my boy to participate in the troubles in Vietnam when our great nation is not willing to give them the all out protection they need for a fighting chance for survival. I know and understand the reasons we, as a nation, are there—I too thought it wise at first. However since then things have not changed in the least—we are the losers—our boys

(American women cannot bear enough baby boys to police the world)—money that is sadly needed here to benefit the country as a whole, instead of taxing the populace to the breaking point—to say nothing of the unrest and violence within our boundaries caused by this "no win attitude."

Tell me, what would we lose if we pulled out—brought all our boys home? A little face? How much is that worth? Thousands and thousands of lives—billions of dollars—so we can boast never defeated. A retreat is not undignified if the purpose is great. . . .

I speak as only one mother—my boy is only one of thousands, but my feelings are for him and all the others—please do what you can to stop this needless waste. . . .

I was happy and proud when he joined the Air Force—I knew it would give him the opportunity to serve his country and make a man of him—but this is not a declared war against our country—as it stands it has not been proved our help has been worthwhile.

My heart goes out to the families of prisoners there—if we pulled out couldn't we buy them back? . . . A payoff! Absurd? Why? We pay kidnappers when there is no other alternative—why not for those who were willing to stand up for their country? The cost couldn't be as great as it now stands! . . .

Mr. Stennis, don't delay another day—each hour brings more deaths, more prisoners, to say nothing of the cost. Help bring our boys home—the time certain is now! Not tomorrow or next year!

Very truly yours,
(Mrs.) H.D.L. (Pascagoula, MS)

41

Dear Mr. [Richard M. Nixon] President,

April 25, 1971

It is unfortunate you do not have a son. Without one it is impossible to understand the special love that exists between a father and his son. My wife and I are preparing for an event which is one we have looked forward to for a long time. Our son is graduating from college next month. This should be a happy event, but unfortunately it is not because shortly thereafter our son will be drafted into the army.

Our son will serve because he has been raised to face his obligations, and will do so, even though he does not agree with the war or associated policies.

However I now question if I have not failed him in his raising. We have tried to raise our son in Christian belief of love and peace. You, and our US laws, will now take him against his will and force feed him with hate and war. He will be taught how to "kill" his fellow man. As a citizen, and especially as a parent, I object to this! If the security of our country was in jeopardy, both my son and I would be asking to serve.

I am probably more opposed to our direct SE Asia intervention than anyone, therefore I certainly object to anyone's son being involved in such an "unholy" war. Already too many sons have given their lives needlessly. No more sons must die, and no more families made to suffer such an ordeal as the loss of a love one in SE Asia.

Please end the present US participation *immediately,* then end the unamerican "forced labor" law known as the draft.

Sincerely yours,
L.L.D. (New Orleans, LA)

42

Dear Mr. [Russell B.] Long:

May 7, 1971

Four years ago my son started to college and received a student deferment. I felt that each year would be the last one in Viet Nam and that surely by the time my son spent four years in college that I would not have this worry hanging over my head. Well, four years later my son is graduating from college, and we are still in the midst of this terrible war.

Mr. Long, we are so tired of this long drawn out war. Our boys cannot start a life of their own with the dread of this thing hanging over their heads. My son once said to me, "Mother, don't worry over this schedule of classes, in a year I'll be in Viet Nam and be killed anyway." Do you know what this does to a mother? I'm sick over it. And, my second son will be 19 in July, so here I go again.

Mr. Long, I (and many others I know here in Lake Charles as well as all over the U.S.) plead with you to do whatever you can to help bring our boys home now. Let us once again have a land where our kids will be proud when they see the American flag instead of wanting to burn it. . . .

Your truly,
Mr. & Mrs. F.LeB. (Sulphur, LA)

43

Sir [Senator J. William Fulbright]:

[December 1971]

Last month my little brother came home from Viet Nam. The Army had no further need of him since he had been killed on Nov. 10, and was therefore damaged equipment. Mr. Nixon promised to bring our troops home, well once again he had kept that promise. SP/4 B.T.D. was twenty-one years old. He wasn't a radical or a hippie, just an average American who saw no reason for our presence in Viet Nam. In his last letter home, he said anyone who dies over here dies in vain. He died for nothing.

Mr. Nixon has bought time and played politics with the life of my brother and all the others who have fought and died over there.

The responsibility for their deaths rests on Nixon and the people who follow and support his policies. How many tears will it take to wash the blood of America's youth from American hands?

Please do all you can to stop another tragedy from taking place, another home saddened by a useless death.

Respectfully,
D.W.D.

44

Dear Senator [Harry F.] Byrd [Jr.]:

June 1, 1972

Enclosed is an article concerning my son, 1st Lt. F.W.W., who was killed in the Vietnam War. It is his and my plea for peace. I do not feel that because he and many other young men lost their lives there, that we are committed to "win" this war which is a total failure for the United States and many times more so for South Vietnam, whether we win or lose. Rather, I feel that the only decent thing that the United States can do at this point is to withdraw all forces from Vietnam before it is totally devastated.

I sincerely hope that you can and will work swiftly and earnestly to end the Vietnam War—and all wars.

Sincerely,
S.H.W. (female, Richmond, VA)

P.S. I urge you to use this article in any way you may see fit.

Enclosed Article

May 5, 1972

Four years ago today, my son was killed in an irrational, insane war—one that he no longer believed in. When F. was sent to Vietnam in September of 1967, he was 20 years old; an infantry officer with 45 men in his command. When he first arrived in Vietnam, he felt that somehow he could help erase the anguish of poverty, pain and misery in that little country. Instead he found that he and his fellow soldiers were doing the complete opposite. He saw that the United States was not helping in the struggle against poverty, pain and misery, but was actually causing it. He felt trapped in a mindless, merciless machine, bent on destroying a helpless country and its people.

On April 22, 1968, thirteen days before his death, he wrote:

"All logical conclusions one can make point to our (U.S) error. Ho Chi Minh, this little character, has been doing more for the Vietnamese people than anyone. Certainly the South Vietnamese have not had anything but corruption and mismanagement for ages. Ho is doing for Vietnam what he believes is right * * * * they certainly don't need what the South Vietnamese Government and the Americans give them. Why can't the U.S. learn to stick to what they are really involved in and make some definite decisions instead of blundering through politics * * * losing everything. America seems to be setting a terrible example. Riots, murders, false peace proposals * * * maybe something will come up to change all this, but I am not tempted to go back to all these depressing scenes."

Despair overwhelms me whenever I think of his photograph, taken just before he was killed and sent back with his belongings. He was so changed, so desolate. His expression was heartbroken and hopeless. His eyes, always so beautiful and sweet, told a bitter, hideous story. It was the devastating face of war.

I brought up F. and my other children as most mothers did then to be "loyal, patriotic Americans." F. believed that to fight and even to die for his country was a noble thing. It wasn't a thing we talked about or even thought about and this was the mistake. It is the way most of us live—not thinking—not communicating; unaware—unheeding. Later I awakened to the truth; that we were not as close as I had believed.

My grief is many times more terrible because of the responsibility I feel for his death. I know now—now that it is too late for my boy—that if only I had been more aware of him and perceptive to his needs that he might be alive today. He might be living the exciting, fulfilling life that was rightfully his and enriching the lives of all who knew him. F. was that sort of person.

Instead, my son, whom I love more than life itself, died a senseless, violent death in an alien land, with no one by his side to hold his head or love him * * * alone * * * alone.

5. Fulbright, Calley, and the Southern Public

Arkansas's Senator J. William Fulbright, the South's most significant dove, and Florida's Lieutenant William L. Calley Jr., whose actions at the My Lai massacre led to his conviction for murder, elicited starkly contrasting responses from their southern neighbors. Those responses afford telling commentary on the South's sense of patriotism and duty during wartime and the region's commitment to the military tradition and ethic.

Senator J. William Fulbright

Fulbright was elected to Congress from Arkansas's Third Congressional District in 1941 and advanced to the U.S. Senate in 1944. From the beginning of his service in Washington, Fulbright took an active interest in American foreign relations, first as a member of the House Foreign Affairs Committee and after 1948 on the Senate Foreign Relations Committee (SFRC). A supporter of containment and early Cold War policies such as the Truman Doctrine and Marshall Plan, he diverged from majority southern opinion by rejecting "an all-out effort in Korea" that might have led to war with the Peoples Republic of China.[1]

The senator departed even more markedly from southern foreign policy assumptions on Vietnam. From his chairmanship of the SFRC, Fulbright harshly criticized both the Johnson and Nixon administrations' Vietnam policies. His questioning of the rationale for war in Vietnam, opposition to escalating

1. Randall H. Woods, *Fulbright: A Biography* (New York: Cambridge University Press, 1995), 166, 217–18, and "Dixie's Dove: J. William Fulbright, the Vietnam War, and the American South," *Journal of Southern History* 60 (August 1994): 533–52; Joseph A. Fry, *Debating Vietnam: Fulbright, Stennis, and Their Senate Hearings* (Lanham, MD: Rowman & Littlefield, 2006), 8–9; William C. Berman, *William Fulbright and the Vietnam War: The Dissent of a Political Realist* (Kent, OH: Kent State University Press, 1988). Woods is the foremost authority on Fulbright.

the U.S. military involvement, and call for a negotiated, compromise settlement and U.S. withdrawal raised the ire of both presidents and the South's prowar majority.[2]

Despite these reservations regarding U.S. involvement in Vietnam, Fulbright played a crucial role in the passage of the Gulf of Tonkin Resolution. He feared that Senator Barry Goldwater (R/AZ), the Republican nominee for president and an avowed hawk on Vietnam and Cold War foreign policy, might defeat Johnson in the 1964 election, and the Arkansas senator accepted Johnson's version of the Gulf of Tonkin incident and assurances that he did not intend to widen the war. Only later did Fulbright learn that Johnson, Secretary of State Dean Rusk, and Secretary of Defense Robert McNamara had misled him and Congress by withholding information regarding U.S. and South Vietnamese operations that could have incited the North Vietnamese attacks on the USS *Maddox* and by presenting the questionable second attacks on the *Maddox* and the USS *C. Turner Joy* as fully confirmed.[3]

After failing to convince Johnson to rein in the U.S. involvement, Fulbright held nationally televised SFRC hearings from January 28 through February 18, 1966, to assess the war. These hearings embodied a direct challenge to Johnson and his war, and they constituted the first true public debate over the conflict's origins, merits, and conduct. Fulbright and other antiwar senators such as Albert Gore (D/TN) and Wayne Morse (D/OR) interrogated Secretary Rusk and General Maxwell Taylor (ret., USA), who had served as chairman of the Joint Chiefs of Staff and U.S. ambassador to South Vietnam. The SFRC chair also called witnesses to bolster the antiwar brief: General James M. Gavin (ret., USA) and George F. Kennan, the foreign service officer who had formulated the containment policy in 1946–47 and subsequently served as U.S. ambassador to the Soviet Union.

The hearings' most dramatic moment came when Fulbright confronted Rusk, a fellow southerner from Georgia. While lambasting the secretary and Johnson's foreign policy, the SFRC chair denounced the cost of the war and rejected the contention that U.S. honor and credibility warranted continued involvement. Since Ho and his followers had begun their struggle with the nationalistic goal of independence from France, it was a gross "oversimplification" to portray the war as an essential facet of the international Cold War. The senator declared, "Vietnam is their country. It is not our country." From the enemy's perspective,

2. Fry, *American South and the Vietnam War*, 103, and *Debating Vietnam*, 9–10.
3. Fry, *American South and the Vietnam War*, 82–85.

"we are obviously intruders" who represent traditional "Western imperialism." Surely Rusk should understand this response to outside intrusion, given the American South's objection to post–Civil War Reconstruction. Fulbright also questioned the national conviction that Americans were peculiarly peaceful and well-intentioned.[4]

When the hearings failed to restrain President Johnson, who further escalated U.S. involvement, Fulbright continued his opposition by speaking out against the war, holding a second set of high-profile SFRC hearings in February and March 1968 to grill Rusk regarding the Gulf of Tonkin incident, and maintaining this blunt antiwar stance during the Nixon presidency.

The hearings may have made dissent more respectable nationally, but, as Fulbright's constituent correspondence demonstrated, majority white opinion in the South sharply disapproved of the senator's antiwar posture and actions. The South's response clearly illustrated the personal trials and political hazards of opposing the Vietnam War in Dixie. Critics of the senator, his hearings, and his persistent opposition to the war accused him of divulging strategic information to the enemy via the open hearings; of impugning the nation's international honor and reputation; of encouraging the Vietnamese communists to believe they could outlast a divided United States; of confusing the American public with spurious information; of inconsistency, given his vote for the Gulf of Tonkin Resolution; of encouraging unlawful domestic protests and demonstrations; of consorting with northern liberals and detested civil rights activists; and of failing to offer a viable alternative to Johnson's or Nixon's policies.

Fulbright's antiwar supporters, who comprised a clear minority in Arkansas and the South, praised his courage and willingness to confront Johnson, applauded the SFRC's attempts to reassert the Senate's central role in foreign policy formation and implementation, endorsed the merits of an open, informative debate on the war, agreed with the need to admit the mistake of intervening and to withdraw as soon as possible, and appreciated the loyal opposition's role in preventing the war from becoming even more costly and dangerous. Many of Fulbright's old friends and supporters warned that his antiwar stance was exceedingly unpopular in Arkansas and faulted the senator for not formulating

---

4. Eric Sevareid, "Why Our Foreign Policy Is Failing: An Exclusive Interview with Senator Fulbright," *Look*, May 3, 1966, 25; Fry, *American South and the Vietnam War*, 127, 130–34, and, *Debating Vietnam*, 70–74.

an alternative to Johnson's or Nixon's strategies. The political warnings were prescient. While not the only relevant factor, Fulbright's antiwar position contributed directly to his failure to win reelection in 1974. Opposing the war also haunted other southern senators. Both Albert Gore of Tennessee and Ralph W. Yarborough of Texas suffered a similar electoral fate, and Thruston Morton and John Sherman Cooper, both Kentucky Republicans, declined to run for reelection.

1

Dear Sir [Senator J. William Fulbright]:

January 31, 1966

Again I am pleased to be assured that there are men of your stature and influence in the Congress who are unafraid of political reprisals or public intimidation when matters of dubious morality and legality become the course of action and policy for our nation, and are willing to voice dissent and opposition with candor and persistence. Reports of your silence were disturbing, but in recent days those of us who share your convictions on U.S. foreign policy, and especially the war in Vietnam, have rejoiced at your open and honest challenge of that unfortunate folly.

For what it is worth, you have this one citizen's vigorous and sincere support in these areas: the indefinite continuation of the cessation of the bombing of North Vietnam; the equal representation of major belligerents, including the Viet Cong, at the conference table; and the absolute requirement of the President of the United States to bring all matters pertaining to the continuation and/or escalation of this war to your committee of the Congress and to that august body itself for review and approval before committing the United States to any definite policy. . . .

Let it be known that many of us in the clergy view this war as immoral and illegal and Un-American to the highest degree. You are a strong and sympathetic voice; speak loud and often!

Sincerely,

D.H.E. (Springdale, AR)

2

Dear Sir [Senator J. William Fulbright]:

February 4, 1966

I feel you are doing a great injustice to the cause of the U.S. and your "open" cohorts can achieve only one thing and that is to aid the Communist Viet Cong position.

I do not agree at all with your position. Everyone I know here is also against it. If you people go behind closed doors and black eyes—go ahead. Don't tell the whole world all of our secrets. Because you didn't lay the egg you want to tear up the nest.

The job of a President is difficult enough without a bunch of "softie," "crying," "bleeding hearts" sitting around and talking of stopping a war that we are already in. You talk like you can make a gangster agree to the rules of society. . . .

I suppose after the war is appeased to death and the rooster comes home to roost and it takes untold millions of lives you will then understand that negotiation with gangsters has always meant death & destruction. Why not fight on our terms for a change. You can kill millions at the present rate.

Yours sincerely,
R.B. (Helena, AR)

P.S. Hope to see you defeated in the next election.

3

Dear Senator (J. William Fulbright]:

February 7, 1966

This is my first letter to a legislator as a supporter or dissenter on any political action. As an ex-serviceman, and as a father and father-in-law of two boys that sometime soon will be in service, I feel that it is now time to speak out on the Vietnam War. . . .

I followed your Committee meeting on TV last week and there were several points made that my friends and I believe should be supported by your Committee. First, Sen. Church said that if we are going to trim our domestic budget, then the aid program should be trimmed also. *Agreed.* Second, your statement, in context, that we had better be trying to improve our relations with China and other countries that are destined to be major powers, is necessary if we are to survive without a nuclear war or at least a major war. . . .

Way off down here in Arkansas may not be conducive to making foreign policy but if we are to help furnish the service men, then we can help formulate some of the ideas. If Vietnam is to cost more then we should take it from the aid programs as well as domestic front. If the millions are needed for that new port-harbor in Vietnam—then the Ark. river needs to be finished for transportation also. We want to be good citizens but we want to be treated as good citizens. Our grand children are mortgaged to the hilt now and yet our aid is trying to buy the world. Thank you for the courage you have shown but more especially for your foresight and reasonable thinking. If it is too deep or profound as some of the radical thinkers slyly hint, then I say we need some deep thinking and some soul searching too. . . .

Senator, I'm a railroad switchman with a school teacher wife. We have three children. . . . I tell you this to show you that we are a family trying to improve ourselves as we improve Arkansas. We are proud of Arkansas and our Country but we feel that there is room for improvement in our foreign policy and that the public should be allowed more knowledge of our position in world affairs for our lives depend upon some of those decisions and sometimes we are capable of wise decisions if we are properly informed. Thank you.

A Constituent,
J.W.P. Sr. (Fort Smith, AR)

4

Dear Senator [J. William] Fulbright:

February 9, 1966

This is with respect to your committee's open discussion of the Vietnam situation. It may be that we have no right being in war in Vietnam, but we are, right up to our ears. You know as well as I do that we can not and will not pack up and walk out now. It seems to me that your interest in debating these issues is a bit late. This should have been done before we became so involved.

Your open debate will not settle anything. It will result in more people being confused as to the correctness of our position in Vietnam. When in war we should unite, not divide. I feel that your open debate of the Vietnam matters is a disservice to the American men who are giving their lives daily in Vietnam. . . .

I feel that your committee should be kept fully informed on the Vietnam situation but in closed session.

Sincerely,
P.B.M. (Little Rock, AR)

5

Dear Senator [J. William] Fulbright:

February 9, 1966

I am writing to let you know that I and many other people with whom I am in contact wholeheartedly support your stand concerning this country's foreign policy with regard to Vietnam.

The whole area of our involvement and our present conduct should be able to withstand a good "airing." Otherwise something must be amiss. We in this country have always been able to openly discuss any decision—major or minor—without fear of undue pressure or criticism. This is as it should be in our type of democracy. Lately, however, in dealing with the present administration it becomes more and more evident that if a person speaks against a Johnson Policy, he is immediately branded as one who is not quite as loyal as he should be—one who does not have the wellbeing of the country at heart. . . .

Again I congratulate your courage in taking this stand. Many of us were almost ready to agree that Congress was in fact the Yes Man for Mr. Johnson. I urge you to continue to act as you have in the past. . . .

Sincerely,
J.B. (Walnut Ridge, AR)

6

Dear Sir [Senator J. William Fulbright]:

February 15, 1966

We wish to register our complete disapproval of the Viet-Nam inquiries by your committee. You are giving aid and comfort to the enemy, by your completely biased testimony by your so-called Liberals—who are morally too cowardly to take a stand for the right against the Communists—Russian, Chinese, African, Cuban or Viet-Cong.

Why do you so often criticize the policy of our government and refuse to support its policy in international affairs when dealing with Communists?

Why do you not speak out against Russia supplying arms and missiles to kill our American boys? . . .

We are ashamed and humiliated of the image you have given of the loyal patriotic Arkansans which you are supposed to represent.

Very sincerely,
Mr. & Mrs. J.T.M. (West Fork, AR)

7

Dear Senator [J. William] Fulbright:

February 17, 1966

I have spent much of today watching with avid interest the televised debate of the Senate Foreign Relations Committee as they have interviewed Mr. Maxwell Taylor. I find myself becoming extremely emotionally involved.

The war in Viet Nam is a subject that we discuss with increasing regularity in this area. Almost without exception, my friends and I agree that we cannot in the interest of this country get out of Viet Nam until we have won this war.

I would not be one to stifle free discussion in this nation. However I have been alarmed when I have heard the remarks of your committee today. Particularly you and Senator Morse. It would seem to me that, in your official capacity, this borders on giving aid and comfort to the enemy. As one of your constituents, I would like to register my vigorous protest. . . . I feel sure that your views are in variance with those of the great majority of Arkansans.

In my humble opinion, the best thing that we can do is to get in there and mop this thing up while we can do it with as little risk as we can today. A few years from now Red China will be armed with nuclear power in operational war capacity, and the world's real paper tiger will be in fact a menacing threat to the world. Communism can and must be contained now. . . .

Sincerely,

J.A.K. (Camden, AR)

8

Dear Mr. [J. William] Fulbright,

February 19, 1966

It is with a sense of frustrated regret that we write to you, knowing that since our views are as divergent as they seem to be, you will neither heed or understand the indignation with which we address you.

We feel, as do others in your state, that you have betrayed your native land to such a degree as to be treasonable, and that criticism for criticism's sake, for which you hold such high regard, is completely out of place in time of crisis.

Your adverse treatment of the efforts of American fighting men in Vietnam is not only in bad taste, it is a means of undermining the efforts of your government and mine. . . . In attacking—openly, publicly, and flagrantly—this policy of the United States at a time when our military forces are under fire is the action of a traitor who is determined to undermine his government, regardless of the cost.

We feel that if perhaps you had been a fighting man, and had known the definite finality of life lived minute by minute, you could better understand the character of your present war against the war in which our own sons are engaged. Since it is obviously impossible for you to have this realization, we implore you to stop giving comfort to an enemy who shoots to kill, and to desist from giving outrage to American men who fight in the face of your blasphemies. . . .

We are in support of the military efforts in Vietnam, and feel that the only solution, at any time, is a military victory that the world can understand. We feel that your hearing is conducted at the worst possible time, and that it should be stopped immediately. This is not the proper moment to wash government linen in view of the world, and if you had felt compelled to criticize, as you often do, it should have been done in private conference. . . .

It is the time for withdrawal, not by the United States fighting forces, but by Senator J. William Fulbright.

Very sincerely yours,
J.R. and Mrs. J.R. (Pine Bluff, AR)

9

Dear Senator [J. William] Fulbright,

February 19, 1966

May I express my support of what you are trying to do in relation to our involvement in Viet Nam.

I do not like to be suspicious of my government's integrity. But I am greatly concerned that in the face of overt and publicized invitations to negotiate, two and possible three overtures made by Hanoi looking toward negotiation were thwarted by premature publicity in this country. It is almost as if we wished to put obstacles in the way of negotiations instead of clearing the way for them.

I am also concerned at persistent references to communist China as if Hanoi were its military puppet. The background reading I do convinces me that Hanoi is trying to resist China's attempts to intervene. . . .

As an American I am thoroughly committed to our assuming a responsible role in the community of free nations, and we ought to cooperate in all honorable measures to resist the advance of communist imperialism; but I do not think this means assuming unilaterally the role of world policeman.

As a theologian I am disturbed by our increasing propensity for playing God; specifically, presuming that we can allow freedom of choice among the emerging nations only when the choice is predetermined in our favor. . . .

Sincerely yours,

W.A.W. Jr. (Springfield, VA)

10

Dear Senator [J. William] Fulbright,

February 21, 1966

I've never written a public official before but as a voter, citizen, and minister I feel impelled to write you and express my feelings on your T.V. hearings on our policy in Vietnam.

First, I think they are ill timed. Why didn't you do this years ago if it must be done? The time is past for debate. I fear that you, Mr. Morse and others of your persuasion are giving aid and comfort to the communists and helping to prolong the war. The enemy predicted we would finally tire and pull out and thus the communists could take over the government of South Vietnam.

The trouble with your group is that they offer no constructive alternative. Communism is the active enemy of the Christian Church and all she stands for. How long will it take us to learn that the Communists are playing for keeps, that they intend to win and dominate the world? . . . They are not interested in coexistence. They have no respect for treaties, agreements or humanitarian ideals. Karl Marx said that the social principles of Christianity are "lick spittle." Let us not be lulled by wishful thinking.

We can win this war with communism only if we realize that we are in a life and death struggle. It is freedom or communism—one will survive; one will die. We will lose by appeasement and retreat. . . .

Sincerely yours,

C.N.S. (Hazen, AR)

11

Dear Bill [Senator J. William Fulbright]:

May 9, 1966

. . . I have refrained from writing you during recent weeks on your many speeches concerning Viet Nam. . . . The time to criticize has ended and unless you can offer specific, constructive criticisms and specific remedies either to cure wholly or partially this ill-advised venture.

If you will recall our many conversations during the past 20 years each of us has had his own premise regarding Communism, the menace it presents, and how the menace can be resisted. I have always respected your viewpoint and still respect it. There is a great need in America for independent views to be presented by unselfish patriots such as you. . . . Whether I agree with you or not will not affect my support for you when you run for reelection to the Senate in 1968. I, together with more than 250,000 other Arkansans, take a personal pride in having Bill Fulbright in the U.S. Senate. But, I do think you have gone far enough in mere criticism. . . .

This is not being critical. As one of your strongest supporters, I am telling you the facts of life. Keep discussing Viet Nam, but do it on a *constructive basis*. Present a program of *specifics* if you have any. Otherwise defer your statements until you have something *concrete* to offer. Personally, I think you will come out on top in the controversy. If they ever have an honest election in Viet Nam, people will tell us to go home. The Oriental does not like the Occidental to interfere.

With personal regards to you and love to Betty from P. and me.
Sincerely,
O.F. (Blytheville, AR)

12

Dear Bill [Senator J. William Fulbright]:

April 28, 1967

Thank you for your fine letter of recent date. I share your pessimism about the war in Vietnam. . . .

I can see so clearly what I believe you can also see . . . that our present COURSE OF ACTION is bringing us closer and closer to World War III and world destruction. You have always been a YEAR and MORE AHEAD of the average man on the street's awareness of what is going on. You have had to go through unpopular phases time and again, in taking the RIGHT STAND, regardless of public sentiment. But the public attitude can CHANGE OVERNIGHT when events finally reach a point wherein EVERYONE can SEE the results of a great mistake. . . .

Sitting out here, in our beautiful Ozark hills, where I have a sense of God and Nature, and at the same time a sickening feeling of what is coming—the bottomless pit our boys are facing in Vietnam . . . the billions being spent for destruction * * * and the BILLIONS yet to be spent * * * I am overwhelmed by feelings of frustration and futility.

What CAN be done to STOP this? . . .

This is a hell of a letter to be writing you. I wish I could be more optimistic. I only hope you have the GUTS, along with some of your courageous associates like George McGovern, to keep the door open for free debate and discussion in our supposedly free country. . . .

Sincerely,

H.S. (Mountain View, AR)

13

Dear Sir [Senator J. William Fulbright]:

December 25, 1967

I note in your letter that for the last two years that you have raised serious questions concerning our involvement in Vietnam. Since you were one of those [who] voted with the rest of the Senate passing the Resolution to give the president the supreme authority to the take "whatever measures were necessary." Now you question this action and wish to shift the responsibility for what you term a tragic mistake.[5]

You also say that you have been "accused of performing a disservice" to the country by asking questions of this kind. . . . I sincerely believe that antiwar demonstrators have been encouraged by your activities and public criticism of the involvement. Your criticism along with other influential men have encouraged much disrespect for our president and country. . . .

You indicate in your letter that there is a difference between supporting our soldiers in Vietnam and criticizing the president, the government and all the war effort. How many lives of soldiers are being lost daily by giving *comfort* and *consolation to the enemy* by influential men like yourself making antiwar statements, such as *surrender! withdraw* the American forces! stop the bombing etc. That is exactly what Ho Chi Minh would say. Such statements lead the communists to think that they *can win* prolonging the war. Unlike Asians, we are an impatient people—and of course this is what Ho Chi Minh hopes: That our impatience will get the better of us and we'll say, "Oh Lets Get Out."

I don't see that the War in Vietnam is immoral anymore than all the past wars in history. Sherman said "War is Hell." You fight a war "for keeps." . . .

5. The reference is to the Gulf of Tonkin Resolution.

We have a deep commitment in Vietnam, one that goes back almost 20 years. . . . Mr. Fulbright "We cannot back out of Vietnam without *invalidating our position as a world leader.*" So many countries are now getting the assurance that America will stand firm in its commitments. If we allow the communists to have South Vietnam, the next step would be to work on Japan, Korea, Thailand, Cambodia, Laos, Philippines, Taiwan, Australia and India, then where would we stand? . . .

Respectfully,

G.D.C. (Ozark, AR)

14

Dear Sir [Senator J. William Fulbright]:

March 13, 1968

Have been proud of your Senate record in most respects but must say that I am and have been in disagreement with the public worldwide stand you have taken on the Vietnam issue and insistence on the televised questioning (or inquisition) in detail of a top level official. I felt the first time that it was a great mistake to air the family wash before the whole world and have found no reason to change. . . . I think that first public hearing and subsequent public criticism did as much as anything to influence Hanoi to refuse to negotiate on any terms but its own, which is all or nothing. . . .

With each Senator having to say something or ask questions for the benefit of his constituents, it was interminably long. . . . Haven't always agreed with Secretary Rusk but will say he did a good job and he did offer to discuss certain things in a private meeting—with which I agreed. That gave me more of a feeling of confidence in him than in those who seem to want to tell the whole world what is planned or going to be done. . . .

I admire a person who stands for what he believes and I want to vote for you again for Senator, but certainly do not want my vote for you on the basis of other things you have done to be considered a vote against President Johnson. In other words, I hope you do not campaign as anti-Johnson.

Sincerely,

M.L.S. (Bentonville, AR)

15

Dear Bill [Senator J. William Fulbright]:

October 16, 1969

You have been so kind and thoughtful to me in recent years that I hesitate in writing you about this Vietnam debate; but surely our relationship is such that it can stand—maybe even thrive upon—sincere difference of opinion. . . .

Both of us agree that we wish we had never gotten so deeply involved in Vietnam. Where we differ is the method of getting out. I cannot refrain from believing that we are encouraging the enemy with all this open criticism of the President and his policies. Don't you believe he would like to get out of there as quickly as he honorably can? Shouldn't we give the President and the military advisers some more time? If I had a son over there—and I have one that is approaching seventeen—I don't think I could sit still if we were not really trying to win the war.

These are my thoughts at "mauretorium day"; these attempts to "pressure" the President or the Congress by demonstrations in the streets are repugnant to me. And I must honestly—but respectfully—confess that I regret seeing that the Senate Foreign Relations Committee will hold these hearings at this time. I believe that the majority of the people are behind the President—as most of us were behind the previous President—in his efforts to bring the war to an honorable completion. And I wish we could all give him some more time. I know many of your friends who wish the same.

I hope I have not offended you. I have tried my best not to write you about this matter—but I had to.

Sincerely,
C.L.D. Jr. (Joiner, AR)

16

Dear Bill [Senator J. William Fulbright],

November 11, 1969

You seem surprised at the hate letters you are getting. It is true I think that the tide of public thinking has been gradually turning against you these past two years. I do not think it is you personally. It is a possibly needed reaction to the "right" while the reading public has seen you as more and more drifting to the left. . . .

Being a member of the group I believe I know how this silent majority thinks.

It deplores the casualties and the expense (and this too is important) of Viet Nam. It does not think of this war as being Mr. Nixon's, Mr. Johnson's, or Mr. Kennedy's. We think of it as the result of many blunders in our international relations and actions since W.W. II, when the hero stepped out to police, feed, educate the world and make it over in our own image. The Marshall Plan worked in western Europe, peopled by a society much like our own ideologically and economically. Therefore, it should work in Latin America, the Middle East, the Far East, and we even tried it in reverse in Africa. It got us into Korea with allies. It got us into Viet Nam alone.

Realizing this, or thinking we do, we ask in fairness, what could Mr. Nixon have said other than what he did say? Trite? Sure. It has been said many times before. But what solution or even reasonable alternative do his critics offer? They object and they march. Neither is even a partial solution. . . .

Sincerely,
AC (Little Rock, AR)

Please to not misinterpret this as a mad letter. It certainly is not. To differ by frank discussion is to find the best way out.

17

Dear Senator [J. William] Fulbright:

November 11, 1969

This is the first time ever, and I am in my fifties, I have felt compelled to write to a congressman about a national issue.

Senator Fulbright I, my family, and many of my friends (a part of the silent majority!) support your position 100%. We think we are good Americans, we appreciate that we live in and are protected by the greatest nation on earth, we want to do everything we can to support the men (and women) who are fighting for us in Vietnam (and too many other places), but simply can see no reason for continuing on in these futile wars.

A lot has been said about why we are involved and why we must continue (honorable peace, prestige, commitments, domino theory, etc.). I hope I am wrong, but wonder if history will not show that we accomplished nothing for democracy. If our position is so noble, why do we not have more enthusiastic support from countries who supposedly are friendly to us. . . .

Keep on with your honest, straightforward, appraisal of what is going on.

Sincerely,

E.A.E. (Little Rock, AR)

(Because of my work I request that my name not be used in any way)

I am not opposed to protests as such, but the ones I see generally seem to be headed by the kind of people with whom I would not associate.

18

Dear Senator [J. William] Fulbright:

November 11, 1969

According to a UPI Article in the Arkansas Gazette this morning it seems that you are under quite a bit of fire from some of the so-called patriotic people of this country. . . . I for one would like to go on record saying that I agree with your assessment of [the] situation in Vietnam and in no way consider this as being unpatriotic in any sense of the word but rather an intelligent grasp of the situation. I do not consider myself anything of a super patriot like some of these people since I don't have an American Flag pasted on the window of my car, nor do I go about shouting my feelings in the market place, but let me say that I did serve twenty years in the service of my country as a United States Marine and that I shed blood sweat and tears for our way of life. I consider this as my credentials to say what I am going to say. If as you say, it is impossible to achieve a military victory in Vietnam then we should get out immediately without further loss of life, because if we start a planned scheduled withdrawal of troops we are going to end up with a situation analogous to what currently exists in Korea or even worse. You are right, Senator Fulbright, it is criminal to waste our youth and resources in a lost cause like Vietnam when there are so many things here at home, especially in Arkansas that could benefit from the infusion of some of the funds. . . . In the vernacular of the colored people, "You tell it like it is," Senator, so don't let all that junk mail sway you in doing what your conscience tells you is right.

Thanks for listening to me, Senator, continue with your task, history will show you to be right in the final analysis. We look forward to seeing you back in Arkansas again.

Sincerely yours,

W.D.F. (Paragould, AR)

19

Dear Senator [John C.] Stennis:

April 27, 1970

I am deeply concerned over the situation in South East Asia. . . . It can be settled quickly by persuading our President to let the military conduct the war. Blast Hanoi and Haiphong off the map.

Simultaneously round up the Fulbrights, the Mansfields—the Churchs—the Kennedys and others of the same breed; and hold them in a concentration camp where the news media cannot find them. . . .

Sincerely,

F.C.W. (Picayune, MS)

20

Sir [Senator J. William Fulbright]:

May 6, 1970

I would like to voice my long standing opposition and disapproval of your position in the struggle against communism in S. E. Asia and elsewhere.

It should not be necessary to point out to a man of your background and experience that the Free World is still in danger of communist ideology with the ultimate goal of conquest. . . .

We are involved in a combat by arms against communist forces in S. E. Asia. This is no seminar on conflicting political views, but simply a matter of whether we or they shall prevail (they have prevailed for 25 years!!). . . .

The deplorable lack of aggressive censure or even concern thru the communications media over actions by the N. Vietnamese forces by your committee are hard to understand. . . . Do you condone the Geneva Convention Violations of Laotian territory that has gone on for years by N. Vietnamese forces? Do you condone the massacres, such as the one at HUE?[6] Why are you not as concerned and vocal over the treatment of American POWs, some of whom have been mistreated for 6 years, as you are over cleaning out N. Vietnamese supply and arms dumps on the Cambodian border? . . .

6. Hue was the location of the bloodiest battle of the 1968 Tet Offensive. The United States and South Vietnamese suffered at least five hundred casualties. The NLF and NVA lost as many as five thousand fighters; and while occupying Hue for more than a month, killed approximately five thousand civilians.

I am thankful that President Nixon is reducing the enemy's war potential along the Cambodian Border, in the DMZ, and just above it; how do you expect our troops to function properly when the enemy can cross an imaginary line with impunity? . . .

The gradual withdrawal of our troops is the only course of action left since circumstances (may you get full credit by historians for many of them) now preclude a decisive win. Please assist our President in completing his plan for withdrawal. . . . I implore you to put American lives and the honor of our country ahead of your own personal sensitivities and political feuds. Arkansas needs you in the Senate to represent the traditional views of this state and our troops need you, right at this moment to encourage and support them.

Sincerely yours,
W.C.M. (Wynne, AR)

21

Dear Senator [J. William] Fulbright:

June 11, 1970

Arkansas and the entire nation should appreciate and be grateful for your efforts to bring about peace in the awful crisis we face. As one of the so-called "silent majority," I want to express my admiration for your views and your convictions on our total foreign policy. If I were President, I would want none other than yourself as my Secretary of State. . . .

It seems that we are playing into the hands of Russia and Red China just as they planned that we should. They want us to be tied down in one small war or another, spilling the blood of our youth, spending our wealth, ruining our economy, and adding to our racial and social unrest which will eventually destroy our country. They can wait with no risks taken, no blood shed! I believe as you do, that we should pull out of these war areas at once, stop policing the world, and begin to spend our billions here at home where the need is truly great. . . .

Respectfully yours,
J.L.McG. (Harrison, AR)

22

Dear Senator [J. William] Fulbright:

June 15, 1970

I am sure that you will consider this one of the oddest letters that you have ever received.

I am a recent graduate of John L. McClellan High School here in Little Rock. I received an academic scholarship to UALR for the fall semester. Further I am of draft age and may be drafted anytime after my nineteenth birthday in December. Yet in spite of this I disagree with your vehement stand on the Vietnam War or more precisely on Mr. Nixon's stand on that war.

I have read your book *The Arrogance of Power.* I debated the question of unilateral military involvements during the past year at high school debate tournaments over our state. I fully agree with many of the points you made in that book and agree that we often try to dominate the world through our good intentions. However, I believe that Mr. Nixon's policy of noninvolvement in foreign domestic crises will prevent recurrence of such woes as the Vietnam War. I further believe that his policy of Vietnamization and slow withdrawal and, yes, even the foray into Cambodia to be thoughtful, well-planned actions which, in the long run, will prove to be useful. Already it has produced an infant Asian alliance against communist aggression which may some day keep American boys from fighting another Asian war.

Now for the really odd part of this letter. After all of that criticism you probably feel that I am pretty much anti-Fulbright. Nothing could be farther from the truth. I disagree with your stand on this particular issue, but on balance I think that you have done a rather exceptional job during your tenure in office. Further, your criticism of the handling of the Vietnam War has been useful, if for no other reason, than to give antiwar sentiment a powerful voice. I think that your loyal opposition in this issue has done more to keep our commitment within the bounds of sanity than any other one force. If you and some of your colleagues had not raised voices of protest I feel sure that we would be heading toward deeper involvement in Southeast Asia, a policy with which I do *not* agree.

Thank you very much for the time you have given me and also for your commitment to the people of this state.

Sincerely,

D.O.B. (Little Rock, AR)

23

Dear Mr. [J. William] Fulbright:

June 24, 1970

. . . It seems to me that you have developed into a professional "aginner," that you are against just about everything except continuing your campaign of assistance to the enemy. . . . You have recently voiced encouragement to the college students, including hippies, yippies and other punks, to continue their demonstrations against the war in Viet Nam, when you know, or should know, that such tactics are exactly what the enemy wants. Surely, Mr. Fulbright, you could not be so ignorant as to doubt this.

It is my honest opinion, Mr. Fulbright, that insofar as your usefulness or effectiveness in the United States Senate is concerned, you are nothing more or less than A GREAT BIG STUMBLING BLOCK. . . .

Your constant weeping, wailing and gnashing of teeth about the President's incursion into Cambodia is sickening. This is the only really constructive action taken in the entire war. I suppose you would like a continuance of the Johnson Policies, that of constantly assuring the enemy that we do not want a military victory, that we have no intention of bombing Hanoi or closing the harbor of Haiphong, creating a sanctuary by forbidding any bombing within a five-mile radius of that capital. . . .

Respectfully,
A.C.McG. (Little Rock, AR)

24

Dear Senator [J. William] Fulbright:

June 29, 1970

. . . From the beginning of the Vietnam conflict I have been in favor of military victory and still am. However after waiting and expecting each of three presidents to take whatever action necessary to accomplish this—even if it required the removal from existence of Haiphong, Hanoi and Peking—I have now reached another conclusion. Perhaps this is the conclusion that you had the foresight to arrive at several years ago. A military victory in this war is impossible. It makes no difference whether the reason for this be political, economic, humanitarian, or plain fear of retaliation on our part. After reaching this conclusion, I found myself considering the available alternatives. Only two occur to me—get out now or continue an indefinite occupation of a part of the Asian mainland. The first choice is still repugnant but acceptable to me when I think of the horrors involved in the second. . . .

At this point in my thinking, I can better appreciate your efforts and what you have been trying to say to us for years. With much regret I now admit that the favorable prognostications of our field commanders and even our Commander in Chief no longer impress me. Their past predictions have not come true and after each request for more time and patience on our part I see only a deeper entanglement. For what little it is worth, I wanted you to know that I now appreciate what you have been trying so hard against so many odds to make me understand. . . .

Yours truly,
M.U.G. (Helena, AR)

25

My dear Sen. [J. William] Fulbright:

March 3, 1971

I heard you on Sunday, February 28 on Face the Nation program.

You were much in your usual form: querulous, critical, unhappy about military procedures *that brought reverses to the Communists, but you were at least, more subdued.*

Still you seemed to think the whole "Establishment" was out of step except you, George, Teddy, Eddy and several others who classify themselves as *Doves. I think "chicken" would be a more apt name.*[7]

The nation became disgusted with you, Senator, with the way you conducted the hearing of Sec. Dean Rusk. If ever anyone was put through a public verbal inquisition, you put Sec. Dean Rusk through one at that hearing.

In contrast, Mr. Rusk remained a composed, gentle, patriot through it all. It was at that time the name J. William Halfbright was coined for you.

You are strong in disapproving the action of U.S. Forces whenever they make *an incursion against the Communists,* but you haven't the good grace to admit you were wrong when the venture succeeds. I remind you of the fuss you made at the clearing

---

7. George refers to senator George McGovern (D/SD), who opposed the war. Teddy refers to U.S. Senator Edward M. Kennedy (D/MA), who opposed the war. Eddy may refer to U.S. Senator Edward Brooke (R/MA), who adopted varying positions on Vietnam. By 1971, he was on record opposing the bombing of North Vietnam.

out of the Communists sanctuaries in the Parrots Beak and other points in Cambodia.

It seems to me that the sooner the free world lets the Communist world know it cannot overrun weak nations with impunity, the less Koreas and Viet Nams we will have. . . .

Very sincerely yours,

Mrs. C.L.B. (Mena, AR)

Lieutenant William L. Calley Jr. and My Lai

On March 16, 1968, the First Platoon of Charlie Company, First Battalion, Twelfth Infantry Brigade of the American Division, commanded by Second Lieutenant William L. (Rusty) Calley Jr. from Miami, Florida, killed more than five hundred unarmed women, children, and old men at My Lai 4, a hamlet in South Vietnam's Quang Nai Province. U.S. intelligence had categorized My Lai as a dangerous area and predicted that U.S. forces would confront hostile Vietcong fighters, but Calley's platoon encountered no enemy fighters—only unarmed civilians who were rounded up and shot at pointblank range. After a military coverup of this massacre unraveled, Calley was the only one of twenty-six soldiers charged to be successfully prosecuted and ultimately convicted of premediated murder by a military court. He was sentenced to life in prison. U.S. press reports of the incident first appeared in November and December 1969. Calley had been formally charged in September 1969, went on trial in November 1970, and was convicted in March 1971. In April 1971 President Nixon directed that Calley be held under house arrest at Fort Benning, Georgia, and in August 1971 a military authority reduced his sentence to twenty years. After several appeals to military and civilian courts, Calley was pardoned by the secretary of the army and released in 1974, having served three and one-half years, all in his apartment at Fort Benning.

The national response was very critical of Calley's prosecution and conviction. An April 1971 Gallup poll found that 79 percent of Americans objected to the verdict; 81 percent of Americans deemed the sentence overly harsh; and 69 percent thought Calley was being made a scapegoat for military policies and the increasingly unpopular war. The Nixon administration reported receiving 5,000 telegrams running 100 to 1 in favor of clemency for Calley.[8]

---

8. Claude Cookman, "An American Atrocity: The My Lai Massacre Concretized in a Victim's Face," *Journal of American History* 94 (June 2007): 161; Howard Jones, *My Lai: Vietnam, 1968, and the Descent into Darkness* (New York: Oxford University Press, 2017).

Although Calley's treatment was decidedly unpopular across the country, no other region matched the South's caustic reaction. A great many constituents (2,900, with 97 percent opposing the conviction) sent letters to Senator William B. Spong Jr. (D/VA); 3,000 wrote Congressman Jim Broyhill (R/NC); and 3,500 contacted Senator Bill Brock (R/TN). Reflecting and influencing their readers' perspectives, local newspapers across the South consistently questioned whether the reported events at My Lai had actually transpired, refused to acknowledge Calley's guilt, portrayed his actions as acceptable under combat conditions, and objected to the verdict. These sentiments contrasted with those expressed by the press in other regions.[9]

Prominent southern political figures were outspoken in their support for Calley. Louisiana senator Allen Ellender declared the defenseless Vietnamese villagers "got just what they deserved"; Representative John R. Rarick, also from the Pelican state, pronounced Calley a "true soldier and a great American." Senator Herman Talmadge from Georgia contended that Calley was "assuming the burden for the entire war, including the errors of his superiors," and the senator was "saddened to think that one could fight for his flag and then be court-martialed and convicted for carrying out orders." Georgia governor Jimmy Carter proclaimed an "American Fighting Man's Day" and urged Georgians to "honor the flag as 'Rusty' had done" by driving with their lights on for a week in support of the American military.[10]

It was against this background of strong regional support of Lieutenant Calley that southerners wrote to their elected officials. Calley's defenders emphasized Vietnam's opaque combat environment and the difficulty identifying enemy fighters among a hostile civilian population. Calley and his platoon had simply tried to obey orders and to accomplish the mission for which they had been trained and sent to Vietnam—to kill the enemy. Even if killing the villagers were a mistake, the biased U.S. media and antiwar liberals should not be allowed to undermine the military or make Calley solely responsible and a scapegoat for the U.S. decisions to intervene and fight in Vietnam. American soldiers should

9. Michael R. Belknap, *The Vietnam War on Trial: The My Lai Massacre and the Court Martial of Lieutenant Calley* (Lawrence: University Press of Kansas, 2002), 196; Dixon, "The Vietnam War and the U.S. South," 196, 203, 205–6, 210; Fry, *American South and the Vietnam War,* 181–84; William Thomas Allison, *My Lai: An American Atrocity in the Vietnam War* (Baltimore: Johns Hopkins University Press, 2012).

10. Fry, *American South and the Vietnam War,* 265–66.

not be tried for murder when killing in a war zone; and if blame were to be assigned, Calley's superiors, U.S. public officials, including the president and his cabinet, Congress, and even the American public should be held accountable. Consistent with their response to Senator Fulbright's hearings, prowar southerners worried that Calley's public trial was compromising the nation's international reputation. Other southerners feared that their sons could be charged with murder for carrying out military orders. Moreover, the failure to afford American soldiers unified national support was a greater atrocity than anything that might have happened at My Lai.

Calley's detractors forthrightly condemned the My Lai massacre and the lieutenant's actions. For the South's antiwar residents My Lai typified an ill-advised, immoral war, and the unwarranted suffering being inflicted upon the Vietnamese. Hardly an isolated, exceptional event, the massacre was all too typical and caused massive damage to U.S. standing abroad. This shameful incident, according to dissenters, solidified the argument for admitting the U.S. mistake and adopting the only honorable course of withdrawing from Vietnam. Other critics of My Lai and the war flatly rejected the pro-Calley qualifiers and excuses: murder was murder; the young officer was not doing his duty or just following orders; he, his platoon, and all his military superiors who had attempted to cover up the My Lai atrocity should be prosecuted. Doing otherwise would leave the United States unable to charge any enemy with committing atrocious actions against the United States or to object to North Vietnamese mistreatment of American POWs, who were as vulnerable as the unarmed villagers at My Lai.

26

Dear Sir [President Richard M. Nixon]:

November 28, 1969

First of all I am not antiwar in Viet Nam. I just want to tell you how I and millions of other American people must feel.

It is a sorry day when the United States charges its fighting men with murder. These men are trained to kill, not to be killed. None of these men asked to go to Viet Nam but were sent by the Government to protect our country. As I look at the way things are today, a man being sent to Viet Nam has only three things to look forward to. Either he gets killed, he gets maimed for life or he comes home safely and faces a court martial.

How are our troops to know which are the enemy and Viet Cong sympathizers or the civilians? They all dress alike and run when ordered to halt. The women and children have been known to throw grenades or shoot rifles at our troops and so they also are the enemy.

Over 39,000 men have been killed in Viet Nam, not counting the ones who were wounded, and more are being killed each day. . . . If the United States calls this an act of war, then all the killings that take place over there should be considered an act of war. To bring charges of premediated murder against our fighting men makes the United States look ridiculous in the eyes of the Communist countries. War is War no matter who is fighting and War is always Hell!

It is easy to criticize the wrong doings of others but you should look at the situation from their point of view. These men are fighting for their lives and it is either kill or be killed so how can we judge, never having been in that situation.

Sincerely yours,
S.S. (Columbus, GA)

27

Dear Congressmen [Bill Nichols, John Buchanan, and Walter Flowers]:

December 1, 1969

My nephew is Second Lieutenant J.S., a platoon leader of the 101st Airborne Division, with a military mission in South Vietnam. . . .

The only thing I ask is that he be allowed to do his duty, carry out the orders of his superiors in a war zone, protect the lives of himself and his platoon by prescribed military procedures. But if in doing this he is to be answerable to the press of the United States, rather than to his military superiors, it is with greatest reservations that I see him subjected to the hazards of active warfare, as he is each day that he is on assigned duty in South Vietnam.

I deplore the actions of the press in prejudging the decisions and actions of any of our servicemen while on hazardous duty in a hostile situation prior to prescribed and proper evaluation by the military structure. I deplore the failure of the United States Army to protect its members from prejudging by the press of actions carried out by Americans in a military situation.

Recent developments in this area call for military censorship, to my mind, until hostilities are terminated in South Vietnam. . . .

Sincerely yours,
J.W.B. (Birmingham, AL)

28

Dear Mr. [J. William] Fulbright:

December 2, 1969

I am writing to you regarding the recent exposé of the alleged massacre of men, women and children and the extinction of the village of My Lai in March 1968 by Company C, 1st Battalion, 20th Infantry, 11th Brigade, Americal Division.

As a citizen and a veteran I am greatly concerned and disturbed regarding the manner in which the entire matter is being conducted. So far, formal charges for trial by General Courts-Martial have been lodged against only one individual, 1st Lieutenant William L. Calley, a platoon leader of the unit allegedly involved and so far named as the prime suspect. In view of the newspaper, TV and coming LIFE magazine publicity there is considerable doubt that this young man can expect a fair and impartial trial, assuming that we still operate under the premise that an individual is innocent until *proven* guilty.

Since the first announcement of charges against 1st Lieutenant William L. Calley many other names have come to light but against whom charges of any kind have not been preferred or mentioned. These are:

Captain Ernest L. Medina, Company Commander of the unit allegedly involved. . . .

Colonel Oren K. Henderson, Brigade Commander 11th Infantry Brigade of which Company C was a component unit. . . .

If the alleged offenses for which charges have been preferred against 1st Lieutenant William L. Calley warrant trial by General Courts-Martial it is my opinion that there are others who should be similarly charged and their innocence or guilt determined in the same manner. . . .

Yours truly,

B.L.S. (Little Rock, AR)

29

Dear Senator [Richard B.] Russell [Jr.]:

December 5, 1969

The news and propaganda related to the charges against Lt. Calley and others at Ft. Benning to me is very disgusting. I am sorry but I am suspicious of the motives behind this affair.

I believe that we have to many nonmilitary personnel in Vietnam who are leftwing reporters, so called news gathers, and commentators and perhaps many others whose real mission is to discredit our own Army and the entire Government and the Country in that area; and as a consequence discredit us around the world.

I noted in one of the early TV broadcasts that the "gooks" were parading and carrying banners accusing the United States of being Nazis and a news broadcaster said that the trials would probably be comparable to the Nuremberg Trials in Germany following World War II. If it is what I believe it is, it is a despicable chapter in our military and civilian life in this Country.

I am of the firm opinion that this matter . . . should be dealt with firmly by the Congress of the United States. We have no other recourse as interested citizens except to appeal to our duly constituted representatives and I am hereby making my request that you devote some time to investigating the discrediting tactics being imposed upon us by our own people. . . .

Sincerely yours,
N.M.P. (Griffin, GA)

30

Dear Sir [Senator Herman E. Talmadge]:

December 5, 1969

Learning of the massacre of civilians, women, and children in Vietnam, and seeing the pictures in Life magazine has been a traumatic experience for me. I wish to here register the strongest kind of protest of this kind of military action, and as a United States citizen and human being I demand that those responsible individuals receive the maximum punishment. . . .

Further I have felt for a long time that this war was woefully unnecessary and representing all that was the worst in America, but I have been "silent" but now I am looking for a way to protest this war in a more forceful way. I feel anger, frustration, and, yes, guilt over this whole thing.

It has now, if anything ever has, GONE TO FAR. I am now fed up and looking for another way.

Sincerely,
R.F.M. (Bonaire, GA)

31

Dear Senator [Richard B.] Russell [Jr.]:

December 12, 1969

I write this letter to you with a lump in my throat and anger in my heart to express my feelings of what is going on in Vietnam.

I have just seen the pictures in the December edition of Life Magazine of the massacre of My Lai. I could not believe my eyes, to see women and little Children murdered by American Soldiers.

I am a family man, having served in the Air Force during the Korean War and received an honorable discharge after four years.

I have a teenage son about to enter in service, but having seen the pictures from Life magazine I will persuade him not to join. Is this the way our country "The Land of the Free" now deals out freedom? Has our country become like Japan and Germany during World War II by killing women and children?

I no longer feel proud to be an American and want to hide my face in shame.

True, to drop an atomic bomb is to kill women and children and is a terrible thing to do, but to actually kill little children one by one and in small groups as pictured in the Life magazine makes any good decent American like myself want to cry.

I beg you to do everything in your power in the Senate to bring out an investigation on the killings that are taking place in Vietnam. . . .

PLEASE DO ALL YOU CAN IN YOUR POWER TO STOP THESE BRUTAL CRIMES.

Yours truly,
D.D.H.

32

Dear Sir [Senator John J. Sparkman]:

December 14, 1969

. . . Sir, if you think the *Red Blooded People of America* are going to sit idly by and see Lt. William L. Calley and Captain Medina tried and made scape goats of this Viet Nam thing you have another thought coming. I don't believe in killing civilians in war time any more than anyone else. In fact, since World War II, I don't think that war is a solution to any misunderstanding by any country. There has got to be another way to settle things more sensibly. But if you will listen, its the very same crowd that put pressure on L.B. Johnson to stop the bombing, and President Nixon to start the withdrawal of troops from Viet Nam that want to try Lt. Calley and Captain Medina for murder. Sir, this crowd is procommunist.

Now if you want to try someone for murder, which they have committed, lets bring back L.B. Johnson and yo yo McNamara. In my eyes they are guilty of murder of 40 thousand American boys. You wouldn't think of such a thing would you? For the simple reason you, the rest of the Senate and Congress sit on your hands and let L.B.J. send close to one half million troops into Viet Nam in an undeclared war . . . .

. . . We couldn't win in Korea, nor can we win in Viet Nam as long as we are dictated to by the procommunist United Nations. . . .

Sincerely,
L.C.D. (Mobile, AL)

33

Dear Sir [Senator Richard B. Russell Jr.]:

January 2, 1970

Several national publications have recently reported a deplorable incident which has become known as the Mylai Massacre. . . . I am sad; I am angry.

Sadness is the natural response to news of the abhorrent, senseless slaughter of individuals who were placed by mere chance in a predicament over which they had littler or no control, and for this they died. Anger toward a government which has relentlessly pursued that ignoble concept that for us to live, "they" must die. A government which invites, yes, even forces, a young male citizen to abandon those national and religious teachings which proclaim human life as valuable and even precious and embrace a concept which demands death and destruction. The anger is deep and healthy. It calls for recognition.

I submit, sir, that those who support and organize the national policy which our present government has launched must also stand in judgment even as the Mylai murderers stand in judgment. . . .

Sincerely,
W.H.K. (East Point, GA)

34

Gentlemen [Senator Richard B. Russell, Senator Herman E. Talmadge, Representative John Davis]—

March 6, 1970

I wish to go on record as opposing the trial of Lt. Calley and of any of the five Marines recently accused of "murdering" Vietnamese women and children. I doubt that any of them are guilty of the offenses of which they are charged. Anything that happens in the vicinity of an as yet "unpacified" Viet Cong village, or village harboring Viet Cong and their families, is an act of war, not a crime!

If our sons are not to be allowed to use their weapons, under orders of their immediate superiors, in what they deem to be their country's or their own, defense, then their weapons should be taken from them. If they are harassed about using their weapons they should throw their weapons down and have done with it.

In my opinion, we should end this conflict by the intelligent use of *superior force*. If we are not willing to do that, we should pack up and get out of Vietnam altogether.

It is only fair that, if any of our men are to be tried for errors of judgment in the dangerous and trying environment of battle, then surely some of our Military Brass, Pentagon officials, Senators and Representatives, and others in positions of public trust should also be tried for errors of judgment in environments lacking the physical pressures of combat. Their high level errors cause far more loss of life. The accusers, whoever and wherever, are more guilty than the accused.

This writer has more than an armchair appreciation of the tribulations of war—he, too, served his country in combat during World War II.

Very truly yours,
J.B.R. (Marietta, GA)

35

Honorable Senator [Albert] Gore [Sr.]:

June 22, 1970

"War is hell!" For several months I have been reading about the alleged atrocities being committed by the American soldiers fighting in Viet Nam. We hear so much about the killings done by our men and yet so little of the slaughtering being done by the Viet Cong.

As a country, we force our men to fight a "political" war; one which our people is not so sure is worth the sacrifice. If our boys refuse to serve, they have the choice of imprisonment or of fleeing the country and giving up their citizenship. We send our soldiers to fight a war in a country where life is held cheaply; a country where women and children fight as savagely as the men; a country where it is almost impossible to tell your friends from your enemies; and where a man must kill for his own survival.

How can we honestly then force our soldiers to live this sort of existence and yet to piously judge them for the so-called "atrocities" they commit? How can we justly sentence a twenty-one year old boy to life imprisonment for a crime we, the United States of America, has forced him to commit? Which is the worst atrocity, the crimes committed by our soldiers or the crime committed by the United States of America for forsaking them? . . .

If we can do no better than to take the lives of our own men, then *let's get out of Viet Nam!*

Sincerely,
Mrs. G.F.S. (Knoxville, TN)

36

Dear [Senator] John [G. Tower],

March 31, 1971

I know you have had enormous comment on the Lieutenant William Calley indictment at My Lai. As a combat veteran of World War II and a member of the local Draft Board in Wichita Falls, it is hard for me to believe that our government can single out one individual and convict him of crimes thousands of us have been guilty of in one way or another. By being a member of the draft board I find that I will be facing one of the most difficult tasks of my life in having to be a part of drafting a young man and having him sent to war under these circumstances. I have a son who is of draft age and now even though I realize that we live in the greatest country in the world, I wonder what his future will be if he has to go into combat knowing what can happen to him under the circumstance in Viet Nam as they are today. I cannot believe that our government will let five men who are on the payroll of our government make the decision as to the right or wrong in Lieutenant Calleys trial.

I hope and pray for your deepest consideration and convictions for this man and all of the other men who are defending our Country.

Sincerely,
J.A.C. (Wichita Falls, TX)

37

Dear Senator [John G. Tower]:

April 1, 1971

. . . For your information, the major problems facing this nation and which should be given priority . . . are these:

1. *THE VIETNAM WAR:* We are sick and tired of committing the lives of our young men to facing an enemy with their hands tied behind their backs. . . . Either conclude this war with an all out "hell for leather" campaign to wipe out this enemy and their supposed stronghold or bring our men home *NOW!*

2. *THE LIEUTENANT CALLEY FARCE*: Only a gutless, sniveling coward of a government would even think of allowing the Armed Forces and their personnel to be subjected to the debasement of trial for doing their duty in time of war declared or undeclared. We demand an immediate rejection of the findings of this comedy of errors, and a public apology to Lieutenant Calley and his comrades in uniform by both the Congress and office of the President. . . .

Yours truly,
M.F. (Tyler, TX)

38

Dear President [Richard M.] Nixon:

April 2, 1971

. . . Tonight's radio broadcasts your "100 to 1" mail against the Calley verdict. I pray you have enough discrimination to know that the majority is not against the *verdict*—rather, it is trying to recognize that Calley is but one among countless who are guilty—how unbelievably horrible it is that this wrongful war has led us to become so calloused—so insensitive to human worth as to accept murder (and atrocities equally great). This is the sort of brutal state of mind against which we pretend to defend.

Calley's conviction is the *only* verdict any conscientious jury could reach. May God keep us from a state where we could call murder anything but murder. However, each of us—you to a degree which increases the longer we remain in Vietnam—share in the guilt.

As to this misguided war, how sad that we have no leader perceptive enough, big enough, unselfish enough, courageous enough to realize that humility is more powerful than armies—to tell us (what the world has recognized all along) the error of our entry into the Southeast Asian War and that the error can be corrected only by admission of our guilt and paying the price for it. Your hollow, tragically narrow pleas suggesting we can make "honorable" what is dishonorable—using tricky devices and euphemisms such as "Vietnamization"—these tactics, I submit, lower us in the esteem of all knowledgeable people throughout the world, and sinks us even deeper in the quicksand of our own prideful stupidity. . . .

Sincerely,

D.D.

39

Dear Mr. President [Richard M. Nixon]:

April 2, 1971

As a combat veteran myself (Korea), and as an American citizen, I can no longer remain silent on the Calley court-martial.

What in God's name have we become in this country when not only the great mass of uninformed or ill informed public opinion, but our public leaders, who should know better, not only condone but seek to glorify as the sacred performance of "duty" the atrocity that admittedly took place at My Lai?

When six honorable and dedicated officers, themselves combat veterans—five of them veterans of combat in Vietnam and both more aware than any of us of the pressures and ambiguities of Calley's situation and more sensitive to what is and must be expected of an officer in combat—are vilified because, after the most exhaustive trial, they find neither moral nor legal justification for this outrage on the name of humanity, we have reached a depth of perverted values that is frightening to contemplate. Like anyone who has been in a war, I can think of a dozen things that might have happened that would explain, even if not justify, his action. But not one was offered in the record, not even by Calley himself.

As far as I am concerned, Lt. Calley has disgraced the uniform I wore proudly, and the nation I love and have fought for.

There is no evidence that I am aware of that Calley was acting under orders to do so when he undertook to slaughter the entire unresisting, captive population of this wretched hamlet. His own testimony, as I read it, was ambiguous. But if he were then those responsible for such orders should also be punished. Clearly there must have been an attempt to suppress and cover up this incident by some who were higher up, and they too should be punished. . . .

To those who rave that this verdict is a "sellout" of the American fighting man, I say nothing could be further from the truth. Anyone who thinks he would want his son to serve under such a man need go no further than to read the reports on the testimony of those poor G.I.'s who did serve under him at My Lai. . . .

To those who say this is simply the way war is, I say war is hell enough without using it as an excuse to justify every possible aberration of sadism and inhumanity. . . .

May God help us find our way back to sanity and humanity.

Respectfully yours,
W.B.K. (Atlanta, GA)

40

Dear Senator [Herman E.] Talmadge:

April 3, 1971

Please allow me to take this opportunity to express my views of the Lieutenant William Calley situation. In order to qualify my opinion, let me say that I am a native Georgian and a retired Regular Army Officer who has served in combat in both Korea and Viet Nam.

It is my opinion that the trial of Lieutenant Calley has been completely justified, and that the verdict reached by a Court of Military Officers is sound. The fact that Lieutenant Calley acted in his capacity as an officer of the United States places upon his shoulders the full responsibility of his actions.

This opinion in relation to Lieutenant Calley in no way is intended to imply that he alone is guilty, for his is only one of many similar acts occurring during this war. It is my opinion, based upon my intimate knowledge and experience during the period from 1964 to 1970, that some of the highest officers of the military have been responsible for misleading the government and the people of this country. . . .

I strongly feel that we Americans should not stop here, but that we should diligently search out the facts, bringing to answer for their responsibility, officers at every level of command who committed, condoned, ignored or covered up such atrocities, and who have misrepresented the situation in Southeast Asia to the government and people. . . .

Yours very truly,
G.P.S. Jr. (Clarkesville, GA)

41

Dear Sir [Senator Herman E. Talmadge]:

April 4, 1971

Only one thing concerns me more than the atrocity of which Lt. Calley was accused, and that is the condoning of the atrocity by so many of the American people. Every nation has people capable of atrocity. . . . I am shocked that the American people see nothing wrong with it.

For centuries it has been accepted that people who have surrendered are not to be slaughtered. . . . When the Germans machine gunned over a hundred of our men in the Battle of the Bulge this country was beside itself with outrage. After the war those involved were prosecuted. . . . When the Japanese were guilty of the Bataan death march our blood boiled. Executions followed the war. It is difficult for me to believe that if our men who are prisoners in Vietnam were all shot and the people involved fell into our hands we would not prosecute. If we approve what Calley was found guilty of doing we can never claim "atrocity" no matter what an enemy may do to us.

If, God forbid, North Vietnam threatened to shoot all our prisoners if we did not meet a demand how could we call on World opinion to prevent it if we have forfeited our moral position by agreeing that wholesale extermination of the surrendered is proper. . . . Some say that in Vietnam there is no way to distinguish the civilians from the soldiers. That is beside the point because we have no right to slaughter surrendered soldiers. . . . To agree that Calley was right is to lose our moral position in the eyes of the World as well as in our own eyes. I simply cannot buy this double standard. When our enemies commit such acts we try and execute them. When we bring one of our own people to trial for the same type act it is persecution.

I am not taking this position because I am a dove. I am sure that I would be rated a hawk. On hindsight we may all agree that getting into the war was a mistake. Once in it I do not see how we can just walk out. I have a son in the army who I am certain will be in Vietnam in a few months. I have another son who may be inducted this Fall. I do not claim that what we do or do not do to Calley will change what our enemies do. I do wonder however how I can protest if one of my sons is captured, disarmed and while a prisoner shot if we agree that it is proper for us to exterminate every person in a town, old men, women, children, and babies after they have surrendered.

Vert truly yours,
J.S.P. (Atlanta, GA)

42

Dear Senator [Harry F.] Byrd [Jr.]:

April 5, 1971

Our eighteen-year-old son, Sgt. L.P.H. . . . is an Airborne Ranger lying in a hospital in Viet Nam with a light bullet hole in him. He was lucky for his ruck sack stopped between 10 and 20 bullets. Recently he wrote us that he understood the reason for this war and intended to do his part. . . .

Senator, we are worried sick about the possibility of his being tried for murder in our courts. We know that he can handle himself well against the best soldiers the enemy can muster under the toughest conditions, but he would be nothing more than a spineless weakling in our courts with a murder charge against him. He is very much in the business of killing people and he has killed them too. It petrifies us to picture what can happen to him in the hands of the courts. . . .

Respectfully yours,

C.H.H. and J.M.H. (female) (Richmond, VA)

43

Dear Senator [Harry F.] Byrd [Jr.]:

April 9, 1971

I wish to make two requests.

1. Please use your influence to have President Nixon give Lt. William Calley, Jr. a complete immediate pardon and restore his military rank. He spent two dangerous difficult years in Vietnam defending our freedom and the freedom of other people. He has spent two anxious years awaiting trial and verdict. There have been too many conflicting stories. The verdict was wrong and because of that President Nixon can give him immediate pardon without waiting for appeals. If he delays he will be accused of playing politics. Whoever is nominated will find this trial a big political issue. Students have been widely divided on many issues. They are together in their wish for Lt. Calley's freedom. There will be no further ROTC career officers and certainly no volunteer army. . . .

T.M.M. (female, Williamsburg, VA)

44

Dear Sir [Senator Herman E. Talmadge]:

April 12, 1971

We find ourselves shocked and grieved by much of the response to Lt. Cally's conviction for his participation in the My Lai massacre.

Can sensitive, rational people fail to realize what they are saying when they suggest not only that Cally's conviction was wrong but that his actions at My Lai were right—even commendable? We share the feelings of those who call for a humane response to Lt. Cally in his plight, but we are also seriously concerned that so many persons and prominent organizations in our Nation seem to feel that any and all killing by our soldiers in war is justifiable and commendable. . . . There is a sickness unto death in our Nation if we can condone such activity, even in war.

Lt. Cally and a few others should not become the "scapegoats," however, for such inhumanity as the massacre at My Lai. It seems to us that the guilt for this and all other such acts must become a matter of shared guilt by everyone in our Nation: the President, the Congress, the Military and each private citizen. Our acceptance of guilt will not erase the stains of the past, but it can serve to unite us in an active movement to stop our participation in such needless waste of human and environmental resources as this war is causing.

We hope that Lt. Cally's penalty for his part in My Lai will be reduced from the one which has been imposed by the court. However, whatever is done in this case, authorities should not fail to take into consideration the feelings of the men who were the jury in the trial. So far as we could tell these men dealt responsibility in Cally's case. . . .

Sincerely yours,
L.C.D., Mrs. L.C.D.. G.D., and [Mrs.] D.D. (Lindale, GA)

45

Dear Sen. [Herman E.] Talmadge;

April 16, 1971

I, too, am outraged concerning the Calley case—outraged that others guilty of similar crimes have not also been brought to trial. . . .

Calley is guilty of a crime committed against humanity, and for that there is no justification! The slaughter at My Lai was not committed in the "heat of battle." These human beings were rounded up like livestock and systematically shot. This took place over a period of not less than one hour. At no time was any resistance offered. Yes there was a horrible mistake, but let us not compound it by "canonizing" Calley.

I note, Senator Talmadge, you are saddened that one could fight for his flag and "be court martialed for apparently carrying out orders." How saddened were you during the Nazi trials at Nuremberg when the same argument was advanced by the Nazi defenses? . . .

I quite agree we should not be in Viet Nam, but we are. Whether or not we should be there, however, is quite academic when it comes to the people of My Lai, as this does not make them any less dead. How can we so eloquently plead for humane treatment of our own POWs and at the same time condone the actions of Calley?

Respectfully,
Mrs. R.T.Y. (Hollywood, GA)

46

Dear Senator [Herman E.] Talmadge:

April 20, 1971

. . . Both of us being legal secretaries, one of us having worked for the Army, Office of the Staff Judge Advocate for four years, we have a working knowledge of the court system of the United States, as well as an understanding of the military justice system. It is a shame indeed that one person has been singled out to assume the responsibility for all the atrocities of this horrible, senseless war. We also, like most Americans, sincerely believe that Lieutenant William Calley is assuming the burden for the entire war, including the errors of his superiors. Understanding the military system, we know that there is a "chain of command." Thus, why should a mere Lieutenant be singled out when his superiors are free to issue more "like" orders to their junior officers with no apparent repercussions to the senior officers, regardless of what their orders entail.

We feel that the United States should withdraw NOW—all troops, advisors, etc. from Viet Nam and surrounding territories. . . .

Sincerely,
(Miss) G.H. and (Miss) B.A.B. (Atlanta, GA)

47

Dear Senator [Herman E.] Talmadge,

April 20, 1971

. . . The whole thing with Calley is sickening. In my judgement, he should not have been brought to trial, at least not until after Capt. Medina has had his day in court and it had been definitely shown one way or the other if he commanded Calley to do what he did. It is perfectly clear that Calley deliberately killed women and children and we cannot condone or justify that. But I think the basic mistake was in the "search and destroy" policy which could be and evidently was applied in an extreme way. My thought is that the higherup officers should have recognized that, censured Calley privately, and modified their policy. The country at home and in the eyes of the world has been hurt immeasurably by all this testimony-taking, and the people who profit from it are the ones who practice wholesale butchery without qualms, as they did at Hue,—the communists. . . .

I lost a nephew there and he did not die for the moddle-coddling kind of thinking and yapping we are having in the country now. Neither did 45,000 others die to have this country surrender to Russia. We need some red-blooded Americans in Congress to get up and talk until Fulbright, McGovern, Kennedy, Muskie, Church, and Hatfield and some others shut up.

Sincerely yours,
E.J.H. (Atlanta, GA)

48

Dear Senator [Sam J.] Ervin:

May 7, 1971

Haven't we, as American, seen enough killing and wounding of American boys in Indochina? . . .

Haven't the tragedy at My Lai and the hundreds of probable other My Lais, which have literally torn at the souls and consciences of each and every American, been terrible enough to cause us to get out of this needless, senseless, idiotic war? . . .

Around Salisbury there has been a complete turnaround in public opinion since the Calley fiasco. The attempt, by many, to picture Calley as a hero shocked many people and caused them to question a man being lionized as an American "hero" to be sit aside the likes of Washington, Jefferson, and Lincoln. People who had never before questioned the war began to not only question the morality of it all, but went on to say let's get out * * * and get out *now!* This is the consensus of the local people, reawakened by the Calley case and the recent marches by our veterans in Washington. . . .

Sincerely,

H.B.P. Jr. (Salisbury, NC)

49

Dear Senator [John C.] Stennis:

May 17, 1971

This letter is to protest the action taken that led to and resulted in the conviction and sentencing of Lieutenant Calley on the charge of murder in the death of certain Vietnamese civilians during the course of combat operations. The stand we take is one of principle.

We in Local 3907, feel that Lieutenant Calley was a victim of circumstances, and due to the nature of combat in this country, he did nothing more or less than any soldier who is doing his job has to do in order to survive and attempt to bring this senseless conflict to an early end.

. . . We want the military to stop intimidating the fighting men regardless of who they may be, for they are defending the truth.

Our plea is to free Lieutenant Calley in the name of justice so men everywhere will be able to know we are not afraid to stand for what is right.

Very truly yours,

W.C.R., President, Local 3907, Communications Workers of America (Mobile, AL)

6. Students, Protestors, and Their Critics

Across the nation and the South, university students comprised the most numerous and most publicly prominent antiwar group. Since 1970 was the highpoint of student activism, this chapter features their correspondence during that year. As the principal antiwar group, students became a lightning rod for critics of the antiwar movement. Examining a sampling of southern student opinions and their elders' responses to antiwar protestors elucidates the generational gulf between younger antiwar southerners and the region's more senior supporters of conflict.

Student Voices—1970

Consistent with their parents' prowar stance, a clear majority of southern students were more supportive of the war and less likely to protest actively than their peers from other regions. A survey for the 1967–68 period found that 36 percent of southern colleges and universities reported antiwar protests, compared to 49 percent in the Northeast, 44 percent in the Midwest, and 40 percent in the West. In November 1969, 60 percent of the South's college students polled approved of President Nixon's handling of the war, while 34 percent disapproved. Midwestern students responded with an approval/disapproval rating of 52 and 43 percent and eastern students reported a 36/58 approval/disapproval margin.[1]

Following the U.S. invasion of Cambodia and the student deaths at Kent State University and Jackson State College in May 1970, a national Harris poll of eight hundred fulltime undergraduates from fifty colleges yielded similar results. A higher proportion of southern students endorsed the invasion; accepted Nixon's argument that the operation would shorten the war; rated the president's handling of the conflict "excellent" or "pretty good"; and believed "expanding" the

---

1. Durand Long and Julian Foster, "Levels of Protest," in *Protest! Student Activism in America*, ed. Julian Foster and Durand Long (New York: Morrow, 1970), 83; *GOI*, no. 55 (Jan. 1970): 18.

fighting was the best policy for ending the war. Forty-five percent of the South's undergraduates gave the president a favorable evaluation versus 55 percent who had a negative response. Nationally, the breakdown was 29 percent favorable/71 negative, 16/84 for the East and West, and 36/43 for the Midwest.[2]

The attitudes of southern male students regarding the draft provided additional perspective on their adherence to the region's military tradition and their response to Vietnam. When asked how they would respond if they were called for the draft, 53 percent of southern men answered that they would "accept the draft call and serve"; 25 percent replied that they would "attempt to avoid induction, but serve if these attempts failed"; and 12 percent indicated they would "leave the country" rather than be inducted into the military. In contrast, 33 percent of midwesterners, 27 percent of easterners, and 23 percent of westerners declared they would abide by the draft call.[3]

Developments on southern campuses, where dissent emerged more slowly and was less extensive than nationally, were consistent with this polling data. For example: In February 1966 the first twenty-three organized protestors at the University of Virginia were greeted by 300 angry prowar students; in May 1967 Louisiana State University protestors were physically attacked by other students. That same month only police intervention saved the thirty University of South Carolina students who picketed General Westmoreland's receipt of an honorary degree from physical attack by more than two hundred prowar hecklers.[4]

2. Lou Harris and Associates, "A Survey of the Attitudes of College Students," (June 1970), 11, 14, 17, 21, White House Central Files (WHCF), Staff Member and Office Files, Robert Finch, box 25, Heard Report [1 of 2], Nixon Project, National Archives II, College Park, Maryland.

3. Ibid., 51.

4. Fry, *American South and the Vietnam War*, 296–99. In addition to chapter 7 in *American South and the Vietnam War*, see the following for southern students: Gregg L. Michael, *Struggle for a Better South: The Southern Student Organizing Committee, 1964–1969* (New York: Palgrave Macmillan, 2004); Jeffrey A. Turner, *Sitting In and Speaking Out: Student Movements in the American South, 1960–1972* (Athens: University of Georgia Press, 2010); Martha Biondi, *The Black Revolution on Campus* (Berkeley: University of California Press, 2012); Ibram H. Rogers, *The Black Campus Movement: Black Students and the Racial Reconstruction of Higher Education* (New York: Palgrave Macmillan, 2012); Mitchell K. Hall, "'A Crack in Time': The Response of Students at the University of Kentucky to the Tragedy at Kent State, May 1970," *Register of the Kentucky Historical Society* 83 (Winter 1985): 36–63; Ruth Anne Thompson, "'A Taste of Student Power': Protest at the University of Tennessee, 1964–1970," *Tennessee Historical Quarterly* 57 (Spring-Summer 1998): 80–97; Stephen H. Wheeler, "'Hell No—We Won't Go, Ya'll: Southern Student Opposition to the Vietnam War," in Marc Jason Gilbert, ed. *The Vietnam War on Campus: Other Voices, More Distant Drums* (Westport, CT: Greenwood, 2001), 150–57.

Even though antiwar students were a decided minority across the South and braved hostile reactions from both fellow students and college administrators, opponents of the war lodged significant protests in 1969–70—first as a part of the October 15, 1969, Vietnam Moratorium Day and later through reactions to the U.S. invasion of Cambodia and subsequent deaths at Kent State and Jackson State at the hands of the National Guard and Mississippi State Police. On Moratorium Day students joined at least 2 million other Americans who stopped their regular activities to protest against the war. Many students (5,500) rallied for peace at the University of Texas; 1,200 University of Louisville students joined the university president in planting a "peace tree"; 3,000 Florida State students sang antiwar songs as they marched around the campus; and 1,500 students participated in a full day of sermons, debates, chapel services, and rallies at the University of Virginia.[5]

The following spring student responses were far less sedate and far more extensive when President Nixon's decision on April 30 to dispatch U.S. troops into Cambodia provoked "easily the most massive and shattering protest in the history of American higher education." Student deaths at Kent State and Jackson State intensified the campus unrest. After the ROTC building was burned and sixty-nine students were arrested on May 3, nervous and exhausted Ohio National Guard troops fired on Kent State students (some of whom had hurled bricks and insults and others who were just on the way to class). Nine were wounded and four killed. Nine days later, partly in response to the invasion of Cambodia and the shooting at Kent State, three-hundred students at Jackson State College, an all-black school in Mississippi, threw rocks at passing cars and attempted to burn the ROTC quarters. The next night, May 14, state police fired on the students, twelve were wounded, and two young women inside a dorm were killed.[6]

In response to the invasion of Cambodia and the deaths at Kent State and Jackson State more than 2 million students demonstrated nationally, and approximately 450 colleges and universities experienced strikes or campus closures. The protests were overwhelmingly peaceful with only 5 percent involving violence and 7 percent requiring the intervention of off-campus police or the National

---

5. Fry, *American South and the Vietnam War*, 304–5.

6. Charles DeBenedetti and Charles Chatfield, *An American Ordeal: The Antiwar Movement of the Vietnam Era* (Syracuse, NY: Syracuse University Press, 1996), 280 (quote); Nancy K. Bristow, *Steeped in the Blood of Racism: Black Power, Law and Order, and the 1970 Shootings at Jackson State College* (New York: Oxford University Press, 2020); Tim Spofford, *Lynch Street: The May 1970 Slayings at Jackson State College* (Kent, OH: Kent State University Press, 1988).

Guard; however, the outbreaks of violence received far greater media attention. Consistent with the relative conservatism of southern students, the South's university and college administrators reported the lowest number (54) and lowest percentage (20.8) of schools experiencing "incidents of campus unrest." Still, the number of reported incidents of disruption on southern campuses more than doubled when compared to the 1968–69 school year.[7]

These southern protests were also sufficient to elicit condemnation from the region's office holders, press, and general public. As many as four thousand students ringed the ROTC building at Florida State and broke several windows; one thousand marched in a candlelight memorial at the University of Alabama; three thousand University of Tennessee students rallied against the war and the Kent State deaths and carried out a three-day strike. In Austin, Texas, 2,500 to 3,000 University of Texas students marched from the campus to the federal building, where they threw rocks and smoke bombs at police, and five thousand students rallied the following day. Five hundred University of Kentucky students protested in front of the administration building; thirty forced their way into a board of trustees meeting; and the air force ROTC building was burned. Separate rallies at the University of Virginia drew 1,500, 3,000, and 4,000 students; protestors occupied the navy ROTC quarters; two attempts to burn ROTC facilities failed; and the university experienced a weeklong student strike.[8]

The antiwar students who took the time to write to their political representative in 1970 echoed many of the arguments made by their peers nationally and by other antiwar southerners. They condemned the war on moral grounds and challenged the United States to live up to its national ideals and self-image as a peaceful nation that promoted international justice and righteousness. They lodged familiar geopolitical objections and urged Congress to end what they considered an undeclared and, therefore, illegal war. Turning specifically to the U.S. intervention in Cambodia, antiwar students contended that President Nixon had escalated the war rather than ending it as he had promised.

These students, who consistently denied being radicals or condoning violent pro-

---

7. Urban Institute, *Survey of Campus Incidents as Interpreted by College Presidents, Faculty Chairmen and Student Body Presidents* (Oct. 1970), 7–8, WHCF, Staff Member and Office Files, Robert Finch, box 27, "Scranton Commission," Nixon Project.

8. Fry, *American South and the Vietnam War*, 308–15.

tests, were distraught over the deaths at Kent State and Jackson State. They blamed the Nixon administration for ignoring peaceful protests, impugning the loyalty of dissenters, increasing the disillusionment and frustration among students, and purposefully dividing the nation. In the wake of Cambodia and the student deaths, antiwar correspondents warned that young people were losing faith in their country.

Prowar students, who were less inclined to write to public officials, also voiced familiar arguments. The war was necessary to halt the spread of communism and to promote freedom and Christianity abroad. President Nixon's policies were succeeding in extracting the United States from the war, and the invasion of Cambodia had furthered that objective by disrupting the enemies' operations and supply lines. The United States needed to unite behind Nixon and the war, and those opposing the war effort were encouraging the enemy and were responsible for the loss of American lives.

As these responses to dissent suggest, more conservative, prowar students were critical of campus protests. Prowar students criticized campus protestors and asserted that campus strikes were simply an effort to avoid attending classes rather than a principled objection to the war. Referring more specifically to Kent State and Jackson State, supporters of Nixon and the war declared that prior violent student actions had led to the deadly encounters with the National Guard and state police. Finally, in a reference that was suggestive of the greater inclination for protests at major southern state universities or more elite private institutions than at smaller state or private schools, one student from Ouachita Baptist University in Arkadelphia, Arkansas, declared that participants in the student "riots" were usually from higher income families, and a Florida junior college leader spoke for the "silent majority" of students who loved their country and refrained from public protests and riots.

1

Dear Sir [Senator J. William Fulbright]:

April 15, 1970

My husband obtained a law degree from the University of Arkansas then came into the Army as a 2nd lieutenant after obtaining his commission from ROTC. He would have been drafted before finishing his law degree if he hadn't gotten into ROTC.

Now we're in the Army and things were tolerable because he had been assigned to the legal branch from his branch of armor. We knew he could be called
back into his combat branch at any time. . . . He was called from Washington
and told he would be going to Vietnam in about six months. In the meantime,
he was to get out of the JAG office where he had been acting as a prosecutor . . .
and report to a unit as soon as possible.

My husband and I have opposed this war for years. Our views have been
strengthened after entering the Army. We've heard of officers bragging about the
way they killed in Vietnam. . . . It horrifies us to see the apathy of the American
people to news of such happenings as Mai Lai. As long it doesn't touch them
personally, they close their eyes and ears.

When we first heard of my husband's orders, an armored branch in Vietnam, our first thoughts were to go to Sweden. After a few hours of torment, we
then decided he should go to jail. After more torment, we finally decided that
we could not do this because my husband would never be able to use his law
degree in the way he wants to, to help right the wrongs in this country. We feel
that is worth fighting for. We also have a baby son who we feel would be hurt
by either of the first two decisions. When my husband gets to Vietnam, we pray
that maybe he can get back without having to take anyone's life. This is the worst
nightmare of all. . . .

. . . If we could see an end, it might be justified, for we too oppose a dictatorial
type of Communism, but will there be an end, and is it worth all the bloodshed
or could it be worse than what is happening to Vietnam now? . . .

Peace,
M.S. (Copperas Cove, TX)

2

Senator [Herman E.] Talmadge:

[May 1970]

The recent slaying of four young students at Kent State University is, to say
the least, a tragic example of what can happen when violence is chosen as a
means of protest. By no means can these slayings be written off as an unfortunate
outcome of an unfortunate demonstration, no more than they can be written off
as the result of a morally sick society. . . . Certainly the killing of four people was
not justified by the amount of provocation received by the National Guardsmen

at Kent State. Nevertheless, it cannot be overlooked that the Guardsmen were provoked, and that they were provoked a great deal. Up until the Kent State incident, demonstrators had generally defended National Guardsmen, saying that they were only young men trying to avoid going to Viet-Nam through the National Guard. The incident at Kent State can only be testimony to the fact that when a traditional foe of the demonstrators, such as the police, is not present, the demonstrators will attack whatever is available at the moment. This is not a condemnation of the student demonstrators. . . . It is, rather a condemnation of the form many demonstrations are taking. . . . It is becoming more and more evident that the personality of mass antiwar demonstrations is more akin to a Hitler or Stalin than to the Kennedys and McCarthys with which the demonstrators pretend to identify. If the antiwar people are really concerned with peace, and their words and actions have not yet convinced me that they are, they will in the future make a sincere attempt to limit the size, character, and timing of their demonstrations. They must realize that violence is a two-way street, and that if they persist in throwing rocks, bricks, bottles, etc. at authorities, they can only expect retaliation. A brick in the hands of a rioting student is just as much a deadly weapon as a rifle in the hands of a National Guardsman; the rifle is only a more efficient weapon. . . .

As a student at the University, one who did not participate in the demonstrations following the deaths at Kent State, I think I am in a position to say that although the majority of students did, in fact, abhor the tragic incident at Kent State, it is a small minority of students who are violently enough opposed to President Nixon's Cambodia policy to riot, demonstrate or boycott classes. In my opinion, the majority of the students who participated in the mass antiwar demonstrations were doing so because they had nothing better to do, and because the organizers of the demonstration used any means available to get people to join the demonstration; I even heard two organizers talk of pulling fire alarms in Russell Hall to get people out onto the street.

I hope you will continue to support President Nixon's policy to attain a lasting and honorable peace in Viet-Nam, and to resist the notion that a majority of the American people desire peace at any cost.

Yours truly,
J.P. (Athens, GA)

3

Dear Senator [J. William] Fulbright,

[May 1970]

I have never been radical in my political beliefs although I have opposed the undeclared war of the U.S. in Vietnam for at least six years and have advocated immediate withdrawal of our troops from that land. But recent developments have made it very difficult to refrain from protesting both U.S. foreign and domestic policy in regards to the war in a more vehement manner.

It was appalling enough when President Nixon scoffed at the U.S. public and the U.S. Congress, the voice of the public, and made a seemingly unconstitutional decision to expand the war into Cambodia; but, when four members of the U.S. citizenry are gunned down by members of a branch of federal military power at the campus of Kent State, one's faith in the workings of constitutionality based democracy is almost completely shattered. . . . What has happened to the American concept of life and liberty? Has the time come when we shall have to write to the parents of those dead four and say "Killed in the line of duty as they saw it, Kent State University, United States of America?"

I do not condone violent demonstrations on the part of students or those designated to control them. Nevertheless, whether the demonstrations be violent or peaceful, the use of live ammunition and lethal bayonets is never and will never be justified. . . .

In short, the incident at Kent State, regardless of the number dead, is as bad if not worse than the My Lai massacre across the waters. Not only is it a tragedy occurring as an effect of the Vietnam war in which innocent and unarmed human beings were mercilessly killed; but it is a far greater tragedy in that branches of the federal military power have turned against the very Americans who enable that power to exist. I ask you, our national leaders, where will the killing end? Have we not brought the war home? Will there ever be a time when future generations of Americans will not be at war? . . .

With all due respect,
P.N.O. (Conway, AR)

4

Dear Senator [J. William] Fulbright:

May 1, 1970

Being 19 and quite ripe for our illegal draft, I'm approaching the hour where I'll be thrown into a situation that I want no part of. Soon I'll have to kill or be killed by a people I have nothing against. Yet, I'm not a free person. Oh, this country is the land of the free and the home of the brave alright, but I'm not free. Either I shoulder a weapon and kill, or I'm thrown into a "prison" (I've read articles on how these Military prisons are run, and I sure as hell don't want to go there). So my only other alternative is to run to Canada. But then I become a fugitive, again not free. . . .

The system doesn't seem to be working. Millions oppose the war, the majority opposes it, yet one man says lets press on to preserve a "proud and just people." Our voices don't matter. We're desperate. Our backs are to the wall, can you really blame us for coming out swinging? ? . . .

Sincerely yours,
J.N. (Arkadelphia, AR)

5

Dear Senator [Herman E.] Talmadge,

May 3, 1970

My home is Athens, Ga., but I am studying for a Ph.D. in political science at the University of North Carolina. I am not, however, a radical in any sense of the word and in fact, consider myself a conservative. I do feel it is important that I and others like me write our representatives in Washington because I think the country is in a bad situation now.

First, let me say that Mr. Nixon's Cambodia and Vietnam policy seems to me to be truly dangerous. We should be extracting ourselves militarily from Southeast Asia, and instead we are suddenly invading another country and resuming bombing of the North. Though Mr. Nixon maintains that this represents no escalation and will shorten our involvement, I think that, clearly, neither is the case. One of the most frightening implications of Mr. Nixon's policy is the almost total neglect of the Senate. I hope that you will agree that the recent trend to increasing the strength of the Presidency and the bureaucracy at the expense of the Congress poses a grave threat to our government.

The problem which most concerns me is the effects of this situation on the people of this country, particularly the young people. Faith in our country and our system of government are at an all-time low. Repression, stricter "law and order," and putting down violence with violence will only lead to further loss of faith, frustration, and disillusionment on the part of young people and I think on the part of many adults also. Name-calling, impugning the loyalty of anyone who disagrees with his policies, and other politically profitable tricks may in the long run cost this country more than Mr. Nixon, Mr. Agnew, Mr. Mitchell, etc., can even imagine.[9]

I have grown up (as have most Georgia boys) revering the U.S. Senate and all that it stood for. I still have great faith in you and the Senate. I hope that you will agree with me that Mr. Nixon's policies and tactics both at home and in S.E. Asia have endangered our country, our government, and our way of life. I hope that you and the Senate will provide the leadership that this country so badly needs to extricate ourselves from this grave situation.

Sincerely yours,

A.B.C. III (Chapel Hill, NC)

6

Dear Senator [John C.] Stennis:

May 5, 1970

I am writing this letter from Columbia University where I am presently enrolled in the School of law. . . .

President Nixon's decision to expand the American war effort in Southeast Asia is both repugnant and illegal. Not only has he failed to rectify the now obvious blunders of past American policy, but he has also failed to learn from them. This undeclared war is beyond the limits of the powers granted to the President by the Constitution. He has clearly preempted your power and every other member of Congress "to make and declare war," a power given solely to Congress. His policy has been so blatant that it has even provoked legislative reaction from state governments: witness Massachusetts' recent "antiwar" law.[10]

Richard Nixon has clearly overstepped Presidential prerogatives in his actions. It is time for members of Congress to respond by ending American entanglement in Asia at once. . . .

Sincerely,

T.W.A. (Meridian, MS)

9. Spiro Agnew served as Vice President (1969–73) and John N. Mitchell as Attorney General (1969–72) in President Nixon's cabinet.

10. In April 1970 the Massachusetts legislature passed and the governor signed a law stating that no state citizen inducted into or serving in the U.S. military could be forced to serve in an undeclared war. The law was meant to force a judicial ruling, but the U.S. Supreme Court refused to consider the case.

7

Dear Senator [J. William] Fulbright:

May 6, 1970

I wish to express my continuing support of the high ideals for which you stand. But the time has come for more definitive action. I refer, of course, to the deaths of four Kent State students, which I feel was made possible by the reactionary political atmosphere engendered by the Nixon Administration. The great tragedy, however, is not simply the deaths of these students, for more Americans are needlessly killed in Southeast Asia each day. Rather, the tragedy is that the American public has become so polarized that they can no longer tolerate peaceful dissent. And this is the fault of the Nixon Administration! I therefore urge you, even at the risk of your not being reelected, to take an even sterner stand against Nixon and to use every constitutionally feasible means of preventing him from prolonging the war.

Yours in peace,
E.G.H. (Conway, AR)

8

Mr. President [Richard M. Nixon]:

May 6, 1970

The student body at Hendrix College and we the Hendrix Young Republicans have been deeply moved by the tragedy of the Kent State Massacre. We cannot understand the senseless overreaction by the Ohio National Guard. We cannot understand your statements that the students were killed because they were violent. We cannot understand Vice-President Agnew's statement calling for an intellectual counterattack against "the smug purveyors of mockery and scorn."

Mr. Nixon, in the words of the father of one of the slain coeds, "What has this nation come to, that a young girl cannot object to a government decision * * * without being killed?"

Your inaugural theme was "Bring Us Together." We feel that your administration is not bringing us together, rather it is tearing us apart. We respectfully ask that you reevaluate your present policies that are alienating so many segments of the American public.

Mr. Nixon, we need a leader we can respect, not a politician who plays politics with human lives.

Respectfully yours,

Hendrix Young Republicans (Conway, AR)

9

Senator [Albert] Gore [Sr.],

May 7, [1970]

. . . I am asking you to join with other members of Congress in condemning and in some way using your power as a duly elected representative to cease the expansion of United States involvement in the land war in Southeast Asia.

I am presently a senior at Dartmouth College and a voting constituent of the state of Tennessee. I am in support of a student strike which this institution has undertaken to, in some way, bring attention to the fact that some considerable portion of the American people do not support this country's policies in the Asian war. This strike we are involved in does not in my mind have the connotations which the media would allow the American public to think. I myself have moderate to liberal views, as do my friends, and we are in no way connected with or under the influence of the radical fringe elements which the media supposes to be the chief voice of dissent. . . . I have known you to be a senator who has always been open to dissent and who has himself stood up for his views of conscience. It is therefore in this mind that I write to you and ask your support. . . .

Respectfully,

J.McC. (Chattanooga, TN)

10

Dear Mr. [Herman E.] Talmadge:

May 7, 1970

I am presently enrolled as an NROTC scholarship student at the University of North Carolina. I am writing this letter in the middle of the night as part of an antiwar protest we have been peacefully waging these past few days. This rally has been peacefully supported either actively or passively by a majority of the students.

This letter is meant to encourage you to do all in your power to extricate American forces from Southeast Asia. This war, I feel, is morally inexcusable. And such being the case, I cannot remain a member of an organization which symbolizes support of this immoral war. I also would request that you help to end the draft.

I would like to assure you that we are not striking for an early holiday. I, for one, will remain here and attend free, extracurricular classes as long as I am allowed, should the school be closed. Why are we striking, you might ask. We have protested continually and have gotten no results. A change must occur, and we must act; in the words of King Lear, "nothing will come of nothing." We do not like to be classified with Homer's "silent majority," the "dead ones."

F.L.S. III (Marietta, GA)

11

Dear Sir [Senator J. William Fulbright]:

May 9, 1970

I am a college sophomore at Harvard University. I come from Mountain Home, Arkansas.

I wish to register my total opposition to recent events in Southeast Asia. . . . If this is government of the people then the government must allow sustained public opinion to affect all aspects of policy. It is not up to the "wise" leadership of the United States to dictate what is "good" for us if the public feeling is emphatic and steady. I think it could be justly said that a large majority of the people are tired of the war and want a "quick" and complete withdrawal. Therefore, Nixon did not have the right to enlarge the war unilaterally. In so doing he violated his office both in terms of Congress and the people. Many of us feel a sense of betrayal.

. . . Destroying enemy sanctuaries that haven't made much of a difference till now and stating that we will stop some twenty miles deep are two ultimately contradictory statements. The Viet Cong will merely reset 20 miles further back. . . . Nixon is making bloody mistakes but it is the blood of people like me and not people like him. I've never had an inclination to die in South Vietnam and I do not wish to die in Cambodia or over North Vietnam. It would not be dying for my country but dying for a President who doesn't want to "lose" a war.

Support for a general strike is growing on campuses. Nixon must respond to the people. Withdrawal from Vietnam with a reorganization of our values and our actions would be a greater victory for the United States than any bloody victory for Nixon could ever be. Does Nixon mean that if he will not lose the war, and if he cannot win, that he will extend it so that another President can solve it?

We must as a people:

1. withdraw immediately from Cambodia and stop the bombing of North Vietnam.
2. continue the withdrawal from Vietnam in good faith . . . as rapidly as possible. . . .

3. much more discretion is needed in the use of Federal troops and the police. Too often they incite violence because it must be realized that the young distrust the powers that be and the police as much as older people distrust the young. Kent State is more than a case of nervous, inexperienced, frightened National Guardsmen. It is a symptom of today—the frustration of a system run by people who have lost their compassion and cannot even see the need for change and for a responsive system. It is too easy to draw analogies between the Boston Massacre and the Kent State murders. Those four did nothing to deserve to lose their lives. . . . There is no justice in beating hundreds to make sure that a few rock-throwers are beaten. Hundreds of innocent people will die this summer unless someone stops this slaughter now. You have the power, I don't. . . .

Yours sincerely,
R.N. (Mountain Home, AR)

12

Dear Senator [John Sherman] Cooper:

May 14, 1970

I wish to express the gratitude that I have for . . . your efforts to stop this unconstitutional and destructive war. Once again there is hope for thousands of young people whose cries have been met by indifference, insults, the blows of policemen's clubs, or the bullets of national guardsmen. As a student at the University of Kentucky who was present at the recent demonstrations there, I would like to convey to you my impressions of the antiwar activities on our own and other campuses.

For months the Nixon Administration has closed its ears to the voices of the very generation whose future and lives it has committed to a futile and homicidal war in Asia. Our protest marches and speeches have been met by malicious slander by the nation's President, Vice-President, and Attorney General. Now four students lie dead as a result of anti-dissent sentiments.

At the University of Kentucky campus Governor Nunn acted thoughtlessly when he sent in State Police, followed by city and campus police, to confront a peaceful gathering on the evening of May 5th. Perhaps some frustrated student in anger of the moment did answer to the invasion by setting fire to the Air Force R.O.T.C. building. But even if every building on every campus in every state were burned to the ground, there would be no killing. Those responsible for sending armed national guardsmen to deal with unarmed students cannot make this claim. Those who have sent thousands of America's young men to their deaths in support of a military dictatorship in Asia cannot make this claim.

When the right to meet was banned at the University of Kentucky, we students sat peacefully before a troop of State Police in protest of this action. When an order to disperse, containing a threat of violence, was read, we did leave, quietly and calmly. Still the State Police charged dispersing students, beating them with clubs. One cripple was shoved to the ground, beaten, and arrested. I can never express to you the horror of the reality of a police riot! It was at that moment that I and hundreds of other students at the University realized the extent of the decay of traditional rights of dissent.

University students continued to meet, however, at Transylvania University and at the Lexington Theological Seminary where we had the support of the students, faculty, and administrators. When the police arrived at Transylvania to disperse U.K. students, the police were asked to leave the campus.

We students are seeking peace through peaceful protest. Some of our brothers and sisters are tired of the years of peaceful protest that have produced nothing. It is the lesson of history, they note, that violent protest produces results when legitimate actions are futile. . . .

Sincerely,
F.C. (Hopkinsville, KY)

13

Dear Sir [Senator Herman E. Talmadge],

May 14, 1970

I am a voting resident of the state of Georgia and a graduating senior at Duke University. I myself am opposed to campus violence. I am not yet convinced that America in general, and American governmental leadership in particular, is morally bankrupt. But I am convinced that the ongoing war in Southeast Asia is morally, economically, and politically wrong. And I am opposed to President Nixon's move into Cambodia.

I urge you to vote to oppose the recent move into Cambodia, and to vote for the upcoming legislation to cut off funds for that action. Furthermore I urge you not to let the Cambodian issue distract you from the plight of American involvement in Southeast Asia as a whole. I urge you to do everything within your power to end completely American involvement anywhere in Southeast Asia and to withdraw all American troops, and all American financial and military aid and support as well.

. . . Americans are tired of leaders in Congress who let an undeclared war drag on for six years without having the courage and the moral character to publically declare, through a roll call vote, their own personal stance on this central crisis in American life. Americans are morally outraged by the continued deaths of Americans and North and South Vietnamese that occur during the long weekends that legislators play golf instead of meeting in special session to end this undeclared war, by whatever means. . . .

I myself shall continue to work within the system. But any system is only as good as the men who run it and the confidence which they can command in the form of respect. Governments do not make good men. Good men make good governments.

Sincerely,
S.H.B. (Durham, NC)

14

Dear Senator [J. William] Fulbright:

May 22, 1970

I am a student at Ouachita Baptist University, and I am very concerned about the current situation in Southeast Asia and the unrest on our college campuses. . . .

I feel that President Nixon is pursuing the best possible course for our country, our armed forces overseas, and for countries in Southeast Asia. I do not feel that the Senate should vote to restrict funds for the Vietnam War. If funds are restricted for the war, it will further endanger the lives of our American servicemen. . . .

The majority of Americans, including many Arkansans, support President Nixon's policy in the present crisis in Cambodia. The lives of many American servicemen have been saved as a result of uncovering and destroying the war equipment that the Communists were planning to use against the Americans.

The college dissenters and protests from our government leaders has caused more casualties of United States servicemen. The headlines they have gained in the newspapers has caused the Communists to feel that we are ready to raise the white flag. These college protestors are making a big mistake, for they do not know how to go about expressing their opinions without being destructive. We can never hope for an end to the war until we can at first have love between our brothers at home.

... We, as Americans, must get together and support the President in the present crisis in order that he might bring the war to an end much sooner. ...

Respectfully yours,
S.A.T. (female, Malvern, AR)

15

Dear Sir [Senator J. William Fulbright]:

May 22, 1970

I am concerned! Our country is in such a turmoil today that I worry about the out come of all the trouble that is happening at home as well as abroad.

I am in my senior year of college and my future in this country looks very dim. Every time I turn on the television there is usually a congressman talking about the war in Vietnam or on the riots on our college campuses. This talking will not help. Why do the congressmen not get together and pass, not submit, some laws to handle these actions.

First of all the war in Vietnam. I am for stopping the Communists at any cost! Also I am of draft age. This draftability does not hamper my thinking in the least on the war. I saw on television a congressman that firmly disagreed with the Presidents actions toward the offensive into Cambodia. If he does not like it, why does he not do something about it on the floor of the senate and not on the steps in front of television cameras?

Finally, the riots are caused by the minority of the students, usually the higher income bunch or the ones whose money is furnished by some one else besides themselves. These people do not really know what they want or what to do if their demands are met.

My opinion on these riots is more power to the police. The students feel that the enterprises owe them the education, jobs, money, and their personal demands. I do not agree with this "you owe me" attitude. No one owes you anything accept what you can make for yourself, through the education you get and the job you earn after you graduate.

Sincerely,
W.H.V. (Arkadelphia, AR)

16

Dear Mr. President [Richard M. Nixon]:

May 28, 1970

I represent a large majority of students, concerned students that care about our countries problems. But we are not different. That is, we do not grow our hair long, we do not have beards, we do not protest in the streets, we do not riot or burn down R.O.T.C. units.

We are the average everyday students that go to classes that try to make good use of our time and constructively work out problems. I believe we are the silent majority, and I think it is time that someone listened to us.

The Media is projecting the loud protestors. They are not even concerned and do not care about the average student who is concerned with our country. We happen to love our country and we appreciate our past history as a small dependent country struggling and growing into a large, almost independent country. It took a lot of backbone, sweat, blood and tears. Yes, we are concerned students that care and who do not want our country at the mercy of loud mouth protestors that do absolutely nothing but criticize and in no way improve our country or its problems. We understand that if there is going to be changes made that there is a right way to do this.

I was a member of the Student Senate and was elected as Vice President and then President of the Florida District IV, Student Government Association, in which I was President of seven Junior Colleges consisting of 45,000 students. I was also part of the Executive Board for this state so I know that there were students all over the state that also feel the way we do.

In conclusion, Mr. President, I think it is time that we were heard. We hope that it is not a matter of who shouts the loudest. . . .

Sincerely,
G.A.M. (Highlands, NC)

17

Dear Senator [John C.] Stennis,

[June 1970]

As a college student, I'm not in a group of protestors and I don't believe in their actions but I do have some questions that I would like very much to have you answer for me.

My first question is this: Why were all the heads of state, etc., . . . sent so quickly to our state when the episode took place at Jackson State College? I truly don't understand their quick action when weeks before other students were killed and demonstrations were taking place at Kent State. There weren't any reports of important people rushing there. Do not misunderstand me, killing any person is wrong but why do the officials jump down our state's throat so much faster than other state's when something like this happens. I know the press have a lot to do with it, they helped make Miss. the scapegoat for years now and it seems they just don't know how to stop. Although I realize the President and Vice President are of a different political party than you, I would like to say I think they're both doing a fine job. . . .

My next question concerns the situation in Cambodia. I know that this is what a lot of the protestors are protesting against but since our troops are there, God knows they need all the help they can get, so why can't the people support our boys. . . . As I understand, our advancement into Cambodia has proven to be a success, if this amendment to stop everything in June passes, will we have really accomplished anything? If we pull everything we have over there out, what is there to prevent the communist from coming back and setting up their forces again? . . .

. . . Since we're already in Vietnam and the North Vietnamese were going into Cambodia to hide, why is Congress trying to get our troops out, when it seems like this is helping to end the war in Vietnam? . . .

Thank you,
Miss A.F.M. (Senatobia, MS)

18

Dear Sir [Senator Herman E. Talmadge]:

June 3, 1970

I am 23 and I don't want to die. It is only a matter of time before I am drafted. I am not unpatriotic, but I do not want to die for nothing. If there was a war being fought in which the enemy presented a threat to my country, I would enlist.

The leaders of the U.S. have attempted for ten years to justify the deaths of my friends in Viet Nam, they have yet to do this.

The ones who have come back are more disillusioned about the fighting than I.

Statistics have been used by Presidents to prove we are winning this war, yet my friends are still dying. President Nixon says he is trying to get the U.S. out of Viet Nam with "honor." What "honor" is there in drafting the cream of this country's resources, its young men, to die while he deliberates?

Please, Mr. Senator, use your influence to stop the war in Viet Nam immediately. My life is at stake.

Sincerely yours,

D.F.P. (Chamblee, GA)

19

Dear Senator [Russell B.] Long,

July 1, 1970

... I'm a junior at Tulane University and I've been doing some thinking about myself and my country, and our relationship with the people of the world. I have thought about how lucky and fortunate we are in comparison to these other people. We have never had a major war fought on our territory outside of the civil war, while whole generations are being raised knowing nothing of peace and happiness in other countries. And when blood was shed on our soil it was never shed for any length of time.

Because we the American people, the American government, have never known the fear and anguish of others and because we are a prosperous and stable nation, we have a great responsibility to the nations of the world whom we can help find peace.

What I do not understand is how and why a nation such as ours, who has been dedicated to the acquisition of peace can claim to be truly seeking peace, yet let its pride stop it from finding peace. Why must we have all nations openly bow down and pay homage to us and tell of our greatness. . . .

What I am concerned about is what exactly is America concerned about. Are we truly committed to helping a people who so desperately need it or are we concerned about how we look to our public?

How much greater would we be if we for once put our goal of peace at the top of our list? How much self-respect could we find if for once we stood up for what is just and right for the sake of justice and righteousness, instead of what is just and for right for ourselves?

Sincerely,

A.F. (Abbeville, LA)

20

Dear Sir [Senator Herman E. Talmadge]:

July 14, 1970

. . . My feelings for President Nixon also apply to his efforts in Vietnam. I have full confidence that he is doing everything in his power to do what is best. All people make mistakes, and those like Richard Nixon learn from those mistakes. I sometimes think we fail to remember that Nixon did not get us into this war, but he has done more than any other president to get us out. I give him praise for this. I would like to see the war in Vietnam ended as much as anyone else. I have several close friends fighting there and my brother is now of draft age. However I feel that it is the duty of a supposedly free, Christian nation to perpetuate our ideals in foreign lands.

As a 20 year old college junior I realize that I am idealistic at times, but if it hadn't been for some idealism I dare say that this country might be wearing the shoes of South Vietnam. . . .

Sincerely,
Miss J.H. (Coolidge, GA)

Southern Responses to Antiwar Protestors

Although southern students were more prowar and more restrained than their contemporaries from other regions, the South's antiwar students were much more outspokenly opposed to the Vietnam War than the general southern public, and their protests elicited a decidedly negative response from their elders. The harsh regional reaction was consistent with national polling. In a 1968 University of Michigan Survey Research Center national poll, respondents were asked to convey their "feelings" toward "Vietnam war protestors" on a 100-point scale with zero being very unfavorable, 50 neutral, and 100 very favorable. Seven of ten adults rated protestors below 50, or unfavorable, and more than 50 percent of respondents who advocated unilateral U.S. withdrawal from Vietnam also viewed protestors negatively. The next year, a Harris poll found that 81 percent of Americans agreed that protestors highlighted important concerns, but 51 percent objected to the dissenters' actions. This dynamic was equally evident following Cambodia, Kent State, and Jackson State when Gallup found that 58 percent of those polled deemed the student protestors at Kent responsible for the deaths and 80 percent believed student protestors should be expelled.[11]

Antiwar students and other Vietnam War critics provoked these negative responses for a variety of reasons. They were challenging many of the nation's most cherished and long-held myths and self-images. By criticizing U.S. military intervention and actions in Vietnam, protestors questioned whether the United States was an exceptional country with a history of peaceful, defensive foreign policies; whether the nation was a consistent force for good and the promotion of justice and democracy abroad; whether America could impose its will militarily when determined to do so; or whether the United States had acted aggressively, selfishly, even imperialistically while ruthlessly destroying a much smaller, weaker country that posed no threat—all the while achieving no geopolitical gains. Moreover, in the South, attacking the war, and in the eyes of the conflict's supporters, the warriors, was equivalent to assailing the region's military tradition and soldiers. In the absence of appreciable military progress and the inability of either the Johnson or Nixon administration to convincingly explain the rationale for the war or the U.S. failure to win, a majority of older Americans held firmly to the more traditional views of the United States and accepted conceptions of patriotism while directing their frustrations at critics of the war.[12]

Conflating antiwar students with other challengers to accepted American norms and institutions reinforced their unpopularity. They were regularly associated with "hippies" or those young and sometimes not so young dissenters who rejected mainstream values and opted for a counterculture. When many college students grew long hair and wore jeans and sandals, even if they did not

11. Schuman, "Two Sources of Antiwar Sentiment in America," 516–17 (U. of Michigan); Susan A. Brewer, *Why America Fights: Patriotism and War Propaganda from the Philippines to Iraq* (New York: Oxford University Press, 2009), 212 (Harris); Christian G. Appy, *American Reckoning: The Vietnam War and Our National Identity* (New York: Viking, 2015), 189 (Gallup, 58 percent); Terry H. Anderson, *The Movement and The Sixties: Protest in America from Greensboro to Wounded Knee* (New York: Oxford University Press, 1996), 325 (Gallup, 80 percent).

12. Appy, *American* Reckoning, 216, 228–29, 334, and *Working Class War*, xii; George C. Herring, *LBJ and Vietnam: A Different Kind of War* (Austin: University of Texas Press, 1994), xii; Dirkson, "More Than a Conservative, Pro-War Narrative," 13, 42; Michael S. Sherry, *In the Shadow of War: The United States since the 1930s* (New Haven, CT: Yale University Press, 1995), 254, 274, 300; Tom Engelhardt, *The End of Victory Culture: Cold War America and the Disillusioning of a Generation* (Amherst: University of Massachusetts Press, 1995), 14–15, 259, 274; Philip Caputo, *A Rumor of War* (New York: Henry Holt, 1996), 353–54.

take drugs or practice sexual promiscuity, middle America was horrified. College students seemed to have lost respect for proper politics, morality, and decorum. Being associated with civil rights workers and protestors was even more damning in the South, where prowar voices often linked antiwar critics to the Reverend Martin Luther King Jr. or Muhammad Ali.[13]

Protestors' ostensible disregard for law and order and seemingly "anti-American" tactics, such as burning the American flag or flying the Vietcong banner, solidified the hostile assessment among the prowar southern majority. Although the vast majority of southern antiwar protests were peaceful, the exceptional attacks on ROTC facilities, the breaking of windows, and the use of off-campus police and National Guards by governors and college administrators left an indelible impression—one that was strongly reinforced by the arrest of 7,200 students nationwide, by the violent confrontations between protestors and the Chicago police and the National Guard at the 1968 Democratic Convention, and by the deaths at Kent State and Jackson State.[14]

The letters from a distinct majority of southerners vividly embodied this array of hostile reactions to student protestors. Southerners castigated student activists as unpatriotic, as communists, and as cowardly draft dodgers who sought to avoid going to class and disrupted the education of their conscientious classmates. By refusing to support the war and by extension U.S. soldiers and by furthering divisions within the nation, the students were encouraging the enemy, prolonging the war, and precluding an American victory. Consistent with the call for law and order, the South's prowar majority sided with the National Guard and their actions at Kent State, arguing that the students had initiated the confrontation and left the National Guard no choice but to defend themselves. Some southerners even asserted the students had deserved their fate. Finally, student protestors who disrupted their institutions should be expelled.

Antiwar southerners were more supportive of the students whom they believed acted from patriotic and principled opposition to the war. By questioning U.S. policies and actions, the students demonstrated faith in American ideals rather than extending aid to the Vietcong and North Vietnamese. Nor were the

13. Joseph A. Fry, "Unpopular Messengers: Student Opposition to the Vietnam War," in *The War That Never Ends: New Perspectives on the Vietnam War*, ed. David L. Anderson and John Ernst (Lexington: University Press of Kentucky, 2007), 231.

14. Small, *Antiwarriors*, 102; Hall, *Rethinking the American Anti-War Movement*, 129–30.

deaths at Kent State warranted or acceptable. Members of the National Guard were in no clear danger, and the loss of replaceable property never justified the killing of students, even disruptive ones.

21

Dear Mr. Senator [Richard E. Russell Jr.]:

October 18, 1965

The apparently communist-instigated so-called "peace-marches" of the past weekend seem a blot upon the name and honor of this, our country and so greatly in contrast to the words of that great and exemplary patriot who declared: "I am sorry that I have only one life to give to my country!"

If we analyze the participants of those deplorable, cowardly and traitorous demonstrations we probably find only a sprinkling of really bona fide Conscientious Objectors. We will find however communist agitators, stooges of Moscow and Peiping, then hoodlums and delinquents, and as majority a bunch of yellow draft-dodgers who are afraid for their precious skin! . . .

It is my suggestion to designate these demonstrations throughout the press of the country as

"Chicken Parades,"

as I believe this appropriate name will best show them up for what they really are! This is a name right from the vocabulary of the participants of these youthful draft-dodgers!

Yours sincerely,
W.B. (Athens, GA)

22

Dear Sir [Senator Richard E. Russell Jr.]:

October 20, 1965

The last few months I have waged a daily battle trying to get "shut of" the Mask of Fear that most of humanity wears, until it can once take a stand on an issue which is right, regardless of how many friends, neighbors, leaders you offend because they think it is wrong. I have Won and I am now Free, not only from myself, but all other humanity. This is not an easy thing to do as the greatest number (Mass) of the population is still hypnotizing and deluding itself by believing that lies are truths. . . .

. . . In last night's (Oct. 19) Atlanta Journal . . . you denunciate OUR YOUTH YOUTH for the same things that our American Ancestors fought for in the American Revolution. Liberty and Freedom which is God granted!!! . . .

You say that our Youth are wrong and sick to riot and demonstrate when they don't even have the right to vote in many of the states until they reach 21 years of age. No, it is we who are wrong, we who conceive them; bear them into a world of strife and violence; . . . rear them in moral and ethical codes, that our own Leaders have buried so deep within themselves that they can make themselves believe that Lies are the Truth; and educate them . . . to help them reach an age when they are at their greatest potential; and have them flung into the deepest depths of Hell by sending them into a World Conflict that they should have no part of. . . . Who is a DISGRACE? Who is SICK?

My Grandfather fought to keep this U.S. together. Was he wrong? My father fought on the fields of The Depression Years to keep government from strangling his Township and County. Was he wrong? I was born in the First World War years and reared and educated in all the unrest of the years between the First and Second World Wars. I was a girl in my twenties in the Second and saw boys I had danced with, bowled with, kissed and yes, loved, come back mangled physically, and yet worse, crippled mentally. And then it was over—We shouted and prayed, knowing it would never happen again because we wouldn't let it happen (I was the Youth then.) . . . My child was born in 1948 about the time elections were being held in South Korea under supervision of the U.N. Commission. Now, these War Born Children have to face a Vietnam. . . .

Don't run down Our Youth! Some of them are picketing and rioting but all of them are fighting, in one way or another, for Freedom which should be theirs. Regardless of what form it may be—Picketing to Protest Morals and Codes that are long outdated—Crying out for Their Identities in the Educational "Factories"—Tearing up draft cards, and on and on, you can believe that they are fighting, not only for their Freedom, but for yours and mine and the whole Worlds. They are also trying to bring all of our 18th and 19th Century Institutions and Laws up to date. . . .

. . . Senator, before you devise more arbitrary and restrictive laws in an attempt to control, remember our experience with all of the UnAmerican Segregation Laws that the Southern Area of the U.S. is still suffering under. Better that you spend your time erasing these Criminal edicts from our history. If we show the world, just once, that we are a just people with a Real Faith in Ourselves, then there will be no reason to worry about any Communist propaganda which may be made from our national activities. . . .

Sincerely,

Mrs. B.M. (Gainesville, GA)

23

Dear Senator [Sam J.] Ervin [Jr.]:

October 20, 1965

As a member of the Selective Service Board of Catawba County, I am filing with you a very strong protest against the antidraft actions which are now prevalent all over the United States. These are some of the most disgusting demonstrations on the part of supposedly American citizens I have ever witnessed. In my opinion, some of these acts may border closely on treason. I sincerely hope the Congress will take some direct action against these people.

What is happening in this country? Patriotism is being called "old fashioned," even by some respected newspaper editors and by others in various media. Fiction TV programs make fun of our military forces, particularly of ... officers (I was an enlisted man in World War II). . . .

Anyone who believes in the principals which have made this country great is now considered a right wing extremist. There is an investigation in Washington now of the Ku Klux Klan. This is a right wing organization which admittedly has some violent tendencies and, no doubt, the investigation is completely in line. But, why not have a similar investigation of the ultra left wing Americans for Democratic Action? . . . [15]

Yours very truly,

T.W.R. (Hickory, NC)

24

Dear Sir [Senator Richard B. Russell Jr.]:

August 19, 1966

On hearing about the group out on the West Coast who send money and donate blood to the Viet Cong, I find myself speechless! Not at the obvious ignorance and disloyalty of this group of fools, but at the men in high of-

---

15. Americans for Democratic Action (ADA) was a liberal lobbying organization formed in 1947. It supported President Johnson's Great Society and Civil Rights legislation and initially supported the war in Vietnam. In early 1968 ADA moved to opposing the war.

fices who sit back and ignore these happenings. And by doing so, actually condone this.

And only this week, the so-called "Student Nonviolent Coordinating Committee" stormed our draft board here in Atlanta. How can anyone say that they have such a right? . . .

We are spending millions of dollars to give Viet Nam it's freedom and look at this country! Don't misunderstand, I have brothers and brothers-in-law and my husband in every branch of the service and I feel that this is only right. Three of them are stationed in Viet Nam.

What I am angry about is the fact that our boys go over there and fight their hearts out to make this world a free place to live while groups of idiots over here help the communists! . . .

How can these Negroes DEMAND, not their rights as we have, but "Preferred" rights (as with this Black Power Movement) and refuse to acknowledge the draft? A white man doing this would certainly not get away with it. But a black man gets a pat on the back for defying the government.

If this is truly a "White Man's War," then the freedom that we fight for should be only for the white! Equal rights should demand equal responsibilities! . . .

Sincerely,
Mrs. S.J.K. (Decatur, GA)

25

Dear Senator [Richard B.] Russell [Jr.]:

April 19, 1967

During my four years of Military Service in World War II I was told that one of the things which constituted treason was giving aid and comfort to the enemy. The same kind of behavior should be regarded as treason when indulged in by a Congressman, a Senator, or, for that matter an ordinary citizen. . . .

In recent months Senator J. W. Fulbright and Dr. Martin Luther King have, by their actions and public pronouncements, given such aid and comfort to the communist enemy in VietNam. . . .

While American boys are fighting and dying to honor the U.S. commitment to the people of South VietNam these two armchair philosophers sit on their derrieres and advocate withholding air support from them and suggesting that everyone become conscientious objectors.

It is one thing to disagree with the prosecution of the war in one's normal understanding of his job responsibilities as a Congressman or Senator. It is another, as James Farley has said, to "indict the character of the American people in terms used by the enemy." Mr. Fulbright has done exactly this. . . .

Dr. King has finally come out and said why he is opposed to the Vietnam War—"Because," he says, "it has diverted attention from the civil rights movement." One wonders if he would be in favor of the war if it focused attention on the civil rights movement. He has equated the failure of our efforts in VietNam with the success of the "civil rights movement" and the so-called "war on poverty," and there is absolutely no question about which he wants to succeed and which to fail. He would rather see some negro in Podunk, Iowa get his "civil rights" than to see millions in Vietnam get their human rights.

Both Dr. King and Mr. Fulbright have, by their disgraceful, asinine and patronizing remarks, given the enemy an increased will to resist, by conveying to him that the nation will not long persevere in its overall war effort. This has prolonged the war and caused the death of countless numbers of American boys. . . .

Yours very truly,
J.W.H. (Elberton, GA)

26

Dear Senator [John J.] Sparkman:

May 8, 1967
. . . By whose authority do the marchers, rioters, mobs, and demonstrators have the right to disturb the peace, destroy property, stir hatred, litter the streets and sidewalks, impose police protection while taxpayers have to be without police protection? . . .

Respect should be a prime factor in our lives—respect for self, others and God. Law and order must prevail as surely as day follows night. How can mistrust be allowed? An education should give an individual a degree of polish and refinement. The image of our college youth certainly is a different one today. The main ones who make the headlines are unkempt, sloppy, uncouth, boorish, and ill-mannered. To the contrast there are some who are self-disciplined, properly motivated, and desirous of a basic education. For this group the routine of study and campus life should be unhampered. Where are the extra curricular activities that enhance one's life and enrich it to appreciate culture and aesthetic things in life? . . .

L.T. (female, Mobile, AL)

27

Dear Senator [Richard E.] Russell [Jr.]:

October 23, 1967

I take this chance, at the end of antiwar demonstrations around the world, to again write you urging reconsideration of our war in Vietnam. I am continuing to read and collect information on this war, and the more I read and the more I learn, the more I am convinced that we must pull out now or be sorry forever! Please note that many of those who demonstrated against the war last week did so out of strong convictions growing out of research and much information. Do not lightly overlook our pleas: we love mankind and see a great wrong to mankind; we have to demonstrate! . . .

Few people love and respect this country more than I and many of my friends who are also against this war. But our love for this country makes us fight to correct her wrongs! Please be assured that I am not against our nation; I seek what I believe to be right for all parties concerned.

Sincerely,
T.C. (Watkinsville, GA)

28

Dear Mr. [Ron] Ziegler [White House Press Secretary]:

January 10, 1969

With your kind permission, I would like to submit to the Pres't.-Elect. a simple idea dealing with termoil in our educational institutions.

Simply this:—A Federal Law, laying down the respective places held by institutions of higher learning and students—and what shall be required of students, who wish to avail themselves of the privilege, etc. Briefly, any infraction of the guide lines by a student, shall result in immediate expulsion, which shall last for one year (and shall include every institution of higher learning in the country). After the year is up, the student may apply for readmission but if his attitude does not indicate repentance, he shall be refused for all time.

We don't need revolutionaries, much less—educated ones and I don't think, our society can benefit by spending any time or any money on them.

One of the things that has to be made clear, is that no student can Demand anything and no student can take over anything or interfere with regular routine any way without being expelled.

You treat nice people nice! You treat rough people rough and you'll get results. Thank you very much.

Sincerely,

L.F. (Fort Smith, AR)

29

Dear Senator [J. William] Fulbright:

May 5, 1970

In a kind of stunned desperation I have put off from day to day writing to you, hoping that something would happen to make some kind of sense out of what we are doing in Southeast Asia. Now, after what happened yesterday in Ohio, I can put if off no longer. . . .

Now I find myself strongly in sympathy with those, especially the young, who protest the course we are taking in our military adventures, and the injustices we tolerate at home. To be sure, there is a radical and violent element with which I could not agree. But if the Administration refuses to listen, even the most serious and restrained students, who have no political power, can do nothing other than demonstrate. If the Administration forces these demonstrators to become violent, or uses violence even when the demonstrations are peaceful, then the students have a very limited range of alternatives. . . .

I hold a most unusually close relationship with the youth of my charge. When they have come to me with their perplexities about the war, I have tried fairly to present the arguments against resorting to military power to settle disputes; but I have tried to be as impartial as I could. Now, I shall urge youth to resist the draft, to refuse induction, and to let their opposition be known. If necessary, I am willing to go to prison with them—and a good portion of our ministers feel the same way! . . .

Most respectfully yours,

J.B.B. (Perryville, AR)

30

Dear Sir [Senator J. William Fulbright]:

May 6, 1970

Am just writing a few lines *in support of* the Ohio National Guard in the *killing of 4 students at Kent State Ohio.* How long do the American people have to stand by and see their property destroyed by rotten communist trouble makers and spoiled brats before any action is taken to stop them. The willful destruction of college property and the Bank at Santa Barbara California are other examples of the extent to which the anti-American forces are allowed to operate and not be punished. It is high time all of this is brought to a halt and I say whatever it takes to do it is justified so hears a letter in support of the Ohio National Guard. They did the right thing and all patriotic Americans should be on their side. . . . Why in the 1st place are not the wishes of the masses of the American people listened to and not those of a destructive minority. It seems that the people who go about minding their own business, obeying the law, living by the American way of life and respecting the rights of others should be listened to more. So lets support our police and National Guard for defending America and the American way of life. . . . Every attempt to take over a college campus should be smashed flat before it gets started. In concluding let me state that those students at Kent State deserve no sympathy they only got what they deserved. Death to traitors.

Yours truly,
W.T.C. (Conway AR)

31

Dear Senator [J. William] Fulbright:

May 6, 1970

I regret this day when as a citizen of the United States my voice counts for nothing, my vote counts for nothing, and my faith in Constitutional Government is dashed by our inability to determine the processes by which we live.

Many of us, of the silent majority, wanted to give President Nixon a chance, the full benefit of the doubt. We had our hopes dashed by former President Johnson, and we hoped that the new President would learn by the reaction of the people that we wanted no more of the War in Southeast Asia. I refrained from writing, and felt encouraged when he announced the withdrawal of troops. Now that is all gone, and I well understand how young people of this country feel—a sense of hopelessness that leads to despair. . . .

Then comes the words of the President that the young people of our campuses are a bunch of bums. How can he ignore the fact that many of them are returned Veterans? The 4 who were killed at Kent State have proved to be anything but bums. Many others that I know are young people agonized with a government that refuses to see that what we want to accomplish cannot be done ever by what we are doing among the poor of the world.

I don't know why I write except there is nothing else to do but pray and write to persons like you and wait. I do all three, but there is little relief when the man who said that he wanted to bring us together has divided us as no other leader in the history of this country.

In God's name, don't you give up!
H.P.O. (Benton, AR)

32

Dear [Senator] Sam [J. Ervin Jr. and [Senator] [B.] Everett [Jordan]:

May 7, 1970

. . . I can hardly write this letter to you without my expressing my extreme regret at what happened at Kent [State] University in Ohio. With no firsthand knowledge of the developments at Kent, my first reaction was one of disbelief and condemnation of the results. . . . Finally, last night on tv, they put in an interview with a few of the National Guardsmen. I was impressed with the fact that these young fellows admitted that they were scared; that they were being pelted with stone, metal, etc., and that they felt the students at the college had an opportunity that they, themselves, did not have at the present time as they were working and had families. This brought to my mind that these young men in the National Guard were rendering a service to their country. They were not at Kent because of any desire of their own, and they would not have been there had the authorities not thought there was some danger and need for their presence. . . .

Now, I hear on the radio that the university presidents have sent telegrams to both of you, condemning the war, and, in some instances, they are expressing protest or leading the students in protest of the Cambodian situation, with some of the students saying that they will not return to college this year.

Just how this group of presidents can undertake to advise the Senators of the United States, the President of the United States, and the military establishment of the United State how to run a war when they cannot control dope peddling on their own campuses, I do not know. . . . On top of that unfortunate situation, now, we come to the students who are trying to burn the ROTC buildings and who are leading strikes to close the universities, and, in any way possible, are disrupting our school system at the cost of millions of dollars and to the disadvantage of thousands of students who are at the universities to get an education and not to mix up with what I would call insurrection, which, in many instances, is led by professors paid by the State. . . .

Sincerely yours,
C.A.C. (Concord, NC)

33

Dear Mr. [Albert] Gore [Sr.]:

May 7, 1970

You say you were shocked by the President's action in Viet Nam.

Let me ask you a question, Sir. Were you shocked by the death of 200 of our boys each week at the hands of a vicious and merciless enemy? . . .

Were you shocked at our young men laying down their lives for their country while their misled and pusillanimous compatriots on college campuses were trampling Old Glory underfoot?

Doesn't it occur to you that our men are facing death on the frontiers of democracy while others of their age are being rabble-roused by hardcore communist sympathizers or actual undercover cell workers?

These lushes should be taken off the campus and put in work camps. The C.C.C. helped many drifting young men during the depression of the thirties.[16]

We need ideas, we need change, but we cannot let the lunatic fringe of society burn our house down. . . .

If we are going to fight a war let's do it all out. If we are not we had better get out and eat crow.

Sincerely,
K.N.G. (Spring City, TN)

34

Dear Senator [Herman E.] Talmadge:

May 9, 1970

. . . We fall into the class of the silent majority that works and pays the major part of the taxes that keeps our country functioning. We feel it is time for us to be heard and let it be known that we strongly believe that law and order must prevail at any cost!

We want it to be known that we fully support our National Guard, Federal, State and City police forces, in what ever measures they have to use in order to maintain law and order in our country. . . .

16. The Civilian Conservation Corps (1933–42) was a New Deal program providing work to unemployed young men during the Great Depression. The CCC improved public forests, parks, and lands.

The Kent State incident is regrettable but if we had demanded that these student demonstrations and militant destruction be stopped five years ago this would not have happened. . . .

Respectfully,
Dr. and Mrs. N.R.C. (Athens, GA)

35

Dear Senator [J. William] Fulbright:

May 10, 1970

I have been a teacher in the Fayetteville Arkansas, school system for seven years. I am a graduate of the University of Arkansas and my husband is still a student and is a Navy veteran. . . .

I am for the war. I am very concerned with your vocalizations proclaiming that we give up the fight and get out of Viet Nam and more recently your statements about the Cambodian involvement. I am appalled that our government had not long ago eradicated the militarily "protected" supply stations on the border. Finally we are attacking. . . .

Secondly, concerning the Kent State happening last week, I pose this question: What would have been the reaction of the students had four National Guardsmen been killed? I suspect it would be just a "sad, sad, thing." I heard on May 8, 1970 over Columbia Broadcasting Company by Dan Rather that we are seeing the "First national campus strike in the history of the United States." I can assure you and Mr. Rather there is no strike here. I also can assure you that students faced with finals welcome any way to get out of them. My experiences as a student just seven years ago at this campus were similar in some respects: this time of year is a "wild" time of year; the weather is warm; we welcomed any opportunity to get outside. I hope the crowds, noise, and wildness do not influence people in your position. These people are idealistic and unrealistic about problems of government.

. . . The younger (than I) people are so concerned about going to Viet Nam because they simply do not want to go. I have talked with many here, and they openly admit this. Fear of dying on a foreign battlefield is a poor reason for tearing our homeland to shreds. . . .

Respectfully—a voter,

P.S. (female, Fayetteville, AR)

36

Dear Bill [Senator William B. Spong Jr.]:

May 15, 1970

I apologize for this long letter. Last Saturday morning I was pleasantly oc-cupied piddling around my yard when the civilian air-raid siren sounded off. This screaking not only upset all the dogs in the neighborhood but reminded me again of the billion dollars plus already piddled away by the Government for this completely useless venture. . . .

I had the great fortune and privilege of being educated in the little public school in Warsaw, St. Christopher's School in Richmond and V.M.I., and I was taught at all these schools and by my parents to obey and respect law and order and that if I did not certain penalties would be applied. I believe my gripes were always heard as they were all directed through proper channels. Why isn't this done today—government leads our youth to believe and behave otherwise. My observation is that all young people are not only completely frustrated but down-right depressed and apprehensive as to where we are headed and how much lon-ger we can keep going. Don't think for a minute that our young people aren't most apprehensive about the unbelievable waste and extravagance of Government. I believe there is a hard core of young people and that they are few in number who need to be told that America is not Utopia and that the Government will not always take care of them and their aim in life should [not] be pleasure without responsibility. These agitators are preventing the 999% plus great youngsters from getting what they properly should have from our Government in the way of the good life you and ours have always enjoyed. I believe that college students who get offside and do not approach the authorities through proper channels should be dismissed. This should be applied to the faculty as well. Every rule can't be spelled out at the colleges. Respect for law and order and respect for those in authority and the decent things in life should automatically be understood. . . .

Sincerely,
S.B.S. (Norfolk, VA)

37

Dear Senator [Sam J. Ervin Jr.]:

May 15, 1970

I have recently been gravely concerned, as I know you have, over what is taking place in our beloved country. Having lived all my life in it, served in its armed forces during World War I, run an essential industry during World War II and enjoyed its many blessings all my life, I cannot sit quietly by and see what is taking place without some protest.

Recently there have been a series of moves, some politically motivated and some pushed by the cowardly young who fear to serve their country that has given them so much. Many of these have been promoted by avowed communist elements and movements among both college students and faculties with the purpose of creating dissention in the country and the wrecking of the institutions that have been built by the American system over the centuries. Thousands of innocent young have been trapped and misled into these subversive movements. . . .

As to the movement among the young college students, unlearned in history, untried in courage and valor, unwilling to risk their lives as have countless of their forbears for the sake of their country, unwilling to work for an education and their own good, unwashed, unshorn and un about everything that has made this country great; the less said the better. For those that lost their lives at Kent State and the similar situations about the country, I feel sorry and even sorrier for their parents to whom they would not listen. Had they, however, have been about the business for which they had gone there, had they heeded the warnings of the authorities against riot and disorder, no harm would have come to any of them. Personally, I feel great sympathy for the men of the National Guard who had left their jobs at the call of their governor and were doing a job to maintain peace and order under most difficult circumstances. Had I have been a member of them under the circumstance with rocks, cement chunks, vile epithets and acute menace being hurled at me, I would have probably have done exactly as did they. I feel they are much more deserving of commendation for a job well done under the most difficulty of circumstances than of condemnation. . . .

Sincerely,

J.R.M. (Greensboro, NC)

38

Dear Mr. President [Richard M. Nixon]:

May 17, 1970

. . . Mine is just one small voice in the wilderness of misinformed, misguided, misanthropic American citizenry * * * * who, in their bewilderment, are now blaming you, Mr. President, for this appalling situation into which our country has fallen.

All thinking people are aware that the events leading to our present crisis are not the fault of one man or two or three men but of we, the American public * * * * many of us too apathetic to assume their responsibilities in the proper fashion.

When I mention the American crisis, I am not referring to your recent actions in Cambodia but to the shocking demonstrations on college campuses and elsewhere throughout our country. We, in Louisiana, are solidly with you in your recent actions which was long overdue. You have displayed great courage and self-sacrifice in making your decision. . . .

I have a son in Vietnam, serving in the U.S. Army for this third (voluntary) year * * * * he is an interpreter and is now on assignment in Saigon. His previous two years were spent in rehabilitation, teaching, etc. among the Montegnards and other tribes who were driven out of their homes. My son is in Vietnam because he is a conscientious American who feels there is work to be done there and that someone must do it to prevent our entire country, ultimately, from being surrounded and overrun with the communists whose insidious progress has already been so largely reflected by demonstrations and riots here at home. . . .

Perhaps you are aware that a demonstration is planned on the campus of Louisiana Polytechnic Institute in Ruston, La., during the forthcoming week * * * a demonstration in reverse this time, because it is in support of your actions * * * * and a protest to other students throughout this country for their recent actions. We pray that this type of demonstration may reach epidemic proportions too * * * * and, who knows in this age of "monkey see, monkey do"?

Thank you for listening, Mr. President.

Sincerely,

Mrs. B.D.J. (Shreveport, LA)

39

Dear Sir [Senator Sam J. Ervin Jr.]:

June 14, 1970

I have received your statement concerning the events at Kent State University. . . .

I deplore the use of force or violence in any form to achieve political or social change. I agree with you that it is unfortunate that the students at Kent State University or Jackson State College did not exercise more self-restraint—many of them were better educated than the guardsmen they confronted, and they should have been better behaved. But I also feel that the indiscriminate shooting of unarmed civilians, be they college students or otherwise, is inexcusable. The only justification for the use of gunfire is a clear and immediate danger to the life of the guardsman himself—and that clearly was not the case at either of these schools. All the news reports I have seen of these incidents fail to establish any conclusive evidence of sniper fire. The guardsmen fired out of frustration, anger, and fear, but that does not excuse their actions.

I do not believe that it is "giving aid and comfort to the enemy" to question in good faith the wisdom of our foreign policies. I do believe that to offer constructive criticism of our country's policies is to express a faith in the ability of our leaders to be guided by reason and wisdom rather that by ignorance and prejudice; to offer such criticism is to express a love for this country and a hope that we can do better in the future than we have done in the past. . . .

Yours truly,
H.M.C. (Raleigh, NC)

40

Dear Senator [Sam J.] Ervin [Jr.],

June 16, 1970

I want to answer your letter concerning the Kent State incident. I have done quite a bit of reading on the subject, and I have found that some of my facts conflict with yours.

You mentioned that the Kent State campus was under the influence of SDS. From my research I have found that SDS had not been active on the Kent State campus for approximately a year, due to the conviction and imprisonment of four of the SDS leader from that area. I have also found that the investigating teams there can find no correlation between SDS and the incidents that happened there this past May.

I do not condone the violence, but had the governor left the students in the hands of the people that know how to handle them (the school administrators), and had he not forbidden them to assemble, there would have been no need for the National Guard on that campus.

I also abhor the rock throwing, but I doubt that it would have done much skull cracking, since the National Guard was in complete combat (riot) gear, which includes a helmet.

Thirdly, the price of a burnt building and broken windows can never equal that of four lives, and none of the excuses given (i.e. the men were there involuntarily, they were hot, hungry) can excuse the fact that they fired *without* orders into crowds of unarmed students. . . .

Perhaps if adults will start listening there will never be another Kent State because the few that resort to violence will not need to be heard that way anymore. You can help this—as can all members of Congress and the Administration—LISTEN TO US!

John F. Kennedy once said, "If we make peaceful revolution impossible, we make violent revolution inevitable." I think that every citizen in this country should weigh this statement very heavily, to decrease the polarizations that exist, and try to save this country before we destroy ourselves.

Peace,

J.A. (female, Greensboro, NC)

41

Dear Senator [Sam J. Ervin Jr.],

June 18, 1970

Thank you for your reply concerning the Kent State killings. Your statement typifies, I think, your attitude towards this kind of incident. You condone the shooting of students who were at worst throwing rocks at soldiers dressed for battle.

I consider this attitude criminal, improper in a public servant, and immoral. I accuse you of condoning murder, and of aiding and abetting further murder. Where is your sense of proportion, of decency, if nothing else? . . .

I have also read your speech in Congress. I further accuse you of aiding and abetting the murder of thousands of our young men, of the murder of hundreds of thousands of innocent people in Southeast Asia, the ruination of foreign lands, the destruction of this country's economy, and the final and complete loss of American's credibility, prestige, and respect abroad. . . .

Yours in peace,

K.A.G. (Chapel Hill, NC)

42

Dear Sir [Robert Finch, Counselor to President Nixon]:

July 19, 1970

. . . Two suggestions: I suggest that more emphasis be put on a study of the *orderly dissenters* and the so-called "straight students" and why they are not destructive and disruptive and how we can encourage and promote that segment (an overwhelming majority) instead of how we can placate that small militant minority. Another Munich is all that will stop them and then only for a short time. To surrender to the militants will only increase the problem.[17] . . .

I also suggest to college and university administrators that their new hires be required 3 to 5 years teaching at the primary and secondary levels before being put to work teaching college students. I think they need it for maturity—as it is they carry their immature student ideas over to the classroom and further confuse and radicalize their students. I contend that a vast majority of the radical or militant professors went directly from one side of the desk to the other; from being parent supported to college supported; and live from theories instead of the practical. . . .

I am 49 years old and the only college connection I have had was in being a university graduate, class of 1942, having worked my way.

Sincerely,

G.D.O. Jr. (Dallas, TX)

43

Dear Senator [Herman E.] Talmadge,

May 11, 1972

The recent escalation of U.S. action in Viet Nam is of grave concern to my family as it is to millions of families in our nation.

As the mother of two teenaged sons, I find this matter growing more serious as the months pass. I cannot help feeling that to continue the useless loss of lives of more of our young men to try to recover our prisoners of war is confounding our involvement in a country which does not appreciate our efforts, anyway. . . .

For several years I was totally opposed to our young peoples' protests over this war, and felt they lacked the patriotism which I had always felt so deeply. I must say that as our involvement continues and nothing is done to bring our sons home, I now find myself in sympathy with those who protest this ghastly, unnecessary war. I shall continue in this vein until U.S. troops are withdrawn from Viet Nam, and I shall do all possible to prevent our sons from serving there. . . .

Sincerely,

Mrs. H.B.F. (Atlanta, GA)

17. At the Munich Conference of 1938 Great Britain, France, and Italy allowed Adolph Hitler and Germany to annex a part of Czechoslovakia in hope of avoiding what became World War II. The Munich Agreement became a symbol of the dangers of trying to appease an aggressor.

SOURCES of LETTERS

The letters in this book were collected from the following manuscript collections and newspapers and will be cited as follows:

Afro-American (Baltimore)

Atlanta Constitution

Atlanta Daily World

Harry F. Byrd Jr. Papers (#16320), Albert and Shirley Small Special Collections, University of Virginia, Charlottesville, VA; cited as Byrd Jr. Papers, box: folder

John Sherman Cooper Papers, Special Collections Research Center, Margaret J. King, Library, University of Kentucky, Lexington, KY; cited as Cooper Papers, relevant box

Sam J. Ervin Papers (#3847A), Southern Historical Collection, Wilson Library, University of North Carolina, Chapel Hill, NC; cited as Ervin Papers, box: folder (all cites to Subgroup A: Senate Records, Series 1)

J. William Fulbright Papers, Special Collections, University of Arkansas Libraries, Fayetteville, AR; cited as Fulbright Papers, box: folder (all cites to Series 48)

Albert Gore Sr. Senate Papers, Albert Gore Research Center, Middle Tennessee State University, Murfreesboro, TN; cited as Gore Papers, series, box:folder

Journal and Guide (Norfolk)

Russell B. Long Papers, Louisiana and Lower Mississippi Collection, Louisiana State University, Baton Rouge, LA; cited as Long Papers, box:folder

Louisville Courier-Journal

Louisville Defender

Thruston B. Morton Papers, Special Collections Research Center, Margaret J. King, Library, University of Kentucky, Lexington, KY; cited as Morton Papers, relevant box.

Nixon Project; consulted in June 2007, when housed in the National Archives II, College Park, MD; since moved to the Richard Nixon Presidential Library and Museum, Yorba Linda, CA. All references are to the White House Central Files (WHCF), Subject Files: Human Rights, Box:Folder

Pittsburgh Courier

Post Tribune (Dallas)

A. Willis Robertson Papers, Special Collections Research Center, College of William and Mary Libraries, Williamsburg, VA; cited as Robertson Papers, drawer: file

Richard B. Russell Jr. Papers, Richard B. Russell Library for Political Research and Studies, University of Georgia, Athens, GA; cited as Russell Papers, box:folder (all cites to Series 16)

William B. Spong Papers (#9838), Albert and Shirley Small Special Collections, University of Virginia, Charlottesville, VA; cited as Spong Papers, box:folder

John C. Stennis Collection, Congressional and Political Research Center, Mississippi State University Libraries, Starkville, MS; cited as Stennis Collection, series, box:-folder

John J. Sparkman Papers, University of Alabama Libraries Special Collections, University of Alabama, Tuscaloosa, Tuscaloosa, AL; cited as Sparkman Papers, series:box

Herman E. Talmadge Papers, Richard B. Russell Library for Political Research and Studies, University of Georgia, Athens, GA; cited as Talmadge Papers, series, box:folder

John G. Tower Papers, Special Collections and Archives, Southwestern University, Georgetown, TX; cited as Tower Papers, box:folder

Ralph W. Yarborough Papers, Briscoe Center for American History, University of Texas, Austin, TX; cited as Yarborough Papers, box:folder

1. PROWAR SOUTHERNERS

1. *Louisville Courier-Journal*, June 7, 1964.

2. Yarborough Papers, 4Zd657:July 14, 1964.

3. Yarborough Papers, 4Zd657:August 6, 1964.

4. Gore Papers, 7, C14:1.

5. Gore Papers, 4, A37:1.

6. Gore Papers, 4, A37:1.

7. Russell Papers, 41:2.

8. Russell Papers, 40:12.

9. Russell Papers, 40:4.

10. Stennis Collection, 4, 85:14.

11. Byrd Jr. Papers, 199:Vietnam, 1965.

12. Stennis Collection, 4, 85:17.

13. Fulbright Papers, 49:6

14. Russell Papers, 38:8.

15. Russell Papers, 37:10.

16. Byrd Jr. Papers, 198:September–October 1966, Vietnam.

17. Stennis Collection, 43, 95:Vietnam Miscellaneous 1967.

18. Stennis Collection, 43, 95:Vietnam Miscellaneous 1967.

19. Byrd Jr. Papers, 195:1967 (October 21–31), Vietnam.

20. Byrd Jr. Papers, 195:1967 (November 11–30), Vietnam.

21. *Atlanta Constitution,* February 16, 1968.

22. Long Papers, 108:34.

23. Russell Papers, 32:8.

24. Ervin Papers, 188:7514.

25. Russell Papers, 32:2.

26. Ervin Papers, 188:8436.

27. Russell Papers, 30:9.

28. Sparkman Papers, 71-A-4217:6.

29. Gore Papers, 4, A47:7.

30. Russell Papers, 29:11.

31. Gore Papers, 6, B47:1.

32. Stennis Collection, 53, 3:134.

33. Ervin Papers, 212:9260.

34. Stennis Collection, 53, 3:130.

35. Gore Papers, 6, B47:7.

36. Talmadge Papers, XI, 103:1.

37. Long Papers, 134:1.

38. Talmadge Papers, XI, 116:1.

39. Ervin Papers, 243:10211.

40. Talmadge Papers, XI, 136:3.

41. Fulbright Papers, 64:1.

42. Talmadge Papers, XI, 139:15.

43. Talmadge Papers, XI, 139:15.

44. Talmadge Papers, XI, 139:1.

45. Talmadge Papers, XI, 144:2.

46. Fulbright Papers, 65:1.

2. ANTIWAR SOUTHERNERS

1. Yarborough Papers, 4Zk657:August 10, 1964.

2. Tower Papers, 284:2.

3. Ervin Papers, 97:4336.

4. Russell Papers, 41:11.

5. Ervin Papers, 112:4981.

6. *Louisville Courier Journal,* July 2, 1965.

7. Russell Papers, 41:2.

8. Robertson Papers, 105:57.

9. *Louisville Courier Journal,* July 28, 1965.

10. Gore Papers, 6, B36:2.

11. Stennis Collection, 4, 85:17.

12. Stennis Collection, 4, 85:16.

13. Gore Papers, 4, A37:1.

14. Fulbright Papers, 48:3.

15. Fulbright Papers, 47:2.

16. Russell Papers, 38:6.

17. Russell Papers, 38:8.

18. Morton Papers, box 19.

19. Ervin Papers, 150:6579.

20. Russell Papers, 34:1.

21. Stennis Collection, 4, 68:11.

22. Byrd Jr. Papers, 195:1967:November 11–30, Vietnam.

23. Byrd Jr. Papers, 195: 1967:October 21–31, Vietnam.

24. Fulbright Papers, 54:3.

25. Ervin Papers, 169:7502.

26. Fulbright Papers, 54:4.

27. Russell Papers, 32:10.

28. Ervin Papers, 169:7512.

29. Fulbright Papers, 56:3.

30. Ervin Papers, 188:8440.

31. Tower Papers, 378:3.

32. Ervin Papers, 212:9259.

33. Stennis Collection, 53, 3:134.

34. Ervin Papers, 212:9264.

35. Talmadge Papers, XI, 103:1.

36. Long Papers, 134:3.

37. Ervin Papers, 243:10225.

38. Long Papers, 134:3.

39. Fulbright Papers, 62:5.

40. Stennis Collection, 31, 11:49.

41. Stennis Collection, 31, 11:49.

42. Talmadge Papers, XI, 131:5.

43. Ervin Papers, 267:11113.

44. Talmadge Papers, XI, 137:2.

45. Talmadge Papers, XI, 137:2.

46. Talmadge Papers, XI, 139:1.

47. Talmadge Papers, XI, 139:1.

48. Fulbright Papers, 65:5.

49. Fulbright Papers, 65:1.

3. BLACK SOUTHERNERS

1. *Journal and Guide* (Norfolk), May 22, 1965
2. *Louisville Defender*, July 22, 1965.
3. *Atlanta Constitution*, January 13, 1966.
4. *Afro-American* (Baltimore), January 15, 1966.
5. *Louisville Defender*, February 3, 1966.
6. *Louisville Defender*, March 17, 1966.
7. *Louisville Defender*, March 31, 1966.
8. *Louisville Defender*, April 7, 1966.
9. *Louisville Defender*, May 5, 1966.
10. *Louisville Defender*, May 12, 1966.
11. *Louisville Defender*, June 16, 1966.
12. *Journal and Guide* (Norfolk), June 18, 1966.
13. *Post Tribune* (Dallas), June 18, 1966.
14. *Post Tribune* (Dallas), July 9, 1966.
15. *Louisville Defender*, July 21, 1966.
16. *Louisville Defender*, August 4, 1966.
17. *Louisville Defender*, September 8, 1966.
18. *Louisville Defender*, October 13, 1966.
19. *Louisville Defender*, November 17, 1966.
20. *Louisville Defender*, January 12, 1967.
21. *Louisville Defender*, February 23, 1967.
22. *Louisville Defender*, March 30, 1967.
23. *Journal and Guide* (Norfolk), April 1, 1967.
24. *Louisville Defender*, April 13, 1967.
25. *Journal and Guide* (Norfolk), May 13, 1967.
26. *Pittsburgh Courier*, July 22, 1967.
27. Louisville Defender, July 27, 1967.
28. *Louisville Defender*, October 5, 1967.
29. *Louisville Defender*, October 5, 1967.
30. *Louisville Defender*, December 11, 1967.
31. *Louisville Defender*, January 11, 1968.
32. *Louisville Defender*, February 8, 1968.
33. *Louisville Defender*, February 23, 1968.
34. *Louisville Defender*, April 18, 1968.
35. *Louisville Defender*, April 25, 1968.
36. *Journal and Guide* (Norfolk), May 25, 1968.
37. *Journal and Guide* (Norfolk), June 8, 1968.
38. *Louisville Defender*, September 26, 1968.

39. *Louisville Defender,* December 26, 1968.

40. *Louisville Defender,* January 2, 1969.

41. *Louisville Defender,* April 3, 1969.

42. *Journal and Guide* (Norfolk), May 29, 1969.

43. *Louisville Defender,* June 12, 1969.

44. *Journal and Guide* (Norfolk), June 21, 1969.

45. *Louisville Defender,* July 31, 1969.

46. *Louisville Defender,* August 28, 1969.

47. *Louisville Defender,* September 11, 1969.

48. *Louisville Defender,* October 16, 1969.

49. *Louisville Defender,* November 13, 1969.

50. *Louisville Defender,* November 20, 1969.

51. *Louisville Defender,* December 11, 1969.

52. *Louisville Defender,* December 25, 1969.

53. *Louisville Defender,* February 12, 1970.

54. *Louisville Defender,* March 5, 1970.

55. *Post Tribune* (Dallas), May 9, 1970.

56. *Atlanta Daily World,* May 17, 1970.

57. *Atlanta Daily World,* July 30, 1970.

58. *Louisville Defender,* December 10, 1970.

59. *Post Tribune* (Dallas), December 19, 1970.

60. *Louisville Defender,* March 4, 1971.

61. *Louisville Defender,* April 8, 1971.

62. *Louisville Defender,* April 8, 1971.

63. *Louisville Defender,* April 8, 1971.

64. *Journal and Guide* (Norfolk), April 24, 1971.

65. *Louisville Defender,* May 20, 1971.

66. *Louisville Defender,* June 10, 1971.

67. *Louisville Defender,* July 22, 1971.

68. *Louisville Defender,* August 19, 1971.

69. *Journal and Guide* (Norfolk), February 12, 1972.

70. *Louisville Defender,* February 17, 1972.

71. *Louisville Defender,* April 20, 1972.

72. *Louisville Defender,* December 7, 1972.

4. SOUTHERN FAMILIES

1. Sparkman Papers, 67A959:9.

2. Gore Papers, 6, B33:2.

3. Stennis Collection, 4, 85:16.

4. Fulbright Papers, 47:3.

5. Fulbright Papers, 47:6.

6. Gore Papers, 6, B33:1.

7. Stennis Papers, 43, 83:8.

8. Gore Papers, 7, C22:1.

9. Fulbright Papers, 48:3.

10. Russell Papers, 33:6.

11. Russell Papers, 35:7.

12. Stennis Collection, 4, 68:11.

13. Tower Papers, 327:1.

14. Russell Papers, 35:4.

15. Russell Papers, 33:7.

16. Russell Papers, 33:7.

17. *Atlanta Constitution*, February 29, 1968.

18. Sparkman Papers, 70A4063:5.

19. Fulbright Papers, 54:2.

20. Long Papers, 108:35.

21. Tower Papers, 372:3.

22. Talmadge Papers, XI, 59:Vietnam War.

23. Russell Papers, 30:8.

24. Ervin Papers, 212:9256.

25. Russell Papers, 30:8.

26. Sparkman Papers, 71-A-4217:6.

27. Fulbright Papers, 56:3.

28. Russell Papers, 30:1.

29. Long Papers, 116:22.

30. Long Papers, 116:22.

31. Nixon Project, WHCF, Subject Files: Human Rights, 36:2/170–12/31/70.

32. Gore Papers, 6, B44:2.

33. Yarborough Papers, 3W149:4/28/70.

34. Ervin Papers, 212:9261.

35. Gore Papers, 6, B44:6.

36. Gore Papers, 6, B44:6.

37. Talmadge Papers, XI, 87:1.

38. Byrd Jr. Papers, 199:1970–1972, Vietnam Condolences.

39. Stennis Collection, 31, 11:49.

40. Stennis Collection, 31, 11:49.

41. Long Papers, 134:1.

42. Long Papers, 134:1.

43. Fulbright Papers, 62:3.

44. Byrd Jr. Papers, 199:1970–1972, Vietnam Condolences.

5. FULBRIGHT, CALLEY, AND THE SOUTHERN PUBLIC

1. Fulbright Papers, 47:7.

2. Fulbright Papers 47:3.

3. Fulbright Papers, 49:5.

4. Fulbright Papers, 49:3.

5. Fulbright Papers, 47:2.

6. Fulbright Papers, 49:3.

7. Fulbright Papers, 48:5.

8. Fulbright Papers, 49:6.

9. Byrd Jr. Papers, 198:1966, February 17–28, Vietnam.

10. Fulbright Papers, 50:2.

11. Fulbright Papers, 48:1.

12. Fulbright Papers, 53:3.

13. Fulbright Papers, 54:3.

14. Fulbright Papers, 55:3.

15. Fulbright Papers, 56:4.

16. Fulbright Papers, 58:1.

17. Fulbright Papers, 58:1.

18. Fulbright Papers, 58:1.

19. Stennis Collection, 53, 3:134.

20. Fulbright Papers, 60:5.

21. Fulbright Papers, 66:1.

22. Fulbright Papers, 59:2.

23. Fulbright Papers, 60:5.

24. Fulbright Papers, 60:1.

25. Fulbright Papers, 62:1.

26. Russell Papers, 42:6.

27. Sparkman Papers, 71-A-4217: 6.

28. Fulbright Papers, 57:4.

29. Russell Papers, 42:6.

30. Talmadge Papers, XI, 78:4.

31. Russell Papers, 42:9.

32. Sparkman Papers, 71-A-4217:6.

33. Russell Papers, 42:9.

34. Russell Papers, 42:6.

35. Gore Papers, 6, B44:6.

36. Tower Papers, 383:1.

37. Tower Papers, 383:4.

38. Ervin Papers, 243:10218.

39. Talmadge Papers, XI, 115:3.

40. Talmadge Papers, XI, 115:3.

41. Talmadge Papers, XI, 115:3.

42. Byrd Jr. Papers, 263:1971 April, Constituent Mail.

43. Byrd Jr. Papers, 263: 1971 April, Constituent Correspondence.

44. Talmadge Papers, XI, 115:3.

45. Talmadge Papers, XI, 118:6.

46. Talmadge Papers, XI, 118:3.

47. Talmadge Papers, XI, 118:3.

48. Ervin Papers, 243:10214.

49. Stennis Collection, 31, 11:49.

6. STUDENTS, PROTESTORS, AND THEIR CRITICS

1. Fulbright Papers, 61:4.

2. Talmadge Papers, XI, 99:2.

3. Fulbright Papers, 68:1.

4. Fulbright Papers, 68:1.

5. Talmadge Papers, XI, 99:1.

6. Stennis Collection, 53, 3:134.

7. Fulbright Papers, 68:1.

8. Fulbright Papers, 68:1.

9. Gore Papers, 6, B44:8.

10. Talmadge Papers, XI, 99:1.

11. Fulbright Papers, 68:1.

12. Cooper Papers, box 456.

13. Talmadge Papers, XI, 98:4.

14. Fulbright Papers, 67:1.

15. Fulbright Papers, 67:1.

16. Nixon Project, WHCF, Subject Files, Human Rights, 29:8/1/70–8/13/70.

17. Stennis Collection, 31, 11:42.

18. Talmadge Papers, XI, 98:4.

19. Long Papers, 123:4.

20. Talmadge Papers, XI, 87:1.

21. Russell Papers, 40:9.

22. Russell Papers, 40:8.

23. Ervin Papers, 112:4984.

24. Russell Papers, 37:2.

25. Russell Papers, 35:5.

26. Sparkman Papers, 69A4119:6

27. Russell Papers, 34:1.

28. Nixon Project, WHCF, Subject Files: Human Rights, 27:Beginning-3/20/69.

29. Fulbright Papers, 68:1.

30. Fulbright Papers, 66:1.

31. Fulbright Papers, 61:1.

32. Ervin Papers, 212:9261.

33. Gore Papers, 6, B44:8.

34. Talmadge Papers, XI, 99:2.

35. Fulbright Papers, 66:2.

36. Spong Papers, 18:1969–1973, June Correspondence.

37. Ervin Papers, 212:9261.

38. Nixon Project, WHCF, Subject Files: Human Rights, 24:6/1/70–6/30,70.

39. Ervin Papers, 212:9262.

40. Ervin Papers, 212:9262.

41. Ervin Papers, 212:9262.

42. Nixon Project, WHCF, Subject Files: Human Rights, 29:11/1/70–12/31/70.

43. Talmadge Papers, XI, 139:5.

INDEX

Abbeville, Louisiana, 262

activism/activists, 114, 158n17, 243–82; southern responses, 263–82; student voices, 243–63. *See also* antiwar movement/groups; civil rights; protests and demonstrations

ADA (Americans for Democratic Action), 268, 268n15

African militants, 64

Afro-American (Baltimore), 115–16, 116n8, 120–21

Agnew, Spiro, 64, 159, 187, 252, 252n9, 253

aid, economic and military, 12, 21–24, 49, 55, 69, 84, 96, 109, 134–35, 190, 207–8

aid and comfort to the enemy, 38, 59, 69, 209, 210, 211, 212, 214, 269, 280

Air Force, 41, 44, 197–98, 230, 246, 256

Alabama, 4, 15, 18, 31, 115, 133, 246

Albertville, Alabama, 178–79

Alexandria, Virginia, 51, 91–92

Ali, Muhammad, 117, 121–24, 121n10, 174, 197, 265

allies (U.S.), 11–12, 19, 45, 51, 58, 74–75, 84, 130, 180, 217. *See also* South Vietnam

Alvin, Texas, 182

American casualties: antiwar southerners, 87; Black southerners, 114, 121, 147–48, 151–52, 155; declining public support for the war, 8–9; prowar southerners, 45, 48–49; silent majority, 217; southern families, 163–65, 170–71, 174–75, 187–95, 200

American flag: flag burning, 117, 137–38, 174, 188, 199, 265; as outward symbol, 183–84; respect for, 62, 144; saluting the, 152–53

American Legion Post #1 (Raleigh, NC), 67–68

American POWs: antiwar southerners, 75, 97, 107, 109, 110, 111–12; declaration of war, 97; escalation of U.S. action, 282; My Lai massacre, 226, 240; Nixon's policies, 67–68,

109, 110, 111–12, 162; North Vietnam ports, 69, 70, 154; and protesters, 65; prowar southerners, 38; Rolling Thunder bombing campaign, 25; settlement of January 1973, 29; and southern families, 198; treatment of, 131, 219

Americans for Democratic Action (ADA), 268, 268n15

Amsterdam News (New York), 115–16

Anderson, Jack, 32, 161

"Another Mother for Peace" group, 156

Anti-Ballistic Missile projects, 16

antibusing, 161

anticommunism, 13, 19–20, 37–38, 133, 164. *See also* Communism

antiwar movement/groups: antiwar southerners, 73–112; Black southerners, 3, 113, 116–17; Calley trial, 214; children, 93; Democratic South, 36; elders' responses to antiwar protesters, 263–82; and Fulbright, 214, 221; and media, 225; Peace Vigil, Chapel Hill, 102; southern families, 165, 174; student voices, 8, 243–63; technology, 25; women, 7. *See also* Gallup polling; Harris polling; protests and demonstrations

antiwar southerners, 73–112; letters, 76–112; overview, 73–76

appeasement, 42, 44, 212, 282n17

Appy, Christian G., 163–64

Arkadelphia, Arkansas, 247, 250–51, 259

Arkansas, 4, 18, 31, 115, 125, 205–8, 218, 220. *See also* Fulbright, J. William; University of Arkansas; specific places in

Arkansas Gazette (newspaper), 168, 218

Armed Forces Committee (U.S. Senate), 50, 50n10

The Arrogance of Power (Fulbright), 221

CPSIA information can be obtained
at www.ICGtesting.com
Printed in the USA
LVHW110024230922
729105LV00004B/278